Diachrony in Psychoanalys

Also by André Green and published by
Free Association Books

The Work of the Negative
Life Narcissism, Death Narcissism
Time in Psychoanalysis

Diachrony in Psychoanalysis

André Green

Translated by Andrew Weller

FREE ASSOCIATION BOOKS / LONDON / NEW YORK

First published in 2003 by
FREE ASSOCIATION BOOKS
57 Warren Street
London W1T 5NR

www.fa-b.com

A catalogue record for this book is available from the British Library

ISBN 1 85343 554 6 pbk
ISBN 1 85343 553 8 hbk

10   9   8   7   6   5   4   3   2   1

Produced for Free Association Books by
Chase Publishing Services, Fortescue, Sidmouth EX10 9QG
Printed and bound in the European Union by
Antony Rowe, Chippenham and Eastbourne, England

Contents

Translator's Acknowledgements

I would like to express my gratitude to the following people who have helped me in one way or another with this translation. In particular, to Monique Zerbib for all the time and assistance she has generously given me with this. I am also indebted to André Green for our meetings and his very helpful collaboration. David Encaoua has also given me assistance with certain passages in this book.

Andrew Weller
Paris
January 2003

To those who, over the course of time,
have had to accept that I could not be with them
while I was writing these works.

*   *   *

I owe infinite gratitude to Litza Guttieres-Green for the help she has given me in finalising the manuscript. I also thank Philippe Kocher as well as C. Bécant, M.C. Pridun and C. Nyssen.

In the night, in your hand
my watch glowed like
a firefly.
I heard
it ticking:
a dry whisper
escaping
from your unseen hand.
Then your hand again
touched my chest in the dark,
sheltering the cadence of my
dreams.

The watch
kept cutting time
with its tiny saw.
As in a forest
chips of wood,
droplets, bits
of boughs or nests
fall
without disturbing the silence,
without altering the cool
darkness,
so
in your invisible hand
the watch kept cutting
time, time,
and minutes
fell like leaves,
splinters of shattered time,
small black feathers.

I eased
my arm
beneath your neck in the dark
beneath the warmth of your
weight,
and time fell into my hand,
then
sleep fell
from the watch and from
your sleeping hands,
fell like the dark water
of the forests,
from the watch
to your body,
from you it flowed toward
countries,
dark water
time that falls and runs within us.

And so it was that night,
shadow and space, earth
and time
something that flows and falls
and passes.

I hear you breathing,
my love,
we sleep.

Pablo Neruda
'Ode to a Watch in the Night'
Elemental Odes.

1 Diachrony in Psychoanalysis (1967)*

Among the recognised theoretical orientations in what is called structuralism, psychoanalysis – it would be more exact to say, a certain trend in psychoanalysis, that of Lacan – is quite often cited. This assimilation generates confusion and, moreover, is rejected by Lacan himself. Psychoanalysis cannot allow its originality to be reduced in the effort to find a common denominator with other disciplines. Jacques Lacan's structural theory only ultimately acquires meaning within the psychoanalytic movement, as is necessarily the case for each of the disciplines which has seen the emergence of a structural current. This means that, inasmuch as Freudian thought remains its principal point of reference, the psychoanalytic structural conception can only find narrow areas of agreement with structuralist thinking. One of the limits of this agreement seems to lie in the problem of history.[1]

Sartre links the notion of the de-centring of the subject with the discrediting of history.[2] However, if the notion of de-centring merely conceals a reformulation of Freud's thought, one cannot reasonably argue that it discredits the notion of history. Insofar as Freud modifies and renews the model of diachrony, he goes beyond the traditional conception which links individual[3] historical development to an activity of transcending, going beyond, governed by the will of a lucid subject who is free to choose and conscious of what he wants – a subject devoid of any real opacity and inhabited by contradictions that can always ultimately be overcome.[4] Psychoanalysts do not recognise themselves in the image of a thoroughgoing historicism any more than they do in that of a certain classical historicism. One might think that the efforts of certain structuralist interpretations[5] to transcend the dichotomy between structure and history would have facilitated a rapprochement with psychoanalysis; for I have already argued that I consider it as the one field in which this has indeed been accomplished, both in psychoanalytical practice and theory. A large gap still exists between this potential

* First published as 'Diachronie dans le Freudism' in *Critique* no. 238, March 1967, pp. 359–85.

rapprochement and the specific nature of the psychoanalytic position with respect to the meaning it accords to these two terms.

For all these reasons, and others, which are inherent to the theoretical discussions that are taking place within psychoanalysis as well as the source of deep divergences and persistent misunderstandings on the theme of history and the so-called genetic perspective, it seems necessary to return to the concept of diachrony in Freud.

Elements of the Freudian Conception of Diachrony

In a previous article,[6] I distinguished between two tendencies in psychoanalysis. The first values history to the detriment of structure, owing to the excessive importance that the latter attributed to the notion of development and, correlatively, to the notions of fixation and regression. The second primarily favoured synchrony by virtue of its dominant reference to discourse and language, which thus took precedence over the historical point of view. The origin of the opposition stems, in my opinion, from the fact that the notion of history was represented too exclusively by the *theory of libidinal development*. The succession of oral, anal, phallic, and genital stages, interpreted in a simplified and easily manageable version, tended to give the impression of defending a predetermined biological maturation. Moreover, the scale of fixations and regressions could implicitly suggest another scale – the values of which are proclaimed by psychoanalysis which has the task of helping the patient gain access to the 'normal' level of the genital stage. This implicit normative thinking was even less justified in that nothing indicates, *a priori*, that the analyst has himself reached this stage of development. One cannot, however, neglect the theory of libidinal development and exclude it from a Freudian model of diachrony.[7] The error consisted in making an absolute identification between history and libidinal development. This is why I wanted to contrast it with the notion of scansion (Lacan) stemming from the compulsion to repeat which Freud attributes to drive functioning. Eros is the fruit of a conquest snatched from the death drive which strives towards the elimination of all tension in a return towards definitive silence. The whole clamour of life comes from Eros, says Freud. But this conquest has a price: at the heart of the life drives, it meets with another tendency towards preservation, a resistance to change and progression at the very heart of development. If this were not so, there would be no explanation for the dragging movement of regression and the fascinating power of fixation. At the same time, it was necessary to distinguish between a progression which is self-evident and carried along by its own movement, and a succession of figures which only become intelligible within the framework of a conception of the subject in which the latter never occupies the centre of a psychical organisation. Rather he is constantly dislodged from the place he invests, being attracted towards an 'elsewhere' where his division is calling him, captivating him, and subjecting him to the mirages of desire. This subject is, then, as I have said, a barred subject, a divided subject, a subject of *Entzweiung*; a subject, when all is said and done, of the unconscious.

Now, according to Freud, the unconscious is timeless. This notion of timelessness is one that has given rise to very little commentary. Freud no doubt wanted, first and foremost, to underscore the indestructibility of desire, its invulnerability to the test of time, its constancy in spite of subsequent experience. The unconscious learns nothing from the lessons of life; it endures at the heart of the signifying organisation of desire. But this permanence, this perennial nature of desire, does not persist simply in continuity. In order to maintain an obscure presence, in order to organise the whole of conscious experience into its fabric – which rationalisations seek at length to justify – it emerges at two particularly important moments. The first of these affects the child's Oedipal complex phase, and the second the genital phase of the pubertal period inaugurating the adult's object-choices. This diphasic character of libidinal development becomes a fundamental mode of sexual life. Only the investigation of the unconscious will make it possible to shed light on the relations between them, chronological dating apart. Repression reigns between these two phases of sexual organisation, more or less completely erasing the traces of the first Oedipal organisation which consigns the time of the first loves to oblivion.

To speak of forgetting is to speak of memory – precisely because of what is never forgotten – that is to say, a system for retaining memory-traces which Freud distinguished sharply from the perceptual system which registers without retaining anything. In the Letters to Fliess[8] (letter 52), he had already asserted that perception and memory were mutually exclusive. When he carried out his theoretical revision with the introduction of the second topography, replacing the earlier systems of the conscious, preconscious and unconscious with the agencies of the ego, the id, and the superego,[9] he recognised the relations between the conscious part of the ego and the system perception-conscious. For Freud, perception implies a discharge, an exhaustion, an actualisation – all of which, in his view, prohibits retention, elaboration, transformation and combination with identical or different elements of the repressed which is the prisoner of repression, the guardian of a past that is living and never over and done with.

Insufficient attention has been paid to the fact that, for the sake of general coherence, the theoretical reshaping of the second topography required the adoption of the hypothesis of the death drive – which many analysts continue to contest[10] – as well as the hypothesis of hereditary memory-traces; that is, of the phylogenesis of the transmission of acquired characteristics. The latter is also rejected by analysts on the pretext that it has been refuted by the geneticists – I mean geneticists, and not psychologists who refer to the genetic psychology of development.

Thus the different elements that should constitute a Freudian model of diachrony may be enumerated as follows: libido development theory and the points of view of regression and fixation it implies; the compulsion to repeat with its phenomena of scansion; the timelessness of the unconscious underlining the permanence of desire; the diphasic development of sexuality which, as the individual progresses, turns the adult's choices into as many returns – without his knowing it – towards the object-choices of infancy, after the silence of repression; the opposition between perception and memory, and their respective connection with the conscious and unconscious systems; and finally, the hypothesis of hereditary memory-traces.

The Oedipus Complex: Structure and History

The question put by the Sphinx to Oedipus, which was not only an enigma but also a question of life and death, has a paradigmatic value. The fact that he understood that it is man that walks on all fours in infancy, on his two legs in adulthood, and on three in the evening of his existence, shows us that life does not unfold progressively but follows a strange order. Four, two, three: this is something that does not exist in any successive system. If we examined the metaphoric meaning, it would point to a way of retracing man's evolution from his animal origins to the upright position and, from there, to his use of tools. Inasmuch as the Oedipus complex institutes the fundamental difference between the sexes and the generation gap uniting parents and children, it could also be said that it divides itself in order to make room for pure difference (duality), engendering a third party on the basis of the simple line of division separating the terms opposed. There are those who will contend that these are nothing but intellectual games; however, they suggest that the solution to the problem of temporal evolution in man will not be found in any ordinary sequential order.

I have already shown how the Oedipus complex seemed to be a suitable model for replacing the idea of a 'full' subject (*sujet plein*) – as in the subject of the Cogito – with, as Freud and Lacan have suggested, the divided subject, the subject of the *Entzweiung*, the subject in relationship to his progenitors. As I have said, the Oedipus complex is simultaneously a structure – a combinatory structure – in the interplay which unites the subject with his parents' sexual difference, the subject in relationship to what is identical and to what is different, and also the subject of history. This implies the generation gap where any reduction of age difference is impossible. It is owing to the reduction of the generation gap that the adult Oedipus kills his father and marries his mother. Oedipus, the child, has no chance of achieving this. The nature of this endless pursuit constitutes the tragic condition of the Oedipus complex. 'When I shall be my father's father ...' one child said.

Anthropologists have regarded the taboo of incest as a very general condition and seem to be satisfied with the explanation they have given for it. It is held to be the precondition of a system permitting exchange or giving. In the past, theories which saw the prescience of the drawbacks of consanguinity as the cause of this taboo were often treated with scorn. Any theory that sees in this rule nothing other than the conditions of a combinatory system seems to me to be equally suspect, as if the search for a formula, governing the system of alliances, could explain a taboo. Less value is placed on the other face of the Oedipal organisation illustrated by totemism, or 'so-called totemism' as Lévi-Strauss calls it.[11] Without wishing to take sides here in the anthropological controversy, I shall simply mention the funeral ritual celebrating the dead father – the father who has disappeared for ever, the father whose favour, a sign of the omnipotence projected on to him in the beyond, has to be won. It could be said that though it is his memory that is revered, it is the capacity to forget him that is desired – that is, to forget the offences, the innumerable instances of vengeance and the death wishes to which he was inevitably subject owing to his position as father. Eros is expressed in the prohibition of incest; but repression erases the traces of the years during which mother and infant were bound together in a unique love of which only the unconscious has a memory. Prohibition will make it impossible to return to it. The death drive will be at work in the funeral ritual, whatever form it takes, totemic or otherwise; and this will bring back the memory of the deceased. The prohibition of incest erases the union with the mother which is averted through marriage with another person; the funeral ritual will appease the separation from the deceased whose memory will be celebrated. Once again the radical difference between structuralism and psychoanalysis is clear. The former took an exceptional interest in the system of kinship because it is evidence of a combinatory system that is unquestionably unconscious. Psychoanalysis turned its attention more to the processes of erasing and resurrecting the traces both of incest and parricide. In *Moses and Monotheism* (1939), Freud says: 'In its implications the distortion of a text resembles a murder: the difficulty is not in perpetrating the deed but in getting rid of its traces.'[12]

The Object: Mourning and Suturing

Mourning is the precondition of memory. The transition from one object to another – the process of suturing which is of interest to structural linguistics in its study of syntax and grammar – is inseparable in psychoanalysis from the concept of the *coupure*.[13] This *coupure* or 'cut' is not only present through the spacing of the sutured terms – pause or suspension – as indicated by a typewriter or printer by means of a sign which has to be typed in order to separate one word from another. This blank of which psychoanalysis speaks is the product of an erasure, a loss. Libidinal development is thus not only punctuated by these blanks between one stage and another – oral, anal, phallic, and then, much later, genital; it is through a work of mourning that the fruitful moments are elaborated. As Freud points out, before the reality principle can take effect, the object, which formerly procured satisfaction, must have been experienced as lost, resulting in mourning for the mother or her breast. If castration anxiety is to be at least confronted, if not surmounted, the female genital organ has to be recognised which implies mourning the mother's penis. And, for the paths of sublimation to be opened up, the mourning of paternal power must be followed by recognition of the Law in which the phallic signifier is resuscitated. Each of these

acts of mourning is the product of a work; and this work of signification is itself the result of a loss. Consequently, re-finding the object
will only be possible through mediations that bring into play
identity and difference. But this loss is the precondition for the
activation of a system of transformations of the signifier and for the
setting up of a complete register of signifiers whether they are word-
presentations, thing-presentations, affects, or bodily states. The
structures in which these find expression – dreams, phantasy, reminiscence, memory, parapraxes – will all be forms of this system of
traces which it will be possible to decipher partially with the help of
a combinatory system. This will never be sufficient to elucidate
them, however, for it will be necessary to search, under the vestiges,
for the erasure of traces.

One of the ambiguities in the way anthropological structuralists
and linguists on the one hand and psychoanalysts, on the other, use
the term signifier is now clear. For the former, it is a homogeneous
system from which any consideration of historical dating or origin
is excluded, the text in question being judged as if it were complete,
without elision and without allusion. For the latter, its elements are
heterogeneous; moreover, the disclosure of the structure cannot
overlook what has been barred, censored, elided, and erased. It is a
lacunary text in which the suture is sometimes more telling at the
level of its blanks than at the level of its discourse.

A certain orientation in psychoanalysis shares with structuralism
a conception of the subject in which the latter is no longer equated
with the person who is speaking. The subject, as Lacan says is
spoken. The subject of the statement and the subject making the
statement (*sujet de l'énoncé, sujet de l'énonciation*) are not the same.
What is involved here is the process of signification, that is, the
operation whereby the suturing of the terms which are meaningful
reveals the subject of the unconscious. There will always remain,
however, the unbridgeable gulf of repression – an operation that is
not just a work of memory. It allows the elements of the suture to be
drawn from its depths; but it also involves the work of forgetting,
that is, of what eludes the suture and is missing from it when the
text of the discourse is constituted. The real discovery of psychoanalysis is not only to have shown that dreams, phantasy,
parapraxes, symptoms and neurosis have a meaning, or that the
essential aspects of the life of a given subject reveal a certain order;
it is in having discerned that this order, this latent organisation also
carries the scar of a refusal, a rejection, a bar. That the mediation of

the system is the path leading to this discovery, and that its law coincides with the law of desire – that is, the rule – does not obscure the fact that the signifying organisation has been constituted at the price of a disguised transgression; and, that disclosure has occurred at the price of yet another transgression (the lifting of resistances).

History: Ontogenesis and Phylogenesis

> What we teach the subject to recognise as his unconscious is his history – that is to say, we help him to perfect the contemporary historisation of the facts which have already determined a certain number of the historical 'turning-points' in his existence. But if they have played this role, it is already as facts of history, that is to say, in so far as they have been recognised in one particular sense or censored in a certain order.[14]

This was Lacan speaking in a text in which he recognised that he was largely in agreement with the structuralist approach. It is fitting, therefore, that we inquire into this order which dictates the course of recorded events and repressions. The inadequacies of a strictly ontogenetic position cannot be circumvented. As we have seen, it gives pre-eminence to what is earliest, to what is oldest. Primitive and primordial are indistinguishable. And one can understand that the fascination for the German *Ur* (*Urszene, Urverdrängung, Urfantasie*) led to this conjunction. One can also understand that certain recent translators have a preference for other terms, replacing 'primitive' by 'primordial'[15] to mark the difference. I have already pointed out that the ontogenetic approach ultimately boiled down to making oral fixation (the earliest) responsible for all evils, by suppressing the interest of the fixations at later stages, thus opening the door to all manner of confusions, both in clinical and theoretical work.

In a letter to Marie Bonaparte, dated 16 April 1926,[16] Freud expresses disdain for the earlier prototypes of castration: birth, weaning and sphincter training. To be more exact, he subordinates their significance to castration, even though it comes after them: 'For only the penis carries the colossal narcissistic cathexis ... .' This invites us to reflect on this order referred to by Lacan which relates neither to the time of clocks nor to that of the calendar. Moreover, Freud had already emphasised the value he attached to the notion of primal phantasies, primitive (or primordial) which, in his view, were acquired by heredity. It is more important for us to understand why Freud insisted on endowing them with such a status than to ask ourselves whether or not such a transmission is acceptable in terms of the current state of scientific knowledge. By placing these primitive (or primordial) phantasies in the position of 'key signifiers' (Lacan), governing the entire system of subsequent repressions, Freud revealed how he conceived of the human order. At no stage in his work had he denied the role of heredity – the memory of the species – and he now found it necessary to enlighten us as to the nature of what was transmitted. We learnt, accordingly, that these memory-traces did not concern 'tendencies' or 'predispositions', but structured themes – namely, the primitive (or primordial) scene, the scene of seduction and castration.[17] More specifically, Freud indicated on several occasions in *The Ego and the Id* (1923) and, still later, in his final works (*An Outline of Psychoanalysis* (1940 [1938]), *Moses and Monotheism* (1939)), that phylogenesis was not confined to the contents of the id, and that the superego was deeply marked by it. The way in which the ego-ideal is formed, as a product of expectation, of nostalgia for the father, as a germ forming the basis for religions, has to be linked up with the phylogenetic part of a cultural factor affecting every individual.[18] What was taken as the mere eccentricity of a scientist, the stubbornness of an old man,[19] has proved, on closer reading, to be evidence of a deep concern for the coherence of the theory. We know in any case that a deep gulf would continue to separate Freud and Jung. What has been traced in the id is never expressed directly outside the circuits of experience: the ego has to take it over and experience it itself, on behalf of the individual. But, for the 'key-signifiers' of which I was speaking, whose metaphorical power is considerable, it is as though the minimum of experience resulted in the maximum of effect.

Freud had already expressed a similar idea in his article on narcissism (1914b) in which he reveals the double existence of every individual who serves his own purposes while at the same time remaining subject to the chain of the species in which he is just a link 'against his will, or at least involuntarily'. He holds sexuality to be one of the subject's aims, and, on another level, sees him is 'an appendage to his germ-plasm, at whose disposal he puts his energies in return for a bonus of pleasure. He is the mortal vehicle of a (possibly) immortal substance – like the inheritor of an entailed property, who is only the temporary holder of an estate which survives him.'[20]

If this assertion amounted to little more than a commonplace reflection on the antithesis between the species and the individual, all this would not have been of great interest. In fact, Freud wanted, at all costs, to point up the inadequacy of a strictly individual 'developmental' perspective, of an ontogenetic type. For he himself is his own most severe critic when he remarks that the actual experiences of the subject are not proportionate to their consequences; and that, consequently, an explanation has to be found to account for the disproportion between causes and effects. Finally, we can see Freud distancing himself from any psychological theorisation that puts the subject at its centre, pulling the strings of desire in order to reach his ends. The individual is subjected in two ways. First, because of the very nature of sexuality which he endures more than living it in a personal way; and, secondly, because the individual serves the species – 'putting his energies at its disposal in exchange for a bonus of pleasure' – as a vehicle, a receiving host, whose function is to ensure the suture of generations.

In reality, what Freud thus establishes, which is reminiscent of the diphasism of the individual's sexual evolution in the diachronic dimension, is the existence of a split at the very heart of the synchronic moment. By opposing ontogenesis and phylogenesis, the individual and the species, Freud introduces into the time of the subject another time which is not the same, and which is deployed in an 'elsewhere' where it remains inaccessible. I mean of course the time of memory, the time of the murder of the primitive father, and, finally, the time of the Other. This time of the Other is manifested by the way in which the subject is barred. The action of repression can be recognised in it in the forms of condemnation, refusal, denial, and rejection in the presence of the Other. The Oedipus complex, therefore, is not at the subject's free disposal; it is lived simultaneously with what is going on in the parent in his/her relationship with the child. This is awkwardly called the counter-Oedipus complex, by analogy with the counter-transference. But it must be repeated that the parent's counter-Oedipus complex towards the child is itself only the repetitive scansion of his own Oedipus complex – that which united the parent, when he was still a child, with his own parents.

The Timelessness of the Unconscious

It is now easier to see what is hidden behind the expression of the timelessness of the unconscious. Timelessness, as I have said, refers first of all to the indestructibility of desire. But to say this is not enough. What does not disappear with the effects of time is thus accounted for; but, faced with this timelessness, there remains the question of how it has become temporalised through the memory of the unconscious while continuing to be qualified as timeless. For if it were only a matter of the durability of the unconscious, Freud would have spoken of the eternity of the unconscious and not of its timelessness. In order to speak of timelessness, the question not only has to involve the future as an end, but also the past as an origin. This is why, in this instance, too, the hypothesis of memory-traces is necessary in order to overcome the impasses involved in the onto-genetic point of view. One cannot speak of an origin because, before a phenomenon emerges, before it is actualised, the programme outlined by the memory-traces was already inscribed in the parents' desire. It cannot be said, though, that by reaching back across the generations, one would find an abstract eternity; for the experience of individual actualisation is irreplaceable and necessary, and it has a value that is not simply revelatory but genuinely founding. It is on the basis of this actualisation, grounded in personal experience, that the origin will take effect, and not through a transcendence which has inscribed it as a fatality. Psychoanalysis should, moreover, undoubtedly be concerned with what is most singular about an analysand. This singularity is nonetheless related to the universal. It is not possible to speak of an origin, since this is different from experience which is itself framed by key signifiers. It is not possible to push this origin back to the level of the species, since without its individual actualisation, it is mere virtuality.

Timelessness is a concept, then, which owes its substance to the fact that it not only escapes the problem of being destroyed by time, but also that of being created by time. Timelessness is free of any link with origins just as it is from any link with ends. It characterises the human unconscious because it cuts right through it in the succession of progenitors and their offspring – who, in turn, become progenitors giving birth to other offspring. This is not to say that the category of time is dissolved in the process; however, it complies with the requirements of a model which is just as open and rich as that of space, as revealed by structure, the organisation of which is compatible with ubiquity and heterogeneity, areas through which the signifier passes.

Stretched between a limit that is not an origin and another that is not an end, the unconscious endures. It is thus 'outside time', while at the same time resisting change. The paradox is that, in analytic treatment, this resistance to change in the form of a refusal to be extinguished becomes resistance to the discovery of the signifying organisation. What desires to be, exists as such, even if this being carries within it the germ of its own end, being of non-being. One can see, then, that even in this duration of the unconscious which brushes aside the question of temporality to the point of annulling its effects, we are dealing with a semantic category which eludes the ordinary model of psychic time, since what endures, here seems only to serve its disappearance by being disconnected from being. Once again it is clear that progress in discussing the concept of the unconscious can only be made by taking into account the dialectic of the life drives and the death drives.

Need and Desire: The Order of the Signifier

The strictly ontogenetic perspective often, if not always, goes together with a biological perspective and attempts to use primary needs to explain the genesis and progression of an evolution towards the psychical realm. This approach, taken as a fundamental model, gives rise to a debate about the spirit of the Freudian *opus*. We know that Lacan laid particular stress on the distinction between need and desire. Without straying from the objective I have set myself of studying diachrony in Freud's work, I will attempt to show that the non-coincidence of these two orders is all the more striking in that they are in fact linked.

Here are two propositions by way of illustration:

1. What is created by the unsatisfied need is not cancelled out by satisfying the need.[21]
2. What is created by satisfying the need is not cancelled out by removing the unsatisfied need.

The aim of the first proposition is not to suggest that need is always unsatisfied, but rather that when the situation arises in which a need demands satisfaction, another field is opened up. With the movement whereby an impulse is given – that created by the unsatisfied need – another field opens up which accompanies it; for if this unsatisfied need is to be perceived, it must be signified by means of signs: cries, tears and agitation. Something of the order of the signifier is manifested here, separately. Immediate experience cannot distinguish them as they seem to be so wedded together; but, in fact, they constitute two heterogeneous fields for each other and the vicissitude of each will be different. Whereas the response which appeases the unsatisfied need will make it disappear, the signs, for their part, will have quite a different future: they will be endowed with meaning by the Other who is led to recognise them and to respond to them.

Here the signifier will neither have the function of a gratuitous luxury – the surplus, or leftover, of need – nor that of a transcendence beyond the facts. It will be the agent, the witness of an organisation of another order which will follow its laws while going back over earlier traces. The latter can only organise themselves if it is this status of the signifier as such that is recognised. It will include categories as foreign to need as incompleteness, absence, fragmentation, reversal (into its opposite or against the self), reduplication, and so on. In any case, it will be derived from the experience of unsatisfied need. Even though it has constituted itself along an independent path, the signifier will nonetheless maintain certain relations with need which will leave their mark on it – notably, the imperative and urgent nature which underpins its necessity and accounts for its function which is as fundamental in the symbolic order as need is in the order of life.

As far as the second proposition is concerned, let us see what happens when the adequate response has been given, removing the unsatisfied need. This is not limited to an abolition of tension, where the subject, in a state of repletion, has gorged himself in a sponge-like fashion on the gift of the Other. For now something else appears that had not been expected, namely, pleasure. There is thus a hiatus here between need and pleasure. It might be thought that pleasure appears when the need is satisfied, and often Freud's formulation suggests as much. In fact, relaxation – when unpleasure ceases – is qualitatively different from pleasure. What is important is that this non-equivalence appears at the moment when they coincide. Here again the two orders of phenomena are so closely wedded together that they are indistinguishable. But the appearance of pleasure creates a homologous field to that of the signifier, for with pleasure comes the virtuality of desire. Let us recall Lacan's definition of phantasy – namely, that which makes pleasure fit for desire – and we will then see the connection between the order of the signifier and that of desire.

The ego is founded on pleasure and the possibility it provides of giving birth to desire. Two simultaneous actions are involved here:

on the one hand the ego is revealed to itself as an excentric formation – here the subject is in the movement alternating centring-decentring – and, on the other, the fact of desiring has a retroactive effect, referring the subject to a past desire. It does not simply gather up what was experienced at the time of satisfaction; it creates the order whereby the subject will be led to expect, wish and aspire to renew the experience which surges up within the psyche independently of his will (phantasy). The extinction of the need will be repeated indefinitely thereafter, as pleasure cannot be reduced to an experience of consumption. Pleasure and desire have created the conditions of an organisation in which the subject and the Other respond to each other. The anticipation of the subject, who experiences himself in the condition in which he desires to be desiring, makes him demand something of the Other. By linking up the sign and pleasure, it is desire which allows the signifier to be 'that which represents the subject for another signifier' (Lacan).[22]

The conjunction between the order of the signifier and the order of desire creates the conditions of the *Entzweiung* of the subject and the constitution of both an ideal ego – a nucleus of idealised satisfaction – and an ego ideal, an agency of self-evaluation requiring renunciation through narcissistic self-sufficiency. The field of illusion, the field of the ideal, is also a field of the first fictions of the ego.

The essential point that I have tried to emphasise here is the solidarity and independence between the order of need on the one hand, and the order of the signifier and desire on the other. Their sequential relationship appears to make one proceed from the other, whereas their temporal relationship is characterised by an ambiguity linking them together. But this is what will make them distinctive and guarantee the full development of the effects which characterise the human order, namely, the signifier and desire.

Experience and Meaning

It seems, then, that the relations between the signifier and desire constitute the field in which Freud intended to place himself. And he wanted to generalise this field 'beyond' the realm of individual history in order to give his designs a broader significance, the limits of which coincide with those of humanity. However Freudian I may be, I will not go so far as to maintain that, today, we should follow Freud against the biology of our own time. Nevertheless, we need to reflect on our genetic models in order to get out of the ruts into which our thinking has got bogged down.

The strictly ontogenetic source of inspiration rests on a conception of psychical phenomena which is interested in their historical dating from a point of view that excludes everything which does not originate in the individual. The question 'When?' which haunts investigators in this domain, stems from the same order of problems as the 'Where?' of scientists who try to follow the links in the chain of cerebral organisation-psychic organisation. Now, in *An Outline of Psychoanalysis* (1940 [1938]), Freud insists on the fundamental discontinuity between the two elements of this chain. Are we not justified in supposing, then, that the theoretical model of the unconscious is one of a temporo-spatial experience which, both for time and space, must be subject to such discontinuity?

Discontinuity, that is, in the relation uniting the subject with the species, as well as in the various phases of individual experience. When it is asserted, for instance, that ontogenesis recapitulates phylogenesis – which is a matter for debate – one would not seriously think of asking the question, 'When does phylogenesis begin?' What matters here is to establish a system of correspondences between related values – which thus acquire a coherence that is reinforced by the element of repetition in them – the meaning of which depends on connections being established. The same relationship emerges, does it not, between the vicissitudes of the treatment and the events of the past, both forming part of a whole in which one series can only be understood in the light of the other?

Even if the psychoanalyst remains within the limits of an ontogenetic conception, what characterises the position he adopts is what he chooses to say about it. This, in turn, can only be apprehended in the repetitive relationship, which necessarily involves indirect listening more than direct observation. For what is involved here is not perceived by the senses, but uniquely through meaning, which implies making connections. Is it not the case that, in listening to the patient, the psychoanalyst is looking for raw events, consigned and buried under the influence of repression? An attentive reading of Freud shows that he was indeed looking for historically dated traumas – the contents of the *Case Histories* provide clear evidence of this – but this calls for interpretation. In a letter to Pfister,[23] he wrote: 'All repressions are of *memories*, not of experiences; at most the latter are repressed in retrospect.' There is good reason, therefore, to recall the importance of structuring, as Freud puts it, *nachträglich*, that is, retroactively, which separates the moment of the experience from the moment of signification. Even if one restricts oneself to the strictly ontogenetic register, rejecting the hypothesis that there are memory-traces in the id of experiences that are renewed from generation to generation – a haven of residues, 'of countless egos' says Freud – we will be able to recognise in the space of an individual life the traces left by 'countless egos' as vestiges of memories of experiences repressed retroactively.

To understand this better, it is necessary to acknowledge that experience and signification are not contemporaneous.

I will illustrate this with an exposition based on two propositions:

1. The moment when it occurs is not the moment when it acquires meaning;
2. The moment when it acquires meaning is not apprehended as a present moment but as an act of restrospection through identity and difference.

The moment when it occurs offers nothing other than a possibility of acquiring meaning. This possibility is no doubt loaded with anticipation, but it is usually imposed, suffered passively, or, if it is actively invested, it is an effect that captures the subject, fixing him in the situation. Something is happening. Something else could happen. But not just anything whatsoever, since something is already happening. There is the possibility of moving on to something else. And, in fact, for something else to happen, what has happened must not be completely past. Between what is still happening and what has already happened, something happens which cannot be the advent of what happened after, for this would totally erase the past (which is what happened with the past) but is only an advance, a credit, so to speak, on the account of the past. It is important, moreover, that this past remains in the past; in other words, that it has marked a place with its presence from which it withdraws, leaving traces of its presence there for other occupants who owe something to their antecedents.

Consequently what is going to happen can only be experienced as a sliding towards this erasure through identity or difference – which will be important in that it is not just anything at all that has happened. Rather, it is this identity or this difference which attributes meaning to the past retroactively. But what follows is not all difference or all identity. In the first case, it would abolish the past by annulling it; in the second, it would coincide with it. What happens next involves, then, the coincidence of identity or the gap of difference which can vary between a minimum and a maximum. But for that to happen other operations of identity or difference are necessary. What happens subsequently happens between what and what? Between identities and differences. Thus these countless egos are constitutive of experience, and the meaning which is attributed to them retroactively is never operative during the experience itself, which is only potentially meaningful. Anticipation, some will say, but anticipation from which half of the couple is missing so that the meaning is underlined. There is a clear attempt here to find a way out of an impasse in which continuity and temporality are frequently indistinguishable. The separation between the moment of signification and the moment of the experience – which overlap constantly – by means of spacing and the demarcation of stages, introduces a situation of discontinuity which is necessary for con-stituting any signifying chain; but it also makes identity and difference function in it as concepts and not just as psychic events.

It is plain that any attempt at dating the vicissitudes of develop-ment leaves aside the question of the relations between the signifier and desire. In a letter to Fliess (no. 125), Freud seems to have abandoned his initial project of making a parallel between the date of a trauma and the different types of neuroses.[24] Likewise, it is no longer relevant to ask oneself if, at such and such an age, a child can reasonably be affected – as psychoanalysts claim – by what is happening around him. The moment of signification is often only fully reached in the signifying chain experienced in the transference which allows for a constructive[25] rather than re-constructive inter-pretation. For, as Freud insists, it is not a question of discovering what is present, intact, hidden under the cloak of neurosis, but of constructing a meaning which, hitherto, has never emerged in its meaningful form.

The Subject and Concatenation

The idea that the subject, in the chain, corresponds to the constitu-tion of the chain by virtue of the movement of representation and exclusion – something J.A. Miller[26] has recognised in the logic of the signifier – is even more applicable to history. If history is not the proud totalisation of a subject who is always in possession of his means and master of his ends – which also involves being the master of his history – nor an incoherent wandering or perseverance with a tradition, and if, on the other hand, this logic is engendered through the act of enunciation, constituting the subject in his relationship to discourse, then a new field lies ahead of us. Although he does not adopt it himself, Lévi-Strauss makes reference[27] to the notion of process, in distinction to that of structure. He establishes the difference between them from the observer's point of view: the latter can only uncover the structure by remaining outside it, whereas the process is conceived as being closely linked with the way in which temporality is experienced by an individual who necessarily finds he is its captive. From the psychoanalytic point of view, neither position is satisfying. Here it is worth recalling the diphasism of sexuality, because it provides an excellent example of Freud's way of thinking. In it we can find discontinuity and spacing, combination and system (since it is possible to establish a correspondence between infantile sexuality and adult sexuality), insistence and scansion (which are different from preserving a tradition or from taking up again a meaning whose sense will only be revealed at the end of time); and one can even observe the transition that is necessary for constituting this diphasism via chains in which there is a succession of erogenous objects (breast, faeces, penis).

As in the syntagmatic chain, causality is at work there in the same way owing to the repression of the subject. The question we now have to ask is: Who represses, and what is it that is repressed? The answer is certainly to be found at the level of the concept of repression; that is, at the level of a model which takes the unconscious into account.

The idea that the subject is constituted as a product of a repression retroactively, that is, after he has himself been repressed by the constitution of the signifying chain, is not easy to understand. And yet this is how it should be understood.

Retrogressive Over-Investment

The lack of simultaneity between experience and meaning explains the fact that the loss of the object occurs between the two, and that subsequently a work of difference and identity will occur. This notion of object-loss needs supplementing, however, with that of the erasure of the trace, as described by Freud in his short article on the Mystic Writing-Pad.[28] Whether it is Freud's model of desire or the model of lifting repression that is in question – and here one could point to an analogous montage for other key points in Freudian theory – what happens to the subject is never simply the effect of a first manifestation, without antecedents. On the contrary, it is by going back over paths that have already been created as a result of over-investing an existing groove, so to speak, that meaning will emerge. Desire, like reminiscence, is above all a movement towards, which, taking a direction that is frequently retrogressive, emerges along the path of facilitation which goes back over earlier traces. At the very moment this re-inscription occurs, this movement has a double revelatory power. It is 'contemporary' because it is a change that is occurring now, whereby the subject constitutes himself in the signifying chain – spoken or unspoken – and yet 'non-contemporary' because this actualisation revives what was 'already-there' which, in some cases, has always been there or, at least, was there at some point in the past. As in the accommodation of binocular vision, it makes the contemporary and non-contemporary coincide in order to constitute the way of looking. Even the anticipatory element in phantasy, which seems to be directed towards a desired future, can also be envisaged as depending on an operation which involves going back over earlier traces. This conception, linking experience with traces that are already present, which places the accent on re-finding the object, on representation, and the return of the repressed, is inseparable from a process which partakes as much of perception-consciousness as it does of the inscription in the unconscious. It only appears to be an operation of connection, linking and suture because the initial recording is subject to a disconnection, a separation, a cut. In effect, Freud understands this initial investment as a discontinuous process, perception being accompanied by an investment of small quantities of energy emitted periodically, gradually losing their conscious quality with the cessation of present perception, carried along by the perceptual flow and transmitting their excitation to the unconscious. It is now clear that signification consists in re-establishing the initial situation along the 'inverse trajectory' of this process.

If, with each operation, the trace of the representation is erased, what does the perceptual operation involve? Can it be argued that, even if there is no longer a trace of the representation, there is, at least, a trace of the investment? Is it necessary to ask ourselves if this charge will be affective (that is to say, that the increase or lowering of its level of investment will be accompanied by unpleasure or pleasure)? Can it not simply be regarded as a newly created path which, once it has been taken, creates the conditions of a state of preparation or alert? It would thus pave the way for a surge of anticipation which, as one might expect, is always to be seen in relation to a past that has been more or less constituted. It is the increase of the threshold of this fragmented functioning of 'small quantities of energy', to use Freud's expression, which justifies the disproportionate relation between a weak stimulus and the extraordinary development to which it can lead. Proust had to write fifteen volumes in order to be able to regain lost time, evoked by the taste of a madeleine. One must also remember that this time was regained only to be lost again definitively in view of what the reader is able to surmise about the writer's imminent death. I mean, of course, the death of the writer and not the author – a death which occurred at a time when he was just beginning to see how he ought to write the work which was the aim of this search, even though it had already been written and read by us, making its end and its beginning coincide.

Primitive repression is a counter-investment. It is the reverse side of the protective shield[29] which absorbs excitations coming from outside, acting in a similar way by setting up a barrier against the irruption of too much repressed material. But it is also a pattern, texture, structure in which all the repressed material of after-repressions, of secondary repressions will be caught, as in a spider's web. This shutter-like functioning will act as an appeal and as a mirror. But it is a shutter which opens and closes like a contracting pupil which filters what impinges on it from outside, thereby awakening what is already inscribed, or what, from within, resurges as if it came from the outside via the projection which imposes on the subject the return of what is foreclosed in him, revealing it to him this time in incandescent letters. In this gradual process of registration which inscribes and erases at the same time, though in two different spaces – that of the unconscious and that of consciousness – it is as though a certain dispersed field, namely, the structure of the subject, had to be preserved. This field is free to attract towards it representations which it then deflects towards its periphery so as to remain available for new perceptual information; and it is ready to reflect only the structure which solicits the return of fresh inscriptions, which, in their turn, are erased and dispatched to an elsewhere where they enter into a relationship with other inscriptions.

The Senses and Meaning

Freud's allocation of perception to consciousness and of memory to the unconscious calls for further remarks. Nothing essential can be learned from an approach that hopes for greater efficiency from our sense organs. Reality – external as much as internal – will always remain unknowable for us. In contradistinction to perceptions, the scientific approach has abandoned the investigation of the world through the senses as a means of acquiring knowledge. It has accepted, so to speak, the discontinuity between experience and meaning, as well as the discontinuity between the elements of meaning, and only authorises the discovery of connections and dependent relations which are present in the external world. The internal world of thought reflects them or reproduces them more or less faithfully. These assertions, which look as though they might have been written by a structuralist, can in fact be read in Freud's dogmatic testament *An Outline of Psychoanalysis* (1940 [1938]). Moreover, during these same final years of his life, Freud was to draw a parallel between the different quality of the subject's relationship with the mother and the father. Whereas evidence for the bond with the mother is attested by the senses, the relation with the father and his role in procreation can only be established by deduction. And Freud concluded that humanity had made a significant advance towards intellectuality when it decided to accord more value to deductive reasoning than to the evidence of the senses. Thus, if the first relationship uniting the infant with the primordial object is that which binds him to his mother, the father is already memory – that is, he is present in the mother's desire because the child is the one she had hoped to receive from her own father (or from her mother) during her childhood; or again, because the father is only present as an absence between the mother and her child, an absence which will echo the real absence of the mother as she leaves the child in order to be with him. He will have a similar function therefore to the barring effect of repression which institutes the cut in the subject, identifying him with the agent who has erased the trace and, in particular, those traces connected with the death-wish towards the father which, when it is given expression, echoes the 'always already-there' (*le toujours déjà-là*) of the murder of the primitive father.

Truth, Murder, History

Who can remain insensitive to the paradox that at the end of his most controversial work – a work in which his deductive reasoning was at its most hazardous and the ideas he was defending against the scientific knowledge of his time quite fantastic[30] – Freud claimed to be the champion of *truth*? And when Lacan opposes knowledge and truth, are we not made to feel somewhat uneasy? What point is being made here? Perhaps that the issue is not really one of defending a truth or of having recourse to the simplistic Pirandellism implicit in certain structural[31] conceptions which say, more or less, 'to each his own truth', making it necessary to establish the conditions under which it is possible to gain access to the truth.

It might be relevant to say a few words here about myth, especially as this question has been the subject of a debate between Lévi-Strauss and Ricoeur/Sebag. How does the psychoanalytic explanation stand in relation to the oppositions which have emerged from this debate, which have been clearly summarised by Sebag?[32] Hermeneutics and structural studies differ with regard to the position of the observer: hermeneutic research operates from within the field it measures, 'that which leads it to recognise the law of its object as its own'. Understanding this object through interpretation, which itself is based on a tradition, serves, says Sebag, 'stretching the terms a little', to help the subject understand himself. On the contrary, someone who uses the structural method decentres himself in relation to his culture. Ethnological 'asceticism' leads to the abolition, insofar as this is possible, of the observer's subjectivity. Psychoanalysis, therefore, should adopt a position between 'meditative thinking' (Ricoeur) and science.

The function of myth can also be analysed from another angle. In the context of meditative thinking, which does not hide its connections with religion, what is expected of the revelations of myth is a construction of man, whereas its structural study – thanks to the dismantling of myths – coincides with the theoretical project of Lévi-Strauss, that is, of 'dissolving man'.

Is our only choice, as psychoanalysts, between a discourse that aims at the total repression (which is impossible, moreover) of the signified, confining us to the purely combinative system of unconscious logic – which, in spite of its name, remains far removed from what Freud meant by it – and one in which knowledge is subordinated to revelation? Is there no place between the symbolic as a system and the symbolic as hierophany?

There is a growing tendency, nowadays, to attribute psychoanalysis, and Freud, with a demystifying function. It is suggested that the Freudian operation of healthy reduction, through a vigorous process of stripping down, reveals a truth that is more difficult to accept, yet more lucid. True enough, but one must be careful here. It is not difficult to see that most of the time what happens after this recognition of debt is that one inevitably sets about demystifying the demystifier – ad infinitum.

This is quite noticeable in the domain of myths – personal or collective – and is especially striking inasmuch as it is widely claimed that the explicative point of view has been abandoned. Myths are not of the same order as history; they have no explicative value – and, for structuralists, they only have one with respect to their function of formalisation. Freudian thought, which, it is true, is very often criticised on this point, does not, on the contrary, abandon the explicative point of view. But its essential difference with hermeneutic thinking is that it does not look for the meaning of the myth in what the latter contains or affirms, but in its link with the unconscious. Conversely, structural thinking is only interested in the manner in which the elements of a myth are arranged, without reference to their meaning. Psychoanalysis endeavours to interpret myths and their logic, taking into consideration what seems to be distorted, omitted, barred and censored. The dilemma between meaning and form is thus transcended, for meaning and form are introduced as mutilated, truncated and reorganised in order to mask this elision. It may well be, then, that the truth of myth does not depend on its being reconstituted in its totality, reconstructed and even constructed, perhaps for the first time. Rather, it is to be sought along the road which has made it possible to rediscover the paths of distortion, omission, barring, and censoring. Meaning should not be seen here independently of its distortions; it is itself a veil, which is only accessible through the operation of unveiling.

This is, I think, what sets the psychoanalytic position apart, beyond the dilemma between hermeneutic and structural positions. Unveiling should be regarded as different from demystification. From this point of view, truth remains suspended and can never be attained. Only those paths that allow us to orient ourselves in the direction of truth should be followed.

The principle of identity long formed the basis on which all truth was supposed to be established. With Freud, non-identity with oneself reveals the truth of desire better than identity alone. The unconscious reveals the diversity of non-identity with oneself. The concept of castration embraces forms that are apparently very far removed from weaning, sphincter training, or castration proper, and places under a common sign breast, faeces, and the penis as the concept of the 'little thing which can be detached from the body'. One can find more fruitful heuristic hypotheses than the sacrosanct notion of identity. This gives us an idea, then, of some of the difficult questions that arise when an unconscious concept is set in relation to truth.

Non-identity with oneself serves as a mask, veiling desire. It is by analysing the paths that demand takes in the transference that desire is revealed. By addressing itself to the Other, demand reveals in the same movement that, if truth is the truth of desire, it is the Other who possesses the code for deciphering it at the same time as it discovers the object capable of responding to it. The truth of the desire of the Other is its law which, by fixing its rules and its barriers on desire, maintains the suture of generations.

At this juncture a new horizon emerges for our reflection. If the truth of desire echoes the Other, and if desire and the law echo each other, prohibiting the satisfaction of desire and permitting only the detours of demand, how is the meaning of this captive truth to be understood? It only constitutes the subject in so far as he refuses to make this renunciation; that is, insofar as he refuses to accept this barrier and to submit to it. And it is only revealed through transgression – a transgression of the law which prescribes the places and territories in the family setting. In psychoanalysis, it is the transgression of the subject who, like Oedipus, wants to know. And this is the only way in which knowledge can be acquired. Had Oedipus not killed his father at Pothnies, had he not shared his mother's bed in Thebes, and, had he not convoked all those who possessed the scattered fragments of what the oracle had to say, we would never have known what the law of our desire was.

Difference is efficacious; it alone recreates the gap that will push us, unsuccessfully, to try and reduce it completely. This failure will, nonetheless, lead us along the paths of truth.

Synchrony, Diachrony – Structure, History

Finally, we should mention the new thinking on the relations between structure and history. Greimas[33] points out that the

Saussurean position rests on a common denominator 'chronic' which is divided into syn-chronic and dia-chronic; and, for him, the way to avoid getting involved in this impasse is to adopt an a-chronic point of view. In this respect, structure retains its meaning without prejudging its spatial or temporal dimension. Structure may be said to elucidate or govern both synchrony and diachrony equally. One could postulate that structure is always the result of an inscription, which is all the more revealing in that it bears the marks of the distortions of the text. Structure is a form of writing, as Jacques Derrida's recent suggestions suggest.[34] In my view, this retention of the difference constituted by the trace only takes on its full meaning when understood as a trace that is always evanescent, always in danger of being erased, and always, at the very least, barred. The fact that here it is once again constitutive of memory is important, because in it we encounter the figure of the dead father, so much does this memory insist on being recognised in the effects of scansion of the signifier. Consequently, it will be less the safeguard of an established text than a movement towards, a facilitation (*Bahnung*), which makes it possible not only to discover what has been repressed, but also to form the latent outline of a writing which, before it can be read and heard, requires a hand and thought to formulate it or simply give it form. It is there, awaiting its accession.

Nevertheless, the irreversibility of the order of the diachronic approach will remain unresolved: the irreversibility of the order of generations; the irreversibility of the succession of the objects of desire; the irreversibility of repressions, albeit after the event; and, finally, the irreversibility of human progress from life to death.

This discursive analysis of diachrony in Freud, which has taken us a long way from our starting point, must now be brought to a conclusion. If the truth is to be found at the junction between synchrony and diachrony, what this interface reveals for the psychoanalyst is the presence of meaning (as symbol and direction) insofar as it is linked to the constraint (repression) which obliges it to transform and disguise itself. On the one hand, a constraint of synchrony, showing that the subject is indeed part of the ensemble which constitutes him at the heart of the links that unite him with his progenitors, and, on the other, a constraint of diachrony in that nothing can reverse the direction of the passage from birth to death, of the condition of childhood to the more or less accepted condition of parenthood. If the removal of one mask is not simply to result in the revelation of another, more than one operation will doubtless be necessary. While it is illusory to entertain the hope of ever encountering the face of truth, the surprise, by means of which the sign of such an encounter can be recognised, will be, during one of these stages, one of coming across a mirror that looks at the subject.

2 The Primal in Psychoanalysis (1991)*

'Your parents – do you know of them?'[1] Tiresias hurled at Oedipus, thereby repeating unwittingly, and years later, the words of a drunken man who had once called Oedipus a 'putative father' at the Corinthian court. Tiresias thus set in motion again the *primum movens* that had once made Oedipus leave hurriedly for Delphi to consult the oracle. This question of origins, which Tiresias was raising afresh, was uttered just when Oedipus was once again waiting for an answer from Delphi about the cause of the plague in Thebes and the remedy to be applied to the City. So we are already faced with the surprising observation that the enigma of the primal emerges through repetition. But it is also, perhaps, just when certain indications suggest that a solution to the enigma is at hand that the question of its mystery engenders the most improbable myth. On learning from the Corinthian messenger of the death of Polybus, and also that he was not in fact his child at all, Oedipus initially felt a premature sense of relief and went into a trance, declaring that he was the child of Fortune, perhaps the son of Pan or even – who knows – of Apollo Loxias. His thirst to resolve the question of his origins made him momentarily intoxicated with the primal phantasy, delaying for a while the obligation to drink the bitter potion of truth.

It was the desire to know that had driven Oedipus to consult the oracle at Delphi; and it was the fear of finding out, just as he sensed he was on the point of discovering what he was looking for, which made him invent this divine origin – though he had just been disappointed to learn from Jocasta that he was not of royal stock! Sophocles, a dialectician of tragic action, would prophesy through the mouth of Tiresias: 'This day will show your birth and your destruction.'[2]

'In my beginning is my end', T.S. Eliot was to write twenty-five centuries later, showing us that the phantasy about origins is not

* First published as 'L'originaire dans la psychanalyse' in *La narrazione delle origine*, Sagittari Laterza, 1991, pp. 133–79.

only about returning to the beginning. It also concerns our relations with death.

As we know, the Oedipus complex not only marks the question of the origins of neurosis, but also that of the origins of psychoanalysis. At its birth, psychoanalysis encountered seduction – in its strongest sense, since nothing less than the threat of incest was involved.[3] The paternal accusation was heavy indeed. For Freud, it even implicated his own father.[4] Was it simply to exculpate him that Freud then decided that enough was enough surely not all fathers are perverse! – and opted in favour of another hypothesis? By turning the projector on sexuality, Freud was ready to recognise the accident of seduction – the trauma – but not generalised perversion. He looked for the cause of this generalisation elsewhere, that is, in the phantasy of seduction. What is not explained, though, is the reason for the choice of phantasy as a support for this generalisation. That was to come later. Let it be said right away that the passages that are frequently cited about the relinquishing of his *neurotica* do not imply the abandonment of trauma as the eventual cause of neurosis, but the theory of trauma – that is, the notion that a traumatic aetiology exists in all cases. Throughout his work, and each time he recalled his famous turning point of 1897, Freud constantly repeated that it would nonetheless be a mistake to conclude that invoking the presence of trauma is always groundless. On the contrary, it is much more frequent than one would suspect. In short, trauma is conjunctural, accidental, aleatory; phantasy is structural, regular and constant. Trauma may exist more frequently than one thinks; in this case, it 'realises' phantasy.

Let us return to Oedipus: if tragedy is the retroactive effect of a trauma,[5] then myth, on the collective level, is to be considered as the counterpart to phantasy[6] on the individual level. As for the complex, it is the theory of it – in other words the articulated, thought out ensemble, incarnated more or less completely in the random events of a singular history. Once again, the Oedipal paradigm will have proved useful. I will come back to it again later on in my exposition. It is not just an illustration. Inasmuch as it exemplifies the problematic of origins, it inaugurates a mutation. After Freud, the status of the subject was definitively changed. It was no longer possible to refer to a transcendental Cogito, the ultimate and inalienable pedestal of subjectivity. Every subject is necessarily defined by his relationship with his 'primal' parental images: he is united with those who have given him life and linked with them by bonds of incest and parricide, sexuality and death. Through his sexuality he manifests the desire to repeat the act which led to his birth; by harbouring a death-wish towards the father he removes the obstacle which could prevent him from doing so, but this in turn exposes him to a threat from which his desire does not retreat. For contemporary biology, sexuality and death go hand in hand; sexual differentiation destines the individual for death. It puts an end to the indefinite perpetuation of a fissiparous monosexuality but, on the other hand, establishes the regime of alterity through difference.

What was modelled in the species by biology, and rewritten in its own way and for its own purposes by the psyche, was to have repercussions on reflection, after the birth of psychoanalysis. 'I' can only be defined in its relation to its origins, and therefore to what is primal. Such a relation, as we shall see, is only conceivable retrospectively, and shows, as Freud says, that each individual is an Oedipus 'in germ' in his childhood. The primal is thus also necessarily related to what is potentiality and accomplishment, raising the question of knowing what paths unite them. Origin of the subject-origin of desire. And yet, to return to the case of Oedipus, the material out of which Sophocles' work was formed – and we have a better idea of this as a result of Marie Delcourt's work[7] – was only a collection of scattered mythemes without any necessary link between them. There was nothing at the outset to indicate that the most famous legend in Ancient Greece was composed of such apparently arbitrary elements. When the intuitive knowledge of a tragedian took possession of it, he legitimised this popular celebrity and created, moreover, quite apart from the spectacle, a work for the mind – a theory 'in the making', resisting the numerous logical inconsistencies that could be detected in it in order to arrive at a truth,[8] the source of infinite commentaries. Myth, tragedy, theory and ... truth, these are the protagonists that will be constantly encountered as we proceed with this study of primal phantasies.

Warning

Just as I am on the point of laying before you my inquiries into primal phantasies, I find I am faced with a certain difficulty. The process of reflection that has governed my writing has constantly pulled me from one pole to the other. Sometimes the findings relate to experience deriving from the psychoanalysis of children or observations of them; and sometimes they are products of the psychoanalysis of adults. Both form the common basis of clinical experience, the irreplaceable source of theoretical work. But to the relatively reliable knowledge which everyone can verify (while enriching it or contesting it), will soon be added unverifiable hypotheses giving rise to controversies that are entirely predictable. What is more, in order to establish the relation between clinical findings and the hypotheses advanced, it is necessary, when returning to Freud's pioneering, primal text, to analyse his reasoning, its innuendoes and epistemological assumptions. This being so, this ensemble needs to be contrasted with our contemporary experience and the ways in which it adds to Freud's experience. The positions held by Freud are likely to be relativised in the process. By the same token, it cannot be maintained that the present state of our knowledge (clinical and scientific) leaves Freud's theses intact; nor that his epistemology is the same as our own. The theoretical points of divergence still need to be identified. But why must each theoretical exposition be preceded by this reference – this reverence, some will say, to Freud? The question is worth asking in relation to the theme of origins. We maintain the same relation to the Freudian corpus as we do towards what is primal in our thinking. Should we say our primal phantasy? There is no need to be ashamed of saying this since Freud himself described his metapsychology as a phantasy.[9] But a certain aspect of the relationship of psychoanalysts to Freud, which smacks of an attitude redolent of that held towards religious dogma, has come in for criticism too often for us to simply disregard it.

I have already had occasion to explain the three aspects characterising Freud's relation to psychoanalysis. He was the founder of the discipline that did not exist before him. He was also its most original thinker, and the coherence, depth, and inventiveness of his theories remain the most powerful of any to date. Finally, the essential aspects of his thought form the basis of an explicatory system, by its reference to a past that is considered, retrospectively, as the primal origins of the subject, his desire, the psyche and so on. These three aspects weigh heavily upon Freud's posterity and the future of psychoanalysis. A discipline often exists before it has been officially named. Its birth simply constitutes the point when it becomes conscious of its object, and a delimitation of the aims that will emerge as it develops. Lamarck baptised biology; he did not create it. Nor is Lamarck considered by his successors as the greatest biologist. Few psychoanalysts today would contest that Freud is the greatest of all psychoanalysts. As a rule, whoever is considered as 'the greatest' is only born after the discipline has already been in existence for a certain time. Though his value is recognised, he does not have the status of a pioneer and will occupy the position of a link in the chain – a very important one, no doubt – but little more than a link. Freud's case is thus a singular one. Nevertheless, electing a biologist as 'the greatest', whether it be Darwin, Claude Bernard, or Pasteur, does not imply that one continues to adhere to his ideas. The recognition obtained is for the progress that his works have made possible, and does not imply an eternal adhesion to his ideas. How is it, then, that even if Freud is recognised as being 'the greatest' psychoanalyst, one still encounters Freudians whose fidelity to the master is such that they think that his ideas remain true in their totality? Even though one is willing to accept that certain of Freud's views are debatable, and even outdated, by continuing to adhere to them, one is paying tribute to the complexity of the founder of psychoanalysis, even if certain points of detail are abandoned. The example of the primal illustrates this rather well. Freud's theory of origins is only intelligible if it is re-included in the ensemble of which it is an integral part – an ensemble that is itself highly contradictory (theory of development, the timelessness of the unconscious, retroactive meaning (*après coup*),[10] repetition-compulsion, phylogenetic memory-traces, and so on). Today, it is clear that this ensemble has not been the object of sufficient exegesis. Its different components have not been theorised, nor have the links between them and their actualisation been examined. Moreover, one tendency (the developmental point of view) has prevailed over all the others, striving, in fact, to present itself as a necessary and sufficient theorisation of the problem of temporality in psychoanalysis. The semantic and epistemological richness of the heuristically fruitful contradictions of the Freudian corpus has been eliminated in favour of a psychological empiricism. 'If you want to resolve the problem of origins, examine their appearance in the chronology of development.' That is to say, go back to the source and do not be satisfied with what the adult tells you *a posteriori* about childhood. Using observation, go back to a point in the past concerning which there is no inscription that will ever permit you to rediscover it through memory. In this way, it is said, you will have more chance of arriving at exact conclusions. To my mind, the examination of the primal should be based on a reflective approach which endeavours, as far as is possible, to take full account of the complexity of the object of study, even if this means disregarding a verisimilitude whose criterion of truth only exists in relation to the rationality of evidence which is based on what is observable, or what is inferred from it; and, in spite of the fact that the hypothesis of the unconscious invalidates what can be achieved by examining sensory data.

It now becomes clearer, perhaps, why this question of the phantasy of origins makes us oscillate between examining facts that can be most readily observed by any psychoanalyst and the most hazardous speculations that will be rejected out of hand by scientists. At this theoretical level, the discussion will draw us into the conflict between those points of view that can reasonably be accepted and the most fragile dialectical constructions. The latter may, nonetheless, be nearer the truth than those that lay claim to verisimilitude, because they try to articulate a greater number of parameters that are not visible on the surface.

Infantile Sexual Theories and Family Romance

At the frontier of this theoretical field, there is a coincidence between what comes first in Freud's work, something that can be most directly observed by the psychoanalyst looking at childhood, and that which is satisfied with an explanation which can be provided by any ordinary knowledge of children, without a lot of needless speculation. Here we are in the specific domain of the phantasy of origins – as distinct from the primal phantasy.

Shortly after the publication of the *Three Essays on the Theory of Sexuality* (1905), the analysis of little Hans plunged Freud into the eternally surprising freshness of the questions which children ask about the world and living entities. Parents, and particularly mothers, have always been familiar with the age when children ask the question 'Why?' indefinitely brushing aside the pseudo-clarification of each attempt by the adult to answer the question. Freud discovered that the main object of infantile curiosity was the question, 'Where do children come from?' along with the corollary questions related to sexual difference, conception and birth. This gave him the opportunity, then, of writing 'On the Sexual Theories of Children' (1908). Would it be stating the obvious to point out that the child of sexual theories has to wait until he reaches an age when the capacities for imaginary synthesis and for the logic of phantasy have been acquired? The sexual theory cannot therefore be equated with a spontaneous activity of phantasy welling up from libidinal functioning. While I do not contest that it can be preceded by a psychical activity of this sort, the age of sexual theories (which is also the age of the Oedipus complex) implies accession to the beginnings of a conception of causality. It could be said that this acquired capacity, which may have benefited from the stimulus provided by these questionings, is trying hard to apply itself to a domain where clarity is lacking. What is the point of such theories if not to look for the cause of the enigmas protected by the parents? Freud is quite justified in calling them 'theories' because their function is to reassure the psyche against the danger of incoherence, that is to say, of chaos, incomprehensibility, and unpredictability. But why fear such dangers? Probably, because of the mystery and lies of parents. However, although this was more pronounced in earlier generations, even the most enlightened parents (among whom Hans' parents may be counted) respond to their children's insistent questions with answers which are less fantastic but, when one looks at them carefully, still contain many more or less intentional ambiguities. The most famous example, to take but one, is that given by Hans' mother.

Mother: 'What are you staring like that for?'
Hans: 'I was only looking to see if you'd got a widdler, too.'
Mother: 'Of course, didn't you know that?'

Nothing is dissimulated here. Only, the lie is there, too, by omission. There can be no doubt that Hans wants to say implicitly: 'a widdler *like mine*'. This being so, the mother's response, which should have been: 'yes, but not like yours', means: 'We are the same' and constitutes a denial of sexual difference. This passage, which has often been commented on, is dissociated from what immediately precedes it, when Hans asks his father if he, too, has a widdler. The answer he gets is, 'Yes, of course.' There has been a tendency to overlook the child's reaction: 'But I've never seen it when you undress.' In short, faced with this problem of the difference between the sexes which activates his intellect, Hans cannot rely on perception. Though he should be able to see his father's penis, he cannot see it (the child's negative hallucination or the father's dissimulation); and, though he should notice that his mother has no penis, he doubts its inexistence, since he puts the same question to both parents, without being able to rely on what he can see with his eyes. In other words, the referent 'penis' cannot be apprehended by the senses alone. The idea that all individuals have a penis has been contested by those writers who wish to stress that feminine sexuality follows its own specific pathways. It would seem however that, in the case of a girl, the specific nature of her development probably leads her to imagine the existence of this feminine penis later; and also because she has to look for an explanation for its absence. It is thus a retroactive 'theory' that is involved here. It is rarely missing, even if the point of departure and the moment of arrival are different. For the question raised by the difference between the sexes concerns the origin of the female sexual organs – there being no question about the origin of the male sexual organ, perhaps on account of its visibility. It is the phantasy of castration which provides the answer, over-determined as it is by the source of pleasure obtained by the child through the penis or clitoris. It is the theory of castration, therefore, which 'explains' the female sexual organs.

Once again it is the enigma of female (or even maternal) sexuality that leads to the construction of sexual theories relative to conception. The verb 'to conceive' is common to both engendering and understanding. Understanding is about grasping the nature of the causality behind the birth of things and thoughts. Engendering involves putting this causality into action.

One is tempted to see a link between the sexual theories of children and the 'antisexual' theories of adults (stork, cabbage, and their modern versions, 'seeds', which, for a child, have nothing to do with sexuality). Except that certain examples – for instance, Melanie Klein's son, who preferred the theory of the stork related by the neighbour to his mother's detailed explanations, which did not fail to make her angry – suggest that the need of children to be enlightened goes hand in hand with a fear of being enlightened and a preference for fairy-tale explanations. The primitive scene is thus constantly interpreted – without exception – as an act of violence and aggression, but never of love. Is this not because there is nothing more intolerable for the child (of both sexes) than to know that the mother obtains pleasure from someone else, and, above all, in a way which it is not possible for him to understand or provoke? It is not easy to accept that the mother loves someone else more than oneself; and, even less easy to imagine what this form of love may be like. Similar questions arise in connection with birth. We know that the explanations given as to how the baby comes to be inside the mother's body leave us perplexed with regard to how it comes out. If defecation is the most common solution (cf. Hans), others are based on an imaginary analogy (between the breasts, under the armpit, through the navel, and so on). Moreover, the cloacal theory has effects upstream, as it were: if birth is like defecation, then conception may be likened to feeding. Here, the sexual theory concerns the structure of the female body. It is the boy's question about his mother. And the daughter? Does she have the same problems? In a different way, no doubt, but she can scarcely escape the issue of the absence of the mother's penis, and even less, since she is directly concerned by them, the mysteries surrounding the conception and birth of children.

The triptych described by Freud, namely, the attribution of a penis to human beings of both sexes, the primitive scene, and conception modelled on sadistic coitus, that is, giving birth via the anus, is very coherent. This, then, is what can be said about these phantasies of origins:

(a) they designate the central domain of the unknown and throw light on its mobilising role for the intellect (the difference between the sexes, conception and birth);

(b) they concern the subject's own sexuality in relation to parental sexuality, within an implicit relationship of historical generation;

(c) they reduce the possible phantasies to a small number which are inter-related and united by a bound meaning;

(d) via phantasy, they have an etiological value: these are the theories of origins;

(e) they constitute a mixture of what is true and false. The truth resides in discovering what is in question: namely, sexuality; what is false becomes attached to the phantasised elaboration owing to a shortage of facts of reality and the barely restrained development of imaginary beliefs related to the pleasure–unpleasure principle. As such, they enact an imaginary anatomy, physiology, and psychology, but bring into play logical mechanisms (causality of pregnancy and birth, as well as sexual difference, castration, and denial of the vagina, and so on);

(f) they are the matrix of perverse, neurotic, and psychotic solutions owing to the defensive elaborations they provoke; and the latter do not escape the logic of denial, disavowal, repression, fore-closure, and so on, either.

The phantasies of origins constitute models of historical explanation: they say 'why', rather like myths which also say 'how things used to be'. One can understand how these theories provide the basis for the conception of the 'primacy of the phallus' defended by Freud. But it seems to me that their value resides, above all, in the fact that the causality of origins is, and can only be, a bodily phantasy about the body and about other bodies, including those of the parents from whom we originate. It is a bodily phantasy because of the pleasure that is felt when sexuality is activated; it is a phantasy about the body based on questions that are connected with the emergence of its own pleasure; and finally, it is a phantasy about bodies in that there is allusion to the feminine and masculine incarnated by the parents. What is experienced, perceived, and imagined, converges in the construction of thought, the source of all theorisation. Linked to the child's own pleasure is the implicit question of parental pleasure (same? different?), as well as their judgement on infantile pleasure.

Observation plays a part in this production of phantasy. But we have noticed that the child's perception is often subject to his desire (or to his anxieties). Perception stimulates the enigma more than it resolves it. It gets the psychic quest going. That the child grows in the mother's womb is something that can easily be accepted. And yet the analyst is always struck by the amnesia concerning the mother's pregnancies preceding the birth of younger brothers and sisters. But how does the child enter and how does he come out? The situation here is contrary to that found in chess manuals where only the opening and closing moves can be theorised, but not those in the middle. Where infantile sexual theories are concerned, it is the opening and closing moves that are the most problematic.

The status of sexuality is highly ambiguous. One cannot fail to notice a strong colouring by anality in these theories. The hypothesis that a woman possesses a penis – a penis she is said to have lost – leads us, it is true, to conceive of the primal scene as a castration of the mother by the father, but also as an anal penetration (hence the frequency of representations *a tergo*), just as the act of giving birth is supposed to occur through the anus. The other conceptions of giving birth can probably be attributed to secondary repressions or displacements.

An enormous psychic work is accomplished in this activity of theorisation. It links up observations relative to the nudity of the female body, its modifications during puberty and, eventually during pregnancy, and to what may have been perceived or guessed about the parents' sexual relations, etc. But, above all, such an activity necessitates an elaboration of the data observed, a synthesis of what is seen, heard and felt in one's own body, of what has been imagined and rationalised, similar to that which has been apprehended intuitively, raising criticisms about the shortcomings or indefensible contradictions of the parents' discourse. These theories are already an intellectual activity, though their source is to be found in phantasies and libidinal impulses. But even at this level a question arises. Let's not cease to be children and let's ask the question: Why? Why, indeed, does the profusion of phantasies make it possible to group them together under the umbrella of certain phantasies that seem to have the property of organising the others? What should their power of attraction be attributed to?

Not all sexual theories are related to origins, nor is everything that pertains to origins expressed by a sexual theory. The same is true of the family romance, which is necessarily connected with the phantasy of origins since it drives us to look for other parents – generally, more illustrious ones. Freud made a shrewd and penetrating analysis of the reasons for this. If the most frequent motive is to be found in the search for consolation for the feeling that one has lost the love of a parent who has been severe, the family romance can also remove the guilt surrounding certain desires by modifying the relation of kinship that one has with a parental object. But what can the family romance of a prince be?

Whereas in the sexual theories it is bodily functions, and the eroticism connected with them, which are surrounded in mystery, in the family romance it is social identities which form the content of the phantasy. In the former, the body is the stage on which the acts of imaginary sexuality are played out. And it is these 'scenes' which will give rise, when they are short-circuited by repression, to conversion hysteria. The 'social' status of the people concerned by infantile sexual theory plays no role. The only thing that counts is what connects the child's body with that of his parents. In this sense, the sexual theory is more 'fundamental' than the family romance. The family romance is a fable: the characters in it are defined by their legendary attributes – king-father, queen-mother, princess-sister, prince-brother and so on, which are mythical in comparison with everyday reality. The amorous or ambitious plot derives its peripeteia from this quality. The sexual theories anchor the child's body to that of his parents; the family romance seeks to accomplish the destiny of the hero by drawing him away from his hearth in a quest for new adventures. It looks as if infantile sexual theories speak of a time when there were still no kings, queens, princes or princesses – a time that is really primeval, prehistoric. The time, perhaps, of a natural history which is unfamiliar with the distinctions of the social order. This might be the cause of the powerful imprint left by the 'artistic' narrative on the family romance, precisely where the 'scientific' explanation dominates the infantile sexual theories. Freud would show, dialectically, that the secret aim of the family romance is to re-establish the idealisation of the 'primeval' primitive parents just when a more realistic appreciation of them is taking shape. In other words, it is the de-idealisation which will encourage a re-idealising change. It can be clearly seen, then, the extent to which phantasies have a function of regulating time, announcing the major caesura of adolescence which will leave behind the remains of the romance in order to inaugurate the new chapter of adult disillusionment.

Phantasies about origins take two directions, probably because they contain them both. On the one hand, there is the theory, that is, the search for a reasoned, articulated explanation which resorts to imagination in order to supply more satisfying responses; and, on the other, there is the story – or the romance – that is, the narrative process which is perhaps the mode of causality specific to history. The causality of sexual theories is considered to be more synchronic; the family romance more diachronic. Theory and romance may be considered as the two sources of phantasy – of all phantasy – the phantasies of origins are just an exemplary form of it. It should be remembered that if Freud understood that metapsychology depends on the activity of phantasising, if he recognised the part played by fiction or romance in his theory, it was because romance is used, in this case, not for its power of distraction or seduction, but because the way it is presented reveals its essential function for the psyche. If the theory is romanticised, it is because the romance also has a theoretical function. And if the two tributaries, theory and romance, flow into the river of phantasy, recourse to the latter offers us the possibility of going back to the sources of psychic activity. Freud thought he had found a 'Caput *Nili*'. Perhaps the analysis of phantasy will make it possible to analyse a primeval psyche that is capable of providing us with the keys to what it is that determines our thinking about origins, so that we can construct adult theories of the psyche. Hitherto, the examination of the question of origins had not taken us back in time beyond the moment when the child begins to ask himself questions about the most serious questions of existence. There was barely any need to go beyond that point. But the questioning mind, hungry for explanations, is already in evidence. 'Why do all children ask such questions? Why do they all come up with the same basic hypotheses?'

Psychic Reality

While infantile sexual theories can easily be detected in the child, they are not always so easy to find in the adult. Frequently, they have succumbed to repression and are inferred from the returns of the repressed. One can imagine that, as a result of being integrated with the repressed, they have exerted influence on the secondary repressions retroactively, and that they play a role in the organisation of the attraction of the pre-existent repressed. In other words, the repressed events are revised and participate in the construction of memory networks or chains constituted around axes which they represent. For this reason, once they have been repressed, the infantile sexual theories acquire new functions. On the one hand, by becoming integrated with memories, they acquire a 'reality' that is borrowed from that of the memory; and, on the other, by modelling the memories and by subjecting them to the order that these theories play a part in forming (around the axes of the distinction between the sexes, conception and birth), they may intervene in distorting memories.

At the ontogenetic level, sexual theories prefigure the properties that Freud would later attribute to the primal phantasies of phylogenetic origin. I will come back to this later. However, the posthumous functions of 'realisation' (reality) and 'distortion' (phantasy) raise, in the sharpest manner, the question of truth or fiction – a question already raised in 1897 concerning seduction. The infantile sexual theories and the family romance, invented between 1905 and 1910, only allowed Freud to rest for a few years. A second stage, whose birth was complicated, was to begin in 1914. The first written account of the analysis of the Wolf Man dates from the winter of 1914–15, but owing to the war, the text was only handed over to the publisher in 1918. In the meanwhile, some of the problems arising from this analysis had been dealt with in the *Introductory Lectures on Psychoanalysis* (1915–17) without making reference to the material that had served as a starting-point for his reflections. The latter were added to the later version of the 'Wolf Man'. Furthermore, the first mention of primal phantasies appeared in 'A Case of Paranoia Running Counter to the Psycho-Analytic Theory of the Disease' (1915).

Everything suggests that it was during the years 1915–17 – when he was also writing his *Papers on Metapsychology* (though they barely mention it) – that Freud's phylogenetic hypothesis took shape.

But this was preceded by the conception of *psychic reality*. What forms the starting point of the theory – even though it is not named as such – is the *material reality* of the facts invoked by the patient during treatment; that is to say, of the fiction or truth of the traumatic infantile experiences to which the libido remains fixed. This takes us back to the situation prior to 1897! Freud concluded that they were neither exclusively real nor exclusively imaginary. Far from constituting a reason to challenge their value (think of how this debate was modernised in terms of falsifiability and of the sterile conclusions to which it would lead), this obliged Freud to modify his idea of reality. The antithesis reality–fiction was to become one of material reality–psychic reality. In fact, this conclusion had become unavoidable from the moment Freud rejected the hypothesis of simulation in hysteria or that of the actual non-existence of hysterical symptoms, judged by the yardstick of neurological and organic causality. The 'reality' which is attached to fictive events has its own form of truth, since the patient believes in it firmly. The analyst's role is not to impugn this reality – a waste of time moreover – but to analyse it; the rectification occurs spontaneously after the psychical construction has been dismembered. In the world of neurosis, as in that of art, what is decisive is psychic reality. The same is true of childhood, probably because it is the source of the two others. Anyway, with regard to this problem and many others, Freud, unlike the psychiatrists of his time who were obsessed by the idea of being taken in by their patients and ready to exchange the doctor's angular hat for the policeman's kepi, never contradicted his analysands' discourse. Whether he was dealing with a hysterical, obsessional or paranoiac symptom, or with any other affection, he always adopted the same attitude. If the patient affirms what he believes forcefully, there must be a reason for it. And the 'cause' must be looked for behind the displacements, disguises and distortions. A 'kernel of truth' can always be found at the navel of the psychic formation. It is like the parasite around which the nacre of the pearl gathers in order to isolate and neutralise it, giving birth to what will constitute the price of a jewel. Insufficient attention has been paid to the fact that the two cases which served as a point of departure for the thesis of primal phantasies were a case of paranoia and a psychotic structure: Schreber and the Wolf Man.

As for the primitive scene, the most primal of the primal phantasies, it is rare for patients to affirm that they have witnessed parental intercourse. On the contrary, when this seems unquestionable for the analyst (for example, when the child has slept in the parents' bedroom until a late age), the analysand has no memory of it. It is simply that clues appear indirectly in screen-memories, dreams, phantasies, and so on. The Wolf Man later shared his scepticism about the primitive scene with Karin Obholzer,[11] in spite of the fact that he himself had shrugged off the doubts which had invaded Freud at one point in the analysis. The impact of reality does not reside, therefore, in the memory of the real scene or in its nature as a phantasy passing itself off as something real. It is deduced from the capacity these phantasies have to be stimulated by whatever can evoke them – sometimes perceptions that are quite insignificant in themselves, but which, by association or by resonance, reanimate them, so that they acquire an explosive significance. This is what gives us reason to suspect that they are of a traumatic nature. It is not because they refer to what has actually occurred; rather it is as though they had left in the psyche indelible scars that are still sensitive, ready to act as alarm signals at the slightest occasion. It seems to me that this disposition for being activated was one of the arguments that led Freud to give them the status of an inscription registered in the memory of the species.

Such a memory-trace would account for a network of characteristics:

(a) the generality of phantasies about the primitive scene and the constancy with which one comes across them, can only be explained, in Freud's view, by referring to acquired experience which varies from case to case;

(b) the capacity for resonating with the constellations which evoke them in reality is, by analogy, such that individual experience at a minimum level results in effects that are disproportionate to their causes;

(c) the elevated value of psychic reality which they are capable of acquiring. Never mind the reference to memory – always suspect of distortion – or to phantasy; what counts, so to speak, is the 'strike force' of the content of the psychic event;

(d) their organising power over the psyche (like infantile sexual theories) makes them temporal markers with a considerable power for cultural appropriation (oneiric, folkloric, mythical themes, and so on).

Many questions remain pending, however, including that of their relation to the infantile sexual theories or, more generally, their passage from latency to effectivity. That is to say, the way in which life experiences make it possible to bring about their 'precipitation' (in the chemical sense) in the individual in the form of a 'secondarised' phantasy, that is, transformed by secondary processes.

It seems to me to be implicit that for Freud these phylogenetic memory-traces are not only the remains of a forgotten past of the human species. Their action is equivalent to the marks of destiny which map out the life-path of any individual, tracing the paths he will take in the future.

Heterogeneity of the Psyche and Reference to the Subject

In making these initial approaches to the question of primal phantasies, we have embarked upon the most uncertain conjectures. I have put forward some of the reasons for defending such a hypothesis. Before testing the latter further, it it is worth noting that the question of origins covers a very wide field. These different perspectives can be grouped together under three polarities:

1. *The scientific pole*
This extends from the origin of the cosmos to the origin of man. Until fairly recently, physics, biology and anthropology were quite separate disciplines, each dealing with its own objects. This is still true to a large extent; however, today, any work dealing with the problem of the human psyche will devote a large amount of space to the evolutionist point of view. It will, accordingly, go back to the origins of the Hominidae. From there, the theory of evolution will lead it back to the origins of life. And from there, the reader will return to the origins of the cosmos. This point of view is based on the use of the scientific way of thinking, the acquisitions of which inspire admiration on account of their exactness and fidelity.

2. *The historico-mythical pole*
A preoccupation that was scarcely different from that of science, and preceded it, gave birth to religious and mythical cosmogonies,

expressing the same concern with reconstructing origins. While cosmogonies differ according to their religious and cultural contexts, I do not think there is any society which has not been concerned to establish a theory of origins – that is to say, of the social group, of culture, of humanity, or of the world. Here we are in the realm of the divine, of the mythical, and of symbolic thought which finds expression in the works of human kind.

3. *The ontogenetic individual pole*
The infantile sexual theories and the family romance have shown us the interest that is taken in these questions, as well as the answers given to them, in each individual's childhood.

Let me make an initial remark: these three poles correspond to three modes of exercising the human mind which gather together all these properties, while allowing for the specific development of each of the three. Everything that is primal refers to a single referent: the human mind which thinks about it. The latter is itself the original crossroads (heterogeneous) from which these constructions originate or to which they lead. To this day, there is no unified conception which accounts for the potentialities of the human mind in the contradictory diversity of its productions: scientific or non-scientific, collective and individual. In other words, no overall conception of causality can cover the relations between these three fields of psychic reality.

The relations that exist between these three fields are only peaceful in appearance. A subdued or noisily expressed state of conflict pushes the different perspectives to fight each other in the name of truth. The mistake is to believe that any one of these perspectives can itself answer the questions raised by all the others. On the other hand, this requires us to understand the demands to which each of them responds in relation to the shared locus of their activity; that is, the psychic activity of man. Resistance to the unknown can be simply passive owing to the mere fact of ignorance; or it can be active in order to keep hidden what is considered to be intolerable. On this point, the individual polarity is more involved than the two others. We are no longer concerned here with metaphysical questions; they are a cause of anxiety, admittedly, but only affect the investigator from a distance. The outline of the origin of worlds, of life, of man, emerges in the distance behind a more personal mystery – that of the origins of the investigator himself. (This is why the Sphinx asks Oedipus a question which makes him reflect on himself.) While it is recognised today that the resistance to recognising the phantasies of origins resides in the repression of infantile sexuality, one may wonder if resistance to the thesis of primal phantasies cannot be explained by the fact that we find it humiliating to think that, if there are organisers of the human psyche which are capable of so many admirable performances, they would be of a sexual nature. The difficulty of presenting convincing arguments on the origin of these supposed organisers stems from the absence of traces that have been left behind, of discernible inscriptions forming a corpus. In the domain of psychoanalysis, the material presents itself in the form of flying words that are gathered by the analyst's approximate and insufficient memory. If the thought contained in myths is similar to that of phantasies, it can at least can be studied at leisure, orally or in writing. It is even the object of continual exegesis, of endless commentaries – theological, eschatalogical, or simply scientific. The wake of the analysand's narrative closes up again in the analyst's memory as quickly as the wake left by an advancing ship.

Phantasy emerges precisely where knowledge is lacking – and where is knowledge lacking more than in childhood? But what memory is less reliable than that of childhood? The lack of knowledge is aggravated still further by the fact of forgetting the memory – not of reality, but of the phantasy itself which gives it shape. However, this persistent retrogressive orientation of our knowledge of origins still remains: 'How long have you been here?' 'Where were you before?' 'And before that?' 'Why did you come?' 'How did you get here?' are all questions we put to others and to ourselves.

This movement towards the primal, arising from the need to know what was 'at the beginning', to assign it a starting point, if not a date, and to describe how events unfolded, inevitably induces the projection of present knowledge into the past, by attributing this retrospective assignation with a causal value. But everything constantly recommences and converges towards me, the source and matrix of the questioning, of that which makes me what I am.

There is never, and there never can be, a coincidence between the primal and the theory of origins. What was, can only be apprehended, to use the analytic expression, *nachträglich*. We are perhaps faced here with the case of a relationship of fundamental uncertainty, caught between the necessity of reconstituting the past reliably, and, in order to do this, of having to rely on the inevitable creativity of the present. Restitution is not possible without creativity, but all restitution depends on creativity, which is not content with just copying – if that is conceivable – what was. Is there not a contradiction between representation, conception, and the theory of origins on the one hand and, representation, concept, and primal thought, on the other, which, precisely because they are primal, are not susceptible to representation, conception, or thought – since all these occurrences require a certain degree of development? When the latter (representation, conception and thought) are in a position to exercise their capacities, the primal will already be far away. It cannot be anything else but a construction, or even a phantasy which is taken for a memory. I am speaking here, of course, of the primal psyche.

Primary Processes, Retroactive Meaning (*Après Coup*), Organisation

In 'Leonardo da Vinci and a Memory of his Childhood' (1910) Freud wrote:

This is often the way in which childhood memories originate. Quite unlike conscious memories from the time of maturity, they are not fixed at the moment of being experienced and afterwards repeated, but are only elicited at a later age when childhood is already past; in the process they are altered and falsified and are put into the service of later trends, so that generally speaking they cannot be sharply distinguished from phantasies. Their nature is perhaps best illustrated by a comparison with the way in which the writing of history originated among the peoples of antiquity. As long as a nation was small and weak it gave no thought to the writing of its history. Men tilled the soil of their land, fought for their existence against their neighbours, and tried to gain territory from them and to acquire wealth. It was an age of heroes, not of historians. Then came another age, an age of reflection: men felt themselves to be rich and powerful, and now felt a need to learn where they had come from and how they had developed. Historical writing, which had begun to keep a continuous record of the present, now also cast a glance back to the past, gathered traditions and legends, interpreted the traces of antiquity that survived in customs and usages, and in this way created a history of the past. It was inevitable that this early history should have been an expression of present beliefs and wishes rather than a true picture of the past; for many things had been dropped from the nation's memory, while others were distorted, and some remains of the past were given a wrong interpretation in order to fit in with contemporary ideas. Moreover, people's motive for writing history was not objective curiosity but a desire to influence their contemporaries, to encourage and inspire them, or to hold a mirror up before them. A man's conscious memory of the events of his maturity is in every way comparable to the first kind of historical writing [which was a chronicle of current events]; while the memories that he has of his childhood correspond, as far as their origins and reliability are concerned, to the history of a nation's earliest days, which was compiled later and for tendentious reasons.[12]

This quotation, while it is rather long, has the merit of giving us an insight into Freud's preconceptions. One can notice his insistence on always drawing a parallel between collective and individual development. Individual history recapitulates that of society just as ontogenesis recapitulates phylogenesis. The account given by memory, both social and individual, is an idealising distortion of the past: imagination prevails over memory. Memory has absorbed phantasy to the point that it no longer recognises it under the disguise of memory. While claiming to act as an archivist, it puts its productions at the service of present preoccupations. But above all, it expresses an aporia of the singular or collective historical approach. Memory only exists in relation to what has already been experienced. By definition, the latter is retrospective and, as such, is necessarily unreliable. Peoples, as well as individuals, construct a view of their past retrospectively, once they have acquired the means to depict it, and the leisure to cast a glance back on the past. The past is always associated, more or less, with the good times. If certain productions of the psyche are dictated by necessity, others, on the contrary, need to free themselves from it. They are like a luxury whose embellishments the observer enjoys from a distance. This would not matter so much if the distortion concerned only the content of the origins. What is more damaging for knowledge of the human psyche is that the image formed of the origins is governed by a rationality which belongs entirely to the present. The necessary clues for determining what kind of causality is at work in the events which are being considered retrospectively are far and few between. There is a great danger here – known as anthropo- or adultomorphic

– of confusing what only deserves to be called rationalisation for reason. Or primal reason? The least that can be said is that there exists more than one version in the writings of historians of ancient times, of mythologists, and anthropologists.

This is how myths arise which seek to re-make not only the history of men, but the history of the world. Marcel Detienne – in the *L'invention de la mythologie*,[13] I think – concurs with Freud on this, at least insofar as Greece is concerned. This, then, is how childhood memories are constructed on the traces of a past that is largely buried. But it is here that the relations between the scientific approach and the teaching of myths become obscure. While myths have something to do with history, what matters here is the way they distort it; and it is worth bearing in mind the common root between myth and mystification. Some will say that myths are only remotely related to history and that their effects are mainly structural. However, we cannot escape the need to think about the meaning of historic causality, particularly with respect to the distortion which seems to be consubstantial with it. The categories of the 'mind' which appear in relation to structure cannot regard this distortion as accidental; on the contrary, it seems to be structural. This is perhaps what drives us to search for this original truth, buried beneath the lie of centuries, and behind the disguises of distortion.

This was once the theme of a symposium held in Urbino, in which I took part, where there was a clash between the schools of Rome, under the direction of Angelo Brehlich, and Paris, led by Jean-Pierre Vernant. When Marcel Detienne said, on this occasion, that 'myth was eating the event', how could any psychoanalyst have failed to agree with him, while none the less remaining concerned not to erase the history behind 'histories'? The fact is, Freud did not regard the historical reality as contingent; similarly, phantasy, for him, was far from being simply a vapour of the mind that needed dissipating before one could awaken to the truth.

Notwithstanding all the distortions and misinterpretations, the latter [the legends, traditions and interpretations supplied by a people's prehistory] still represent the reality of the past. They are what the people have formed out of their primal experiences, under the sway of motives that were once powerful and which are still effective today; and if, by being aware of all the forces at work, one could only annul these distortions, one ought to be in a position to discover the historical truth behind this legendary material.[14]

Freud was clearly not driven by the same scepticism or caution that has since overcome historians and psychoanalysts. The phantasies of origins, via the sexual theories of children, are to individual childhood what myths are to cultures. They contain a 'part of the truth', which means that our task of interpretation has to be continually renewed.

Phantasies about Origins – Primal Phantasies

We have now come to a turning-point in our consideration of the question of the primal. Establishing the relationship between the effects of structure and history is as necessary as it is difficult to determine. It should be clear by now that I will make a contrast between phantasies of origins, which relate to infantile sexual theories (and to the family romance), and primal phantasies which will be understood as organising schemes – or, in Freud's sense, phylogenetic – the action of which can only be explained by their conjunction with the subject's individual experience. Up till 1910, with the infantile sexual theories and the family romance, Freud had remained within a strictly ontogenetic perspective. The investigation was limited to determining the respective roles of fiction and truth. The phantasies of origins provided an explanation for the enigmas relating to sexuality. But what was the explanation for these explanations? In other words, why did these fictions appear with such regularity and constancy? In 1897, Freud had opted for phantasy instead of trauma because he accorded phantasy with a status of greater generality. In 1915, he opted in favour of primal phantasies over and against phantasies about origins (infantile sexual theories and family romance), that is, he opted for the phylogenetic origin against the ontogenetic origin, because he thought that by grounding the primal category in biological heredity, it would overcome the uncertainties of the accidental, i.e, of the particular history of an individual. In short, he chose structure against history, apparently. This appreciation is highly approximate; for how are we to understand that the Wolf Man was written by Freud precisely with a view to opposing Jung? In it he says:

I fully agree with Jung (*Die Psychologie der unbewussten Prozesse*, 1917, published too late for it to have influenced my *Introductory Lectures*) in recognising the existence of this phylogenetic heritage; but I regard it as a methodological error to seize on a phylogenetic explanation before the ontogenetic possibilities have been exhausted. I cannot see any reason for obstinately disputing the importance of infantile prehistory while at the same time freely acknowledging the importance of ancestral prehistory. Nor can I overlook the fact that phylogenetic motives and productions themselves stand in need of elucidation, and that in quite a number of instances this is afforded by factors in the childhood of the individual. And, finally, I cannot feel surprised that what was originally produced by certain circumstances in prehistoric times and was then transmitted in the shape of a predisposition to its re-acquirement should, since the same circumstances persist, emerge once more as a concrete event in the experience of the individual.[15]

It is noteworthy that Freud was not defending a conception that accorded phylogenesis a quasi-transcendental primacy, as Jung claimed. He was simply returning to a theoretical axis to which he had always, or almost always, adhered. Just as phantasy and traumatic experience form a part of his aetiological conception – the effects of each intermingling with each other and merging into psychic reality – the phylogenetic and ontogenetic form a complementary series. The phylogenetic fills the gaps of the ontogenetic; but, by repeating analogous circumstances, ontogenesis is necessary in order to actualise phylogenesis. The latter is a 'predisposition to re-acquirement' and not *deus ex machina*. If we return to the *Introductory Lessons in Psychoanalysis* cited above, we will find the complex diagram of the aetiology of the neuroses, which can only be understood as a repeated interlocking of complementary series: childhood and adulthood. The effect of a disposition to neurosis originates in the former, and is combined with an accidental traumatic factor occurring during the latter. This disposition is itself constituted from the sexual constitution and the factor of infantile experience. Clearly, the problem is first and foremost an epistemological one. In this respect, the theoretical strategy adopted is to base causality on a complementarity and, to a certain extent, on a contradiction. This highlights the conflict in the theory: not only as it is apprehended in the individual, but also as it is apprehended in the opposing sources of causality which doubtless act in synergy and also partly in antagonism. In this respect, there is a complementarity between that which has its origin in individual experience and that which is thought to derive from hereditary organisation. In other words, between that which has its source in the questionings of childhood and that which arises from the depths of the ages.

There is, then, in Freud's work a complex vision of the primal phantasy. Certainly, the latter possesses properties which make it the equivalent of the 'philosophical categories' and, no doubt, the Kantian *a priori*; but individual experience is indispensable to the intelligibility of causality. They are *Szenen*, *Urszenen*, but they are also schema: 'schemes-scenes'? Rather, they are schemes that will quickly become scenes. I will come back to this in due course.

At this point, the question arises of the relationship between infantile sexual theories and primal phantasies. The former concern the penis as an organ common to both sexes and conception, that is, the parental coitus, the birth of a child from the mother's body. The latter are related to seduction, castration, and the primitive scene, to which Freud added the return to the mother's breast and the Oedipus complex.

Ontogenesis confronts us with the questions posed in childhood and with the answers that are proposed; phylogenesis – according to Freud – explains, as it were, the predestination of these responses, which accounts, so to speak, for their constancy. If we take Freud's reasoning to its logical conclusion, it is necessary to recall that, for him, the primal phantasy represents the internalised schema of actual events – of acts – which are thought to have taken place during the prehistory of the species. Let us set aside today this explanation related to the prehistory of the primal phantasy, and only allow for the hypothesis insofar as it has value in classifying individual experiences, which makes it a symbolic matrix. It will then be possible to compare infantile (ontogenetic) sexual theories and primal (phylogenetic) phantasies. What they both have in common is the primitive scene. In addition, the infantile sexual theories include the generalisation of the attribute penis and the conceptions of birth. Primal phantasies include seduction, castration, the return to the mother's breast, and the Oedipus complex. The following diagram [see Figure 2.1] illustrates these relations.

It is immediately noticeable that the primal phantasy of Oedipal castration corresponds to the universality of the penis prior to the castration complex. Similarly, theories of birth can be compared with phantasies of returning to the mother's breast. Seduction remains

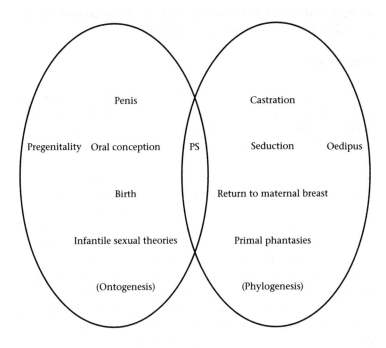

Figure 2.1

on the side of primal phantasies. Laplanche's hypothesis of the theory of generalised[16] seduction can be admitted, but the latter is a consequence of the primal phantasy of seduction. There is no primal phantasy of generalised seduction. To the ensemble of infantile sexual theories, I propose to add the hypothesis of oral conception corresponding, upstream, so to speak, to anal birth.

Finally, I would say that primal phantasies tend towards the Oedipus complex as the articulation which gives them a global meaning; whereas the infantile sexual theories are in danger of regressing towards a pregenitality which retreats in the face of the embryonic intellectual organisation they represent. Should the hypothesis of primal phantasies – many aspects of which are debatable – be considered as unserviceable, as Laplanche and many others are inclined to think, on the grounds that the infantile sexual theories provide adequate answers to the theoretical problems raised? In order to understand what underlies this question, certain theoretical axes will first have to be established.

Prima Summa

There is, then, in Freud's work, in the sphere of ontogenetic–phylogenetic relations, an implicit historical–structural problem, which forms a complex. One can disregard the idea that phylogenesis preserves the traces of the historical evolution of the species; Freud only envisaged its action from the angle of a 'disposition' which, nonetheless, still has to be acquired individually. This remark has not been thought about sufficiently. It is our current ideological preoccupations that push us to interpret Freud's thought. This is an implicit or latent issue whose fruitfulness in other domains of knowledge can be seen from recent developments. Georges Dumézil has successfully summarised the relations between history and structure in relation to the question of origins. He pointed out in passing – showing that he was well aware of their relevance far beyond the specialised contexts in which these oppositions were played out – that these relations could be of some interest to the philosopher. For the psychoanalyst, at any rate, there can be scarcely any doubt.

When one approaches the domain extending 'from prehistory to protohistory', where reasonably reliable data cannot be established due to a lack of facts, the attitudes of historians are divided. For some, it is a question of determining the origin of the elements which their object of study comprises. Determining the nature of eventual structures is secondary in all respects; and often they are the fruit of chance encounters, or ones that it has been necessary to conciliate. The intelligible value of the structure is only a matter of limited interest. For others, the model of a situation of continuity in which nothingness, birth and progressive growth follow in succession, is the result of an oversimplification. On the contrary, it is asserted that what we are dealing with is a complex situation at the outset in which the elements appear in a form that is already organised, articulated, and complex – this is the structural point of view. There is no doubt that what is being emphasised here is the inexact nature of a point of view which sees the human mind as being subjected, passively, to the unfolding of facts and events.

In every era, the human mind has intervened in and on the fringe of the sequences imposed upon it, often proving itself to be stronger than them. The human spirit, however, is essentially organising and systematic; it experiences multiple events simultaneously so that, in any age, apart from successive complexes which can be explained by the successive contributions of history, *primary complexes* exist which are perhaps more fundamental in the hardiest civilisations.[17]

As for the origin of these primary complexes, should they be regarded as innate? Or, since the origin of history is situated way back in the mists of time, can one not suppose that they have acquired the force of inductive agents by virtue of an organisation which has structured them, giving them stability, without necessarily accepting the hypothesis of an innate form of psychic organisation? The question is no longer just one for the historian; it concerns the formation of structures and their origin.

It would seem that the notion in question here is that of a theory of origins which starts out by designating a simple origin, followed by a progressive accumulation of experience which, in itself, is thought to have an explanatory value that is self-sufficient. We are in the presence of a historical mechanism or, if you prefer, a mechanical history, which is entirely satisfied with the arrangement of elements reduced to their simplest form of expression. Now Dumézil is concerned with a problem – that of the first god – which cannot be a matter of indifference to anyone who has a general interest in origins. Far from regarding him as a primeval god, that is to say, a god who is at the origin of the development of the series to follow, he is the god of beginnings who is unconcerned by what happens thereafter – not responsible, I would say – for engendering future events. But, what is not by any means the least interesting point is that this first god one comes across in various mythical contexts (Vayu, Janus) is an ambiguous, mysterious god, representing values of the unknown. He is much less a figure of primeval Oneness than of a bidirectional duality towards the future and the past, bicephalous or bifrontal, representing the values or moral options of good and evil, in parallel contexts. A primeval god, but one of an indeterminate, dyadic origin. Far from imagining this duality as a division of Oneness, this primal category is translated from the outset by a dual structure of opposites, a 'pair of opposites' as Freud would say.

Thanks to this 'first' god, in relation to 'the first thing', which is neither the best nor the greatest, other divine values will be opposed; namely, those which do not originate in him, but impose themselves after him and independently of him. Think, for instance, of the opposition between the well-known deities of Jupiter and Janus. The god Geminus, the god of the Prima, the Initia, the Primordia, the initiating god who is a god of duality, even multiplicity, and, to a certain extent, confusion and chaos, will be followed – though it does not originate in him – by a principle of order Jupiter–Varron referred to by Saint Augustine who defines the problem as follows: 'The Prima are less important than the Summa for, though the Prima come first in time, the Summa excel by dignity.'[18]

As strange as it may seem, it is not difficult to transpose the debates that have arisen from the distinction between Prima and Summa to the psychoanalytic field. It may come as a surprise that such a comparison is possible. This is less astonishing than it would seem initially, though, because what is involved is two opposing attitudes of mind which can be found in many domains. In psychoanalysis, there is a movement known as genetic psychoanalysis which has its equivalent amongst those historians who are suspicious of structures and convinced of the virtues of an approach which strives to take origins as its starting-point, giving the picture of a cumulative development which, without vain speculations, accounts for an ontogenetic evolution. For them, it is no longer appropriate to speak of Freud's primal phantasies, structures to which others refer in order to defend a structural conception.

Though history – including the system of traces on which it rests, which makes chronological dating and the succession of events possible – is lacking, we will be satisfied with what can be learnt from the observation of development and the gradual recording of events, as well as the changes they bring about. There is no point in insisting unduly on the possible objections to this point of view, concerning not only the question of the organising interpretative criteria and the way in which sequences and events are cut up, but also the different types of classification of experiences: in short, the referents of this history which would prefer not to take structures into account.

This way of thinking, which is often characteristic both of child psychoanalysts and a variety of investigators (psychoanalysts or not) who are interested in the study of psychic development, needs to be contrasted with that of psychoanalysts of a structuralist inclination. The former, who always get a little carried away by the impression they have of witnessing *in statu nascendi* the origin of meaningful constructions, whether normal or pathological, seem to be satisfied with the conceptual tools offered by referring to the origin and the continuity of development – as if succession were, in itself, a causality that was self-sufficient. On the other hand, the latter who, moreover, usually work with material presented by adults, are struck by the multiplicity and diversity of singular experiences which resist the imposition of a code of meaning on them aimed at making them intelligible. And it is noteworthy that these principles are not those of a theory of origins, even if reference is made to the primal.

As far as the infantile sexual theories are concerned, therefore, I would be satisfied with a vision that is not simply ontogenetic; but I think it is unnecessary to postulate these complex hypothetical organisations, known as primal, which intervene in development like structured ensembles. In their milestone study, 'Fantasme originaire, fantasme des origines, origines du fantasme' (1964),[19] Laplanche and Pontalis point out that primal phantasies are in fact concerned with origins: the origins of sexuality (seduction), of the difference between the sexes (castration) and of the birth of the subject (primitive scene). But here they make Freud say what they themselves think. For Freud, seduction is certainly not the origin of sexuality; and it does not follow, where the primitive scene is concerned, that the subject makes a direct connection between what takes place there and his birth. These observations are more philo-sophical than psychoanalytic – which, moreover, is the note on which their article ends. Laplanche rejects outright the phylogenetic thesis, contenting himself with the infantile sexual theories.

Now primal phantasies are like complex structures with a variable geometry. For instance, it can be argued that the primitive scene and seduction function according to reversible modalities; or again, that there is a relation of cause and effect between the primitive scene and castration. Or that castration is the sanction for seduction, and so on. This is what is meant by the expression 'symbolic matrix' which supposes the mutual reverberation of different primal phantasies. For it is clear, as Laplanche and Pontalis indicate, that it is necessary to have recourse to a larger ensemble if we want to understand the meaning of primal phantasies. They point out that the Oedipus complex can be seen as the geometrical locus at which they are situated. But where does the Oedipus complex come from? Are these authors going to take us back to the 'genetic' conception of the Oedipus complex, or are they going to refer to the structural thesis which was one of Lacan's hobby-horses?

Is this structural conception of the Oedipus complex not the one that Freud himself defends in the case of the Wolf Man? Speaking of phylogenetically inherited schemata, 'precipitates from the history of human civilization', he writes: 'The Oedipus complex, which comprises a child's relation to his parents, is one of them – it is, in fact, the best known member of the class.'[20] The path that Freud followed is in fact the one he recommends: that is, he emphasises the need to take into account the facts of individual prehistory along with the infantile sexual theories, to recognise their epistemological limits, to invoke phylogenetic structures, and to treat the relations between ontogenesis and phylogenesis dialectically. If, then, time is necessary for a theory of origins to take shape – the questions it raises necessarily emerge *nachträglich*, in retrospect – even more time is required to realise that a theory of the primal is necessary, and even indispensable, and that ultimately it has little in common with a theory of origins. In effect, the theory of the primal does not in any way translate an inquiry into origins. It is not the fruit of the child's curiosity. On the contrary, it comes from an examination of the data supplied by the adult in order to explain the regularity of certain themes. It no doubt inquires into the origin of this regularity, and the cause of its regulatory power, and responds to this question by positing the idea of a primal fund, or reserve, assumed to lie at the beginning of all development. But the origin in question here is one that refers to the history of the species. Primal phantasies are vestiges, or memory-traces, of the account given of origins.

From now on I shall distinguish, in this examination of the problem of primal phantasies, between two questions: first, their connection with phantasy, and secondly, their relation to the primal.

Phantasy? Primal?

The reference to phantasy as a support for the primal corresponds to what might be called the speculative background of Freud's thought. The question is not, strictly speaking, one of psychoanalytic theory, but rather of its implicit foundations.

Just as authors today who are investigating the psyche go back to the origin of the cosmos, Freud left us a manuscript called *A Phylogenetic Phantasy – Overview of the Transference Neuroses*[21] in which his taste for phantasy was given free rein. He readily conceded that the theory of origins has the character of a phantasy. This freedom of expression did not go as far as publication. Freud simply communicated the content of it to Ferenczi, a great enthusiast for the genre. 'You can throw it away or keep it', he wrote to his correspondent – an indication of the altogether relative value he accorded to this metabiological novel. In it Freud's reverie forges links between the constitution of the neuroses and the stages of mankind's prehistory, referring to the effects of the Ice Age, the putting to death of newborn babies for lack of food, sexual restriction, the development of language, castration practised by the jealous father, the sons' rebellion, and parricide. In this fresque, each one of these events corresponds to the appearance of a neurosis. It is clear, then, that even the neuroses are transmitted phylogenetically; their individual origin is attributed to another causality. 'Archaic constitutions' make their return in new individuals, are combined with present claims and facilitate the genesis of neurosis.

Freud's conception of phylogenesis rests on the idea that the important or frequently repeated events and acts are transmitted through heredity and are modified from generation to generation: these facts of material reality, these actions – in the beginning was action, says Freud, echoing Goethe – are internalised. This, in part, is the explanation for the instinctual nature of the sub-layers of the psyche (instinctual drives were once actions). But, although instinctual impulses represent a form of memory, they do not transmit any contents or histories. Freud argues, then, that if something analogous to the instinct of animals exists in the form of inherited psychic formations, it is what constitutes the nucleus of the unconscious.[22] He was probably referring to primal phantasies. Freud defended a similar opinion at the end of the Wolf Man where he sets out his ideas on this matter.[23] Nevertheless, the question is less about the primal phantasy than about the 'instinctive knowledge' of animals. One might as well say that this instinctive knowledge is itself subject to the influence of the primal phantasy. Freud stresses the imaginative structure of primal phantasies as '*Urszene*'. Yet when he employs the word 'scene' at the beginning of his work, it is applied indifferently to a lived event, a memory, or even a phantasy. The typical '*Urszene*' is the scene of sexual intercourse between the parents. It is not in this sense, however, that Freud employs the expression in the letters to Fliess, where he only refers to the primal phantasies of neurosis. Apart from its allusion to the primal, the denomination 'scene' seems to me to refer, above all, to the manner in which psychic events appear before the mind; that is, as enactments (the hysterical attack would be their equivalent), or representations. For Freud, the primal does indeed present itself in the shape of a phantasy, of an elaborated scenario, transmitted as such, which are activated by perceptual indicators, thereby setting the hereditary montage alight. But what, then, is the primitive scene? Is it a scene that is actually experienced by the child? Is it a scene imagined by the child (the fact that it is always remembered in the position *a tergo* pleads in favour of this hypothesis)? Or is it a schema of the intimate encounter between the father and mother, between the masculine and the feminine? It is all this, in fact, ranging from the version that claims to be the most realistic to that which is most abstract.

For Freud, the thesis of the predominance of psychic reality refers to a material reality belonging to a past time, a phantasy belonging to present time, and a schema belonging to all periods of time. Moreover, these scenes do not take on the form of memories; they have to be inferred, constructed 'step by step, and laboriously on the basis of a certain number of clues'. One should not conclude too hastily that their origin is more a matter of phantasy than of memory. Is it not the case, anyway, that phantasy is a relic of a forgotten memory? Dreaming is also a way of remembering. Unconscious phantasy, like the scenes, also has to be deduced, constructed, and inferred from indicators. Are primal scenes primal phantasies, that is, phylogenetically inherited imaginary scenarios? And finally, are primordial schemes necessarily expressed in the form of phantasies?

The question constantly arises as to what comes first (*prima*). But, as we have seen, it is ambiguous, and confused with what is the most important – that is, what has the power to sort, classify, categorise and place in a hierarchical order (*summa*). This confusion hangs over the term primal: what is first is what comes at the beginning and is first by rank.

As we have seen, the primal is related to the hypothesis according to which there are formations in the psyche which the individual is believed to carry in him at birth, which then act in synergy with individual experience in order to classify experiences and to serve as an organiser in psychic construction. They are thus assumed to govern a schema of development in such a way that the latter gives a general direction to destiny and governs the variations, deficiencies, and irregularities of individual life in the face of common destiny.

We know that the choice of this translation for the German prefix '*Ur-*' has prevailed in French. Initially it was translated as 'primitive', 'primary'. The possibility of confusion with factors related to an ontogenetic point of view meant that 'primal'[24] was preferred.

For my part, I propose to make a total dissociation between the epistemological requirement and the phylogenetic theory: the former makes the theoretical hypothesis of factors which play the role of organisers and account for the generality of certain themes – notwithstanding the particularities of their history – necessary, while the latter explains the origin of these formations. I propose, then, that the ensemble designated as primal phantasies, that is, seduction, castration, primitive scene, the return to the mother's breast, the Oedipus complex, be called *primordial schemes*. In this way, we shall free ourselves of the link these formations have both with phantasy and with the phylogenetic origin.

Freud's opinions are in complete disagreement with science, since all geneticists reject the idea of an inheritance of acquired characteristics. What is more, it is debatable whether heredity is transmitted in the form of imaginary scenarios. It should be noted, however, that it is not clear how science can demonstrate the erroneous nature of Freud's ideas. While there is nothing to prove them, it is also difficult to prove the contrary, that is, that they do not exist. Nevertheless, the epistemological requirement is still there. It is possible to attribute the organisation of human desire to a mutation. The latter could be translated by the presence of schema which have been sensibilised by perceptual configurations. When the existence of IRM (Tinbergen and Lorenz's innate reflex mechanisms) was demonstrated; when the attachment behaviour of certain fowl towards man was provoked by making the latter imitate, even crudely, the global behaviour associated with the general shape of an adult animal specimen, and when it was discovered what drove other species of birds to flee from a bird of prey, these reactions were linked up with schemes. Thus, to take the case under consideration, the bird that flees its raptor innately has not conserved an internal trace of the scene of its ancestors being devoured by a predator, any more than it immediately recognises the eagle, the sparrow hawk, or any other bird of prey. What it carries within it is the reflex reaction of flight when faced with the configuration 'eyes close together/short neck'. Likewise, it does not recognise its mother at birth, though every form vaguely resembling her is invested as object/mother.

Primal phantasies might resemble such a schematic organisation at the beginning. The encounter between these perceptual configurations and perceptions arising from individual experience would thus give birth to these symbolic forms shaped by the imagination, endowing them with the status described by Freud as primal 'phantasy'. This would be enriched by a narrative created by the structure 'primal phantasy' which then, and then only, would acquire the quality that would make a scenario out of it. In other words, only the 'phylogenetic' substratum would be linked to the sensible schema (a triggering perceptive configuration); everything else (phantasy, scenic dramatisation) would result from the encounter between the scheme and experience. Experience in itself would not be sufficient to explain the scope of its significance. The schema would account for it, but would only be an empty abstraction if experience did not supply it with the appropriate 'primary' material for stimulating the imagination and the discursive form attached to narration.

In the postface of *The Fabric of Affect in the Psychoanalytic discourse,* 1970–73, I was exploring the questions of what is structurable, what is structure *in potentia*, and what is structuring potential. I concluded that 'primal phantasies are not representations, still less contents, but mediations. Contrary to everything we might expect of the rules of traditional logic, they are that by which representations and contents occur.'[25] They are inductors which encourage actualisation in the form of phantasies, invested with a high coefficient of psychic reality. In the general script of phantasies, these particular ones can be read, apparently, just like the others, but they are printed in bold characters.

Thus the aleatory circumstances of individual experience are reinforced and marked by regular structure so that meaning is stamped by what is significant. Furthermore, the reference to the primal does not disappear completely, for the primordial schema play the role of temporal markers. They assign historically dated events with a range which situates them on the temporal scale, since they are not limited to the moment of their appearance. Their relation to infantile sexual theories contributes to giving some order to origins and no longer only to that which is primordial – primal. They help the past to become past, and to constitute itself as such. The primordial schemes condense a system of harmonic resonances, allowing them to communicate between themselves, and to explain, retroactively – in a causal manner – what has already existed, just as its networks will be ready, in the future, to be sensitive to experiences which continue to have relations with them, or with the forms that existed before they manifested themselves.

An Alternative to the Hereditary Hypothesis

As we have seen, the theory of the primal phantasy can itself be regarded as a phantasy. Metapsychology – the witch, according to Freud – nourishes itself on phantasy in order to progress. It is not only the 'beyond' of psychology, but also what connects psychology to its biological origins. The 'before' of psychology is a sort of psycho-psychology or imaginary biology. Freud would have preferred not to have to leave the cohort of biologists, but they rejected his allegiance and suppressed him as an author of fiction. Thus, contrary to its author's intentions, metapsychology does not refer to biology, but to an equally imaginary discipline: metabiology. While Freud put a lot of biology into his psychology, it can equally be argued that he put a lot of psychology into his biology. Is it possible to avoid referring to phylogenesis altogether? Here it is necessary to distinguish between our ignorance and our prejudices. At a time when so many facts which used to be interpreted as the results of environmental effects are today put down to genetic determinism, there is a total absence of data capable of explaining a genetic transmission in the psychic realm. Although psychiatric illnesses are still attributed to genetic causes, we are completely in the dark as to what might constitute an individual or collective heritage. It is through an act of transmission, repeated during each generation, that culture maintains its patrimony, giving birth to an authentic social heredity (Lacan). The existence of so-called primitive societies raises the question of a state which, if not prehistoric is, at least, protohistoric, even though no one is in any doubt that there is a certain historicity in the evolution of these societies. But here theory rests perhaps on more solid grounds.

Today, societies without a written tradition are no longer qualified as primitive – and no doubt one should applaud the desire to do away, once and for all, with the humiliating and condescending undertones of such a description. But are there not other reasons for abandoning this formulation? Is there not a case for being sceptical about the motives which encourage us today to regard these societies, and our own, as comparable, and as being separated merely by certain differences? Is it not so that what is thereby suppressed is our suspicions about what is inferior, undeveloped and savage? Is it not also true, that by getting rid of the primitive, we evacuate in the process what is basic and fundamental – in short, *primordial*. The purpose in so doing would be to mask the power that such societies have of making us aware of the parameters of the psyche whose organising value is more apparent and visible here, but whose fundamental weight and perennity, which can be inferred from the resonance they still have for us, even today, is difficult for us to accept.

Not that one is entitled to think that the primordial can be grasped via direct expressions which are immediately decodable; for, here as elsewhere, it is only perceptible through a veil of disguises and mediations. No form of transparency spares us the effects of repression. But it is the relationship between these mediations and the hypotheses that account for them which is more enlightening, though it by no means rests on obvious facts. A large number of anthropologists employ a wide array of intellectual means in an effort to remain insensible to it. When one places oneself in the mythological or sociological field, what makes it possible to pass from an ontogenetic perspective to an ontological inquiry is the existence of definable, tangible and analysable productions which are all symbolic formations, projections – condensed, displaced, dramatised – of what could be called the implicit, or the potential element at the base of ontogenetic development. What is then revealed may, from the ontogenetic angle, be present, but it remains invisible and can only be thought about in a latent form. Individual ontogenesis is reflected through mythical and social productions in social ontogenesis – that is, in what can be inferred from taking into consideration the evolution of an individual, from his birth to the moment he acquires an identity in the social group. Myths also give an account of the genesis of society through the history of their heroes – the very ones who are supposed to have taken part in the creation of a social order. The social nature of the object, its general-isation, allows us to comprehend that which, in an individual, and even in a series or collection of individuals, may be suspected of being aleatory, accidental and contingent. The social dimension gives depth, substance and desubjectivation to a subjectivity that seems to get dissolved in collective life. There, the narrative does not so much relate a history as a condensation of histories that are fused, individual and social, real and mythical. This quasi-guarantee of cred-ibility offered by de-individualised social expression perhaps allows us to be satisfied with a causal hypothesis which attributes the result to the articulation of a set of phantasies and elementary affects, supplying the elaboration of the cultural work (myth, rite, cosmology) with the key signifiers which form its basic material. Here I would say that the visibility of the labour of the work is enough to justify, for its part, the causal approach; whereas the reference to ontogenesis is only supposed to provide the starting-point.

But when one turns towards the individual, and when socio-cultural references – that is, the body of mediations which make it possible to notice retrospectively what the human mind has done and, in turn, to analyse its structure after it has given birth to its substantial productions – become indirect, what are we to do? It is here that the hypothesis of the primal arises, fitting into the gap separating individual and social ontogenetic productions. On the one hand, the aim is to provide a firm basis for the coherence of the ontogenetic and, on the other, to try and explain its projective power at the collective level which, it should not be forgotten, cements the relations between individuals and creates an order of its own.

This explains why an anthropologist can safely write: 'We do not believe in the persistence in society, as such, of a phylogenetic memory of repressed collective childhood from which the group is still seeking today to free itself: childhood can only be individual, and it is its trace in adult psyches which allows it to be reformulated in social and evolutionary terms.'[26] And yet it is the same anthropologist who postulates a pre-social semantic and symbolic layer to account for myths and rites. How is this layer organised? The question is referred back to the psychoanalyst – in the hope that he will see no need to resort to phylogenesis.

In any case, phylogenesis is in fact always retroactive, built on the insufficiencies of ontogenesis – not simply on a deficient memory, but, conversely, on the excess of meaning that goes beyond the verisimilitude of an acquisition through learning. This very excess needs to be grasped by a minimal signifying organisation. Phylogenesis is not the recourse to a plethora of themes that add something to individual experience, but an attempt to determine what might provide a model for its possible reduction. The history of the individual, society, life, and the universe is not only interlocking, but gives birth retroactively to implicit categories which can be identified in the narrative truth. As the latter unfolds, it reveals the gaps between the different universes it comprises.

We are perhaps better equipped today to grasp the richness and complexity of the signifying combinations and how they are transmitted intergenerationally, intersubjectively and interpsychically. Can it be assumed that, during the process of raising children, messages, governed by key signifiers, are communicated, which silently transmit from one generation to another these organisers which I call primordial schemes? On this view, the primordial is not to be seen as the product of a hypothesis of biology-fiction; rather, it is re-transmitted, re-communicated , 'decanted', so to speak, to each human being in each generation. By distinguishing between what has been acquired and what cannot be acquired, Freud remained far too confined by a conception of how experience is communicated that is limited to effects that can be made explicit. Today, we are in a position to explain both the invisible and silent character of what is transmitted – which depends on organising structures – and to understand the effects of this transmission via the constitution of networks of communication which are assumed to maintain secondary or derivative formations under their control. This empirical vision, which does without Freud's speculations, is itself based on hypotheses that are no less audacious than those of the primal phantasies. The differences between cultural variations that produce multiple forms of upbringing are held to be invalid in the sphere of the primordial which touches on the fundamental questions of the difference between the sexes and generations, conception, birth, the act of giving birth ... and death. This is what some anthropologists maintain. Can we genuinely decide on which side our preferences lie? All that can be said is that such a conception fits in better with our epistemological horizon, but that it is scarcely more assured. The best solution, as Freud found, would be to come to the conclusion: *non liquet.*

Another question that has not been raised is this: does the experience that has been acquired since Freud confirm the limitation of the primal phantasies to those that he described, or does it require that others be proposed? It seems to me, in effect, that the epistemological requirement necessitates the conception of 'organising schemes of disorganisation', if one may put it like that. In other words, basic models from which multiple and variable forms of destructiveness can develop. The experience of borderline cases, where destructiveness plays such an important role, makes it possible to infer these symbolic matrices of destructiveness. They concern the relation to the object, the limits of the psyche, and, finally, the partial or total death of the ego. Furthermore, it seems to me that the links between these primordial schemes of destructiveness and the primal phantasies cause forms of opposition or symmetry to emerge between them, which in turn give the psychic conflict its full measure.

A Plea for Transitional Concepts

Freud's thought is always informed by that of the child Sigmund who was constantly asking the question 'Why?' and who only stopped doing so when he had found the adult equivalent of the infantile sexual theories of which he was reminded by little Hans. We have reconstituted the theoretical fresco – of which primal phantasies are only a part – which brought Freud the relief of having found an answer that satisfied his curiosity, and we have had no difficulty in recognising its status as biological fiction. But, in spite of that, it has not been possible to jettison these scientific fairy tales because, like the infantile theories, they correspond to a logical necessity. What I have called the epistemological requirement has not disappeared, however, even in the face of scientific criticism. The speculative aspect of these theories at least has the merit of taking seriously the problems posed by the psychical organisation. As I have already said, the theory of the primal phantasy has itself become a primal phantasy.

Let us remain, then, with regard to what is primal in the psychic or social sphere, within the framework of the irreproachable scientific vision. It is accepted today that the prohibition of incest has the status of a 'rule of rules'. It is regarded as constituting a demarcation line between nature and culture. Freud had already understood this a long time ago. But the eternal child in him asked: 'Why?' And if he had lived long enough to hear the explanation given by Lévi-Strauss who accounts for the phenomenon in terms of the necessity of establishing modalities of exchange, he would certainly have seen this as one of the disguised forms of a new parental lie: a fable of the stork for scientists. It was necessary to wait a generation before Maurice Godelier was to propose an interpretation that was closer to Freud's, in which he suggested that the prohibition of incest was a necessary step towards the creation of society. Nevertheless, the Freudian thesis was seen as the typical example of a non-scientific explanation.

The process of investigating the primal generates primal phantasies. The theory of primal phantasies certainly gives the impression of being a phantasy because, once it has begun investigating the individual's past, it cannot stop, and goes right back to his origins, that is, to the generation which gave birth to him as well as to the generation before that, and so on, until all the real and imaginary genealogies have been exhausted.

In a discussion on Piera Aulagnier's ideas,[27] I said that I felt the concept of the primal, in psychoanalysis, was quite untenable. I pointed out that any idea of the primal linked to the individual alone was illusory, since such a conception alluded to a symbiotic situation between mother and child, an indivisible couple, linking the child's psychical apparatus to the mother's, making the construction of the first exchanges between them depend on the latter. This directed us away from the primal of the One to the adult state of the Other, itself a vehicle of the primal (the primal of the Other) depending on its relation to its own ascendant, and so on. From the moment there is intergenerational transmission – and this is the inescapable case of human beings – the primal no longer exists except as a convention which, for practical reasons, fixes more or less arbitrarily a limit to the theory that is more arbitrary than logical.

Other Primordial Schemes?

The primal phantasies in Freud's work date back to the first topography. The invention of the second left them intact. That is to say, sexuality continued to be their sole concern. It may come as a surprise, then, that the introduction of the death drive did not lead to any significant change as far as they were concerned. At the risk of being reproached for increasing still further the amount of speculation in the theory, I propose to add another series of primordial schemes. The first, those which Freud proposed, had an organising value for sexuality. The second, of which I am going to speak, underlie, in my view, the disorganisations that are due to the death drive.

I therefore propose to take into account the following disorganising primal phantasies (to continue to use the current terminology):

- *Phantasies of separation and loss*: these concern all the anxieties which appear during ego–object separation and which involve the threat of losing the object in the most extreme cases – a threat which is nonetheless present in germ during separations of short duration.
- *Phantasies of destructive penetration*: these are connected with the infringement of all the limits of the body, the ego and the

psyche, breaking down the protective barriers and introducing into the now vulnerable space intrusive, destructive agents of all sorts.

- *Phantasies of expelling and emptying*: they express the fear of an evacuation of internal contents leaving the psychic space drained of its possessions and its contents.
- *Phantasies of autonomy and autolysis*: they represent a desperate measure of partial self-amputation or self-annihilation (suicide). These forms of self-destruction correspond to the pure unbound destructivity postulated by Freud at the end of his life. They are linked to the disobjectalising function whose existence I have postulated.

Intergenerational transmission requires that two causal series be taken into account: first, the individual primal world of the *infans* and, second, the parental 'discourse' – which is transmitted via the relationship with the mother's body – which resonates from the *infans* that she was to the *infans* to whom she has now given birth. The limits of the individual primal world are overwhelmed from all sides. Referring simply to the mother as the point of origin is not the solution. For this 'origin' also seeks its own origin by going back to the mother's own mother. Nevertheless, this ceaseless quest for sources does not succeed in doing away with the difficult question of the primal. This depends less, however, on finding a single source than on finding indicators that constitute limits or signs of what should be considered as primordial. There is no origin without primal markers. Once it was clear that psychoanalysis was a discipline which set value on the role of past events, working silently in the lower levels of the psyche, it was faced with an immense task; namely, that of constructing a psychic temporality on the basis of new facts, that is, symptoms, such as reminiscences, screen memories, infantile amnesia, the repressed, and so on. With infantile sexuality which had been very efficiently denied during thousands of years, Freud – notwithstanding the amnesia of analysands and the denial of adults (parents, educators, and so on) – brought to light a dynamogenic factor of development, an inductor of psychic activity, a polarising agent of experience. Owing to the fact of sexual diphasism, temporality found that the quality of continuity that was traditionally its own was now being contested. The *coupure* or 'cut' of latency severed the thread of Ariadne which might have led – as far back as memory permitted – towards the origins of erotic pleasure. This retrogressive orientation of erogeneity towards the most distant[28] past of childhood comes up against the discovery of another causality than that of history and takes another approach – that is to say, of an imaginary origin, as a response to the questions that are asked by children. The infantile sexual theories corresponded to the child's need for causality faced with the puzzling questions of life. Psychoanalytic theory discovered its ancestors in the infantile sexual theories; but the latter were phantasies with theoretical pretensions. In its retrogressive movement, therefore, theory had to take account of theorisation as a consequence of development. The child thus revealed its capacity to theorise. And though the theory could be nothing but a phantasy, conversely, phantasy was inhabited by theorisation.

It was only when Freud had completed the journey leading him to 'Analysis Terminable and Interminable' (1937a) that he was in a position to recognise clearly the link between theory and phantasy. For there is a paradox that psychoanalysis can only escape with difficulty: when theory recognises the place and the function of phantasy, and then attempts to build a theory of phantasy, driving the latter into its last lines of defence, it will be forced to ask itself: is the theory not itself a phantasy?

There are those who will say that it is precisely against such confusions that science takes precautions. The problem is that science – on account of its own limitations – shows that it is incapable of providing a scientific theory of phantasy.

I have tried to get out of this dilemma by according more or less space to phantasy in the question of origins; more precisely, by not bringing phantasy into the picture until after the encounter with experience. I have postulated the concept – even more primal – of primordial schemes. Their function is to provide markers for what governs later developments, and to act as organisers of temporality since they make it possible to think, retroactively (après coup), about what happened before; and to recognise in the anticipation of the future only what is part of the same problematic. Given that the matter cannot be resolved, I have suggested two possible versions: one pertaining to biological heredity, the other to social heredity.

Rather than making a hasty decision about what cannot be decided, we can recognise the epistemological requirement of the primordial schemes and suspend all judgement as to the origin of the primal. To do this, I propose the creation of a new category, that of *transitional concepts*. These concepts would be endowed with 'negative capacity' (Keats cited by Bion): they would be related to Winnicott's intermediate area of experience – that is to say, the opposition true/false would not be applicable to them. They would have a similar status to hypotheses – though the latter are tested and consequently accepted or rejected after they have been put to the test. These transitional concepts would be created purely on the basis of logical requirements related to the degree of complexity of the object to which they apply. In the case under consideration they would account for the way in which the primordial schemes organise themselves into categories of signs which accompany the passage of time and contribute to structuring it.[29]

Psychoanalytic reductionism often comes in for criticism. Yet all knowledge is reductive. What is important is the choice of the reductive parameters, ensuring that the object of study is not mutilated by a flattening distortion and that its 'reduced model' continues to bear witness to its complexity. We have no hang-ups today about speaking of the origin of the cosmos, the origin of life, or the origin of man. It is more embarrassing, however, to speak of the origins of the psyche. We therefore prefer to hide our ignorance by confusing psyche and brain. It is difficult, however, at the present time, to imagine how the study of the brain can shed light on the question of the primal seen from the angle of primordial schemes. But where does this difficulty come from, if not from the fact that the examination of such an issue requires the coexistence of such diverse modes of psychic functioning, bringing into play the most rigorous as well as the freest aspects, the most defined as well as the most indeterminate objects, the most rational modes of thought as well as the most ... imaginary?

At the beginning could there be ... primal phantasy?

3   Repetition, Difference, Replication: A Re-Reading of *Beyond the Pleasure Principle* (1970)*

> Look in thy glass and tell the face thou viewest.
> Now is the time that face should form another,
> Whose fresh repair if now thou not renewest,
> Thou dost beguile the world, unbless some mother.
> For where is she so fair whose uneared womb
> Disdains the tillage of thy husbandry?
> Or who is he so fond will be the tomb
> Of his self-love, to stop posterity?
> Thou art thy mother's glass and she in thee
> Calls back the lovely April of her prime;
> So thou through windows of thine age shalt see,
> Despite of wrinkles, this thy golden time.
> But if thou live, remembered not to be,
> Die single, and thine image dies with thee.

> William Shakespeare, *Sonnet III*

Between two points, *a* and *b*, whether they be in space or time, between *a* and *b* I have to say no: No, I do not want to belong to the devil, no I do not want to go to hell; no I do not want to be his mistress. Between these points *a* and *b*, either I am unable to say no because there is someone in me who says yes in my place, or because there has not been time to say no; or because I have been unable to say no at this particular moment, which amounts to a quarter of a second. One second after I have accepted to belong to the devil, I am assailed by frightful, frightful, frightful pangs of torment and remorse. In order to repair the error, it is necessary to abolish time. I call this negative entropy, since the error does not exist. So the same action has to be continually

* First published as 'Répétition, différance, replication' in *Revue française de psychanalyse*, XXXIV, 1970, pp. 461–501.

repeated, i.e. one has put oneself back in the same conditions in the reverse direction, while repeating, 'No, I do not want to belong to the devil'. I tell myself that, if this is to mean no, if what has happened is to be erased, the same action has to be repeated under the same conditions – something that is impossible. Consider how through a microscope one can always manage to notice differences ... you can never repeat the same action, or express it again in exactly the same way: so I start doing the same thing over and over again, I try to put myself in the same conditions; but it is just that my obsession tells me, my anxiety tells me, that no, it was not exactly the same thing ...

This was the prelude to an obsessional patient's discourse, where the compulsion to repeat is clearly in evidence.

Compulsion involves constraint; repetition involves returning to the same past in order to abolish time, which for the psychoanalyst is the time of prohibited desire. The time of desire is projected onto the space of objects, onto the path between two objects in the external world, two points in a libidinised space. There is a sexualisation of the objects of thought which negation must desexualise. The re-emergence of difference cannot be erased in spite of the efforts to do so. If, for us too, time were not limited, it would have been possible to show how, in the hundred or so minutes that the session lasted, three repetitions occurred in succession. First, the time of the symptom, illustrating the compulsion to repeat. Secondly, the time of phantasy, expressing the themes of a novel worthy of Queneau, in which the terms of the obsessional theme (possession by the devil) are repeated. And thirdly, the time of history in which the themes of symptom and the fantasy converge, the devil appearing in the three figures of the father, the husband and the son, in fact, as the one who possesses the phallus which the patient is lacking. The meaning of repetition here is therefore one of repeating the lack and obsession with its object.

The notion of repetition has always been on the horizon of psychoanalytic research. From the moment he affirmed that hysterics suffered from reminiscences, Freud knew that something was being repeated through the symptom. This emergence of repetition is not peculiar to neurosis; it is linked to the very structure of psychic mechanisms. In Letter 52 to Fliess, Freud wrote:

As you know, I am working on the assumption that our psychic mechanism has come into being by a process of stratification: the material present in the form of memory traces being subjected from time to time to a *rearrangement* in accordance with fresh circumstances – to a *retranscription*. Thus what is essentially new about my theory is the thesis that memory is present not once but several times over, that it is laid down in various kinds of indications.[1]

Repetition is thus an integral part of the constitution of memory. By repeating the memory in the symptom, the latter reproduces the constitution of its memory, continuing to make, in a different style, new inscriptions. It pursues the project of inscribing within and without that which is unsaid, and therefore still remains to be said. The different kinds of signs by which the repressed expresses its return can be seen in repeating, remembering and working-through.[2] The intrapsychic signs are supplemented in this text by the register of the act. In 1937, 'Constructions in Analysis' would detail once again the different kinds of signs that are repeated in the analytic material – like exhumed products of a psychic reality whose vitality persists through the traces it brings to light.

Thus no sign is primal and unique in itself; whatever it is, it is the product of repetition, to which no absolute genesis can be assigned. Its repeated manifestation and its insistent nature are signs of a process of repetition, and it is pointless to look for its source in a first trace. What it emphasises is that there is repetition, that there has already been repetition, and that there will be more of it to come.

The Wooden Reel Game: A First Reading

If, having referred to a few of the precursory texts on repetition, we now turn our attention towards the game of the child and the wooden reel, it is not so much in order to determine its origin – either in Freud's work or in the child's life – but because it is the paradigm of the manifestation of repetition. It is what attracted Freud's attention to the fact of repetition and invited him to give it its conceptual importance.

The fact that it has already given rise to innumerable commentaries will not discourage me from adding my own.[3] It is important to comment first on the conditions of the game. This game was the activity of an ordinary child who was in no way distinguished by a precocious or exceptional intelligence.[4] Though nothing makes it worthy of special interest, its ordinariness holds our attention in so far as it refers to an 'order of things' which pertains to childhood. The child's development was normal; he was brought up, nourished and looked after by his mother. This observation seems to me to be important. For the significance of repetition to be uncovered, it is essential that the symbolic organisation has not been altered too much in development by the effects of a serious trauma. An abandoned child, or a child suffering from hospitalism, would very probably not have played like this. Instead of throwing a wooden reel and then pulling it back again, uttering a cry as he did so, he would perhaps have started rocking or banging his head against the walls in a stereotyped way. Freud says that the child with the wooden reel accepted the necessity for instinctual renunciation precisely because of his mother's love. That is to say, he accepted the inevitability of losing his mother temporarily when she went away. It might be said that he was symbolising in accordance with his submission to necessity. Here, in Freud's writing, Logos and Ananké are seen to be inseparable.

However, in spite of the submission to instinctual renunciation, to 'this fact of life', the game, owing to an unforeseen effect, is instituted as an unconscious analogous representative structure. I say 'structure' because the emerging symbolisation unites three categories of phenomena:

(a)   a motor pro-jection (the act of throwing away/pulling back);
(b)   a representative-perceptual activity (seeing/not seeing the wooden reel);
(c)   a linguistic 'inter-jection' (*o-o-o-o-da* for *fort-da*).[5]

It follows from the foregoing that this symbolisation appears at the heart of a set-up which justifies the extremely detailed description Freud gives of the whole game.

On the one hand this set-up includes:

• a wooden reel (the object),
• a piece of string which is tied round it – long enough so that, however far the wooden reel is thrown, it can be pulled back to the child (the 'throwing action' of the drive),
• a curtained cot, the sides of which are high enough so that the child cannot see the wooden reel once it has been thrown (the screen separating inside and outside).

And, on the other, a child endowed with:

- a hand,
- eyes,
- a voice,

plus a witness not directly involved in the game: Freud the grand-father.

There are two ideas underlying my analysis of this description. The first is that the set-up as a whole forms a montage whose elements are interdependent and grouped together in a functional assemblage. The second is that this assemblage is the product of two complementary halves: one belongs to the child and the other to the inert elements of the assemblage, that is, the instruments of the game.[6] Now we need to come to the interpretation of the game. This calls for a series of responses on different levels and raises conceptual difficulties of an increasing order.

From the outset Freud was faced with the following question. Since what was being repeated was a painful situation, how could the fact that the child was repeating a distressing experience in the game be squared with the pleasure principle? We know what the answer seemed to be for Freud, even though he was not satisfied with it: the child transforms an overpowering situation that is experi-enced passively into an active situation of mastery. He pulls the strings activating the wooden reel-marionette.[7]

This 'abreaction' can be recognised in experiences that are unmis-takably disagreeable, as in the game of playing the doctor,[8] which Anna Freud was to describe as identification with the aggressor. If we extend this interpretation and include Melanie Klein's perspec-tive, the aim of the game would not only be to defend oneself against a painful situation, but also to allow for a discharge of aggressive impulses. On this view, the game is seen as the disguised expression of vengeance towards the mother who is killed and resuscitated endlessly. What Freud was struck by was the undiffer-entiated character of the repetition in which both what is agreeable and disagreeable is repeated. Children repeat – and make adults repeat – the same stories, whether or not they have left an agreeable or disagreeable impression on them, while at the same time demanding scrupulous respect for the slightest detail and rectifying any variations on an earlier version. There is no doubt that, in itself, this repetition can be an object of pleasure. But the transformation of unpleasure into pleasure, which is no longer linked to the theme but to the repetition in itself, assigns the latter with a function that is problematic. The game itself cannot demonstrate the thesis that the compulsion to repeat goes beyond the pleasure principle, under the auspices of the drive; other examples will be necessary (traumatic neurosis, transference).

We need, however, to return to the game and to approach it at another interpretative level, which is implicit in Freud's approach. The game is presented here as an analogy for instinctual functioning. I have just pointed out that, for Freud, repetition is the essence of the instinct or, as Pasche says, is 'the instinct of the instinct'. In this experience of throwing away and pulling back the wooden reel, we can detect a metaphor for the activity of the instinct, the movement of which is directed towards the object it cannot reach. This creates anxieties of losing it which are quickly overcome through the pleasurable experience of finding it again.

These initial reflections now take us on to another level, which is the one I am interested in. I am referring to the way in which the relations between subject and object are determined by the game. What we are dealing with is a double object; in fact, it is doubled twice over. There is the wooden reel and there is the mother. Each of these two objects is duplicated: the wooden reel is both lost and found; and the mother both goes away and returns (*fort-da*). The object's position in this symbolic organisation suggests that it is important, to paraphrase Winnicott on the transitional object, that the wooden reel both is and is not the mother. The object here is subject to splitting – a split between the wooden reel and the mother which echoes the split between part object and whole object. The part object, that is, the wooden reel, assumes the value of the whole object; the whole object is represented in its entirety in the part object. The partialness of presence-absence invests the whole object. This split is reproduced within each of the terms: the absence-presence of the wooden reel and the mother who is both far away and here. The two terms of this correspondence are mediated by perception and representation (visible-invisible object), and language (*fort-da* in *o-o-o-o/da*) which each repeat the motor act by imitating it and splitting it off from its expressions on other levels.

This double and split status of the object may be set alongside a double and split status of the subject. There are two opposing interpretations of the subject here. In the classical interpretation, the subject is the child understood as the active pole of the game, as the agent of the game. It is the child who stages the game, throwing the wooden reel away and pulling it back again; it is the child who notices the object's absence or presence; and, finally, it is the child who articulates the different phases of it by uttering the words *fort-da*. The child is thus the subject as 'I'. If he could speak, he would say: 'I (the child) am playing with the object. I am playing at making my mother disappear and return.' But the child does not say this; Freud says it; for if the child could say it, he would perhaps no longer need to be captivated by the game. In fact, such a subject can only be the subject of consciousness. He plays at making his mother disappear and return, whereas he is played by her, so to speak, in her absence. He only plays to the extent that he is played, however much of a feat he accomplishes in reversing this situation of passivity into activity. Here, then, we have the modern interpretation of the subject. On this view, the subject here is no longer the agent, but that which, owing to the circumstances, can only sustain the pretension of manifesting himself as such by passivating his activity. Which does not mean that he is a victim of the situation, but that he must make this passivation[9] his own by externalising it again at the level of a third party situated in the position of observer. The subject is rendered passive by a situation which dominates and places constraints on him, that is, desire for the object in the experience of lack following its loss. This constraint forces him to make an interpretation and a distortion which give rise to the game. On the one hand, the constitution of the sequence constituted by the game binds together the diffuse effects of the situation of absence; this now becomes part of a series whose essential property is its capacity for reproduction. On the other, this situation creates a certain amount of play which in turn allows the series to be inscribed on several levels in which the drama of absence becomes a diversion. What the game was trying to divert, however, makes its return at the heart of this diversion. Why is there this expression of joy when the wooden reel returns? Play not only creates illusion; it deludes itself through allusion.

I have described the conditions under which the game is possible (normal child, instinctual renunciation), the role of the assemblage, the montage, and lastly, the circuit realised by the game; for the game is a circular one – the reappearance of the wooden reel calling for its disappearance again, which is then followed by its reappearance, thanks to the possibilities offered by the set-up. But it is necessary to stress the importance of absence, of negativity. The mother has to be experienced as lost for the child to have a need to repeat something by playing the game. This dimension of absence forces the subject to manifest himself, just as the absence of food and hunger force the wolf to come out of the wood. This negativity must, however, remain within tolerable limits and contain the hope of return; it must not be disastrous (for otherwise it merely engenders a catastrophic reaction).

From this point of view, the subject no longer manifests himself simply by actively creating the game. The subject is the process which includes all the elements of the set-up. This process is constituted by all the elements on which it depends: not only the hand, the eyes and the voice, but also the wooden reel, the string, the cot, the surrounding space and the circuit which is created in it. The subject comes into existence in this circulation which includes projection accompanied by interjection in the oscillation 'disappearance–return', leading to the retroactive introjection of the game. This submission to the elements of the whole set-up, this construction of an assemblage, constitutes an *analogon* for a psychical apparatus that puts itself at the service of the trend towards extinguishing a tension. The subject is thus defined by all the elements in the process constituted by repetition aimed at extinguishing tension. For one operation of the apparatus alone is not enough. The circulation, the trajectory of the circuit requires the operation to be reproduced in order to stabilise the process. The trace left by a single operation has to be continuously passed over again if the subject is to be able to constitute himself. Played just once, the game has no meaning. It was in seeing it repeated that Freud concluded that its function was to abolish the lack created by his mother's absence. The subject constitutes himself through the repetition marking the new passage over earlier traces. It is a trace that is not primal, but only antecedent; and it can only be spoken about at the moment when the pathway returns towards the appeal that it has inscribed. Here it appears retrospectively as an insistent sign, revealing a trace that has been brought back to life, immediately erased again, and is now capable of playing the role of a new trace the novelty of which is abolished by its antecedent. In the material of our analyses, a psychical constellation is only significant when it is repeated – this is our best indicator. Thus one can say with Lacan: the One is engendered through repetition.

The subject of the unconscious stands in opposition here to the subject of consciousness. There is, in fact, a duality in the subject arising from the split between conscious and unconscious. For by adhering to the interpretation of the subject as an active agent of the game, we abandon the specificity of the unconscious position of the subject caught up in a network of operations to which he is subject rather than being their initiator. For many psychoanalysts the subject can only be the subject of the drives and the desires that inhabit him, even if he is unaware of it. What can be questioned in this approach is whether such a subject exists as an intentional subject. For me, the subject, like meaning, emerges retrospectively, as a result of the operation of the process. In fact when he is playing, the child does not know what his play is about, otherwise he would not be playing and he would not be captivated as he is by the game. The discovery, retrospectively, that the game can be invested with meaning makes the subject emerge as 'I' in the course of the game, which is a process of absence.[10]

It is tempting, then, to fill the gap of this split with unconscious phantasy. This would be seen as the *primum movens* of the game. Is phantasy a constitutive, organising factor of the game?[11] In fact one should say that phantasy is constituted retroactively by the game. Phantasy is unconscious, not only because it hides 'behind the game', but because it is constituted by it. At the outset desire is the leaven of phantasy, but only the execution of the game allows phantasy to structure itself. The game is first and foremost a projection of the drive, an impulse of phantasy. This impulse, of which unconscious phantasy is the retroactive representation, has the aim of binding the unpleasure of the lack or absence of the mother.

Above all, the game reproduces, repeats, this matrix of the loss and rediscovery of the object which are closely bound up here in a single operation comprising two phases in which the second follows from the first. As it constructs itself, structures itself, phantasy will make it possible to achieve various combinations by means of a system of variable permutations – as can be seen from the example of 'A Child is Being Beaten' (1919). Thus the wooden reel may be seen both as the mother herself and as the servant who takes the place of the mother, that is, the father. The child as such is not a subject but a term entering into relationship with the other terms of an ensemble to which he is subject and which can only be thought about as an ensemble. The result of the game is to institute this ensemble which functions as an *analogon* for the situation of losing–refinding the mother and for the operations of the psychical apparatus. The child is himself a part term (part object), the totality (provisional) having no other significance than the (open) ensemble of relations established between the related terms.[12] There are two aspects of repetition here. The repetition of the game itself – that is, the endless process of starting all over again which the game involves, and the game as repetition, as a symbolisation of what is happening on another stage. But the result surpasses the realisation. As a result we are drawn towards a different space from that which constituted the game.

To understand this repetition in the chain it forms with similar experiences, one only has to refer to Freud's work itself. One of its first forms can be found in another game, related in *Inhibitions, Symptoms and Anxiety* (1926 [1925]), where the mother is playing with her child by hiding her face in her hands and making it reappear repeatedly. The game is over-signifying to the extent that the hidden face also evokes an expression of sadness, whereas its reappearance is accompanied by an expression of joy on the face of the one who both creates the game and mimes the reactions of the spectator to whom it is addressed. Here the set-up is reduced to the minimum, but it nonetheless requires the screen formed by the mother's hands.

In another game mentioned by Freud, once again in *Beyond the Pleasure Principle*, the child had found a way of making himself 'gone', that is, he could make his mirror-image disappear by crouching down below the lower edge of a wall mirror. But it would be wrong to think that only two terms – the child and his image – are present here; for the mirror as a reflecting surface and the wall panel which continues to the floor as a non-reflecting surface are also necessary to the set-up. Without them the game is not possible.[13]

The child makes himself disappear in the game, just as the game with the wooden reel allows him to split himself into an agent of the game and an element of the process that he constitutes.

The Mythical Prototype of the Wooden Reel Game and the Psychical Apparatus

The meaning of the game is thus to provide a visible *analogon* for the functioning of the mental apparatus. Among Freud's texts concerning this apparatus, there are two that seem particularly suited for defending this comparison: 'A Note Upon the Mystic Writing-Pad' (written during the autumn of 1924) and 'Negation', written in July 1925. These two articles are very closely connected. If 'Negation' roots the function of judgement in instinctual life, it is because the

'Mystic Writing-Pad' had already laid the groundwork indicating that the work of thinking had to be apprehended through the structures of a mental apparatus.

When, in 'Negation', Freud discusses the function of judgement and its relation to the original pleasure-ego, he defines its properties: 'what is good and useful should be eaten, taken inside myself (introjected); what is bad or harmful should be spit out or kept outside myself (projected)'.[14] Eros marks the first of these, whereas the destructive instincts underlie the second.

As in Freud's metapsychological construction, the child with the wooden reel distinguishes between inside and outside; his limits are duplicated by the second frontier formed by the edge of his curtained cot. By making this comparison, I want to stress that the distinction inside–outside is not limited to the ego and the external world but that, in the interpretation of the game as structure and process, this first distinction occurs again at the heart of the inside and is transposed to another space which is an outside within the internal space as distinct from the outside of the external world. There is, so to speak, in this first approximation of the inside, in its very space, an inside and an outside. The game allows an outside to be established which ceases to be confused with the indefinite 'far away', the elsewhere that is pushed away indefinitely, in order to become this particular 'far away' from where the wooden reel can return. The whole theory of representation is involved here, but this paradigm helps us to understand that it does not so much evoke the object statically as it evokes a movement. It is by means of this return that the inside qualifies itself in that it is no longer opposed to an outside of exclusion, but re-includes this exclusion at the heart of the inside itself. It is not that the outside is in this way entirely reconquered; it subsists as a field of possibility to be determined at a later stage. By virtue of this internalisation, a part of the past of this rejected outside finds its place by designating itself as a future in waiting. Thus the *coupure*, the cut, is displaced from the space it divides towards this elsewhere whose new affectation shifts the frontier of what will now have to be delimited between the subject as agent of the game and the game as constitutive of the subject in process. It is, then, by pulling back the object, which both is and is not the mother, that the game holds the subject in its net as a process, quite independently of its playful intention. It determines him not only as desiring the mother but also as allowing himself to desire her and to save desire from the rupture of bonds threatening the relationship.

Throwing the wooden reel away is not only about suffering the loss of the mother; it is about throwing the substitute for the bad mother or the bad breast far away, outside. Pulling the wooden reel back again is about re-finding the good breast, the one that is within reach, at one's disposal, which can be used as one wishes, introjected and preserved. Later on, it is the mother as a whole object who will be alternatively lost and found again in the depressive position which involves mourning the object. I have already mentioned the interpretation of the game as an act of vengeance towards the mother. The wooden reel game is repetitive, not because it is indefinitely repeated in the act, but because the act itself symbolises the effectuation of the passively experienced situation of the loss of the breast. While actively symbolising, the game captures the child in this symbolisation where he only figures as one of its terms, displacing the subject from his pseudo-activity to the process of the structure as a whole. The mythical event of the loss of the breast is the matrix of symbolisation to the extent that it splits the good and bad object in two and, correlatively, the introjecting and projecting ego. As a result, the game finds a solution to absence.

Unlike Melanie Klein, Freud makes a radical separation between the two qualities: good and bad do not hang together as the two halves of a single unity. The bad is lost (like the object that engenders it); it is rejected, excluded and, one can even say, foreclosed.[15] The bad will be the matrix of the repressed (bad for the subject or bad in the eyes of the Other). In this respect, the unconscious is indeed circumscribed by repression, since even that which is good for the subject but bad in the mother's eyes will suffer this fate. Ego and object are thus split into two separate halves – which will require symbolisation to repeat itself in the search for the missing part that is always lost.

The conception of the lost object – even if it is that of a mythical event or one apprehended as such *a posteriori* – which is so pronounced in Freud, was minimised in Melanie Klein's work and destined, ultimately, to disappear from her theory. For though the lack of the object is indeed, as she says, the cause of what is bad, everything is present, positive, coexistent, without loss; good or bad share the psychic space between them. The depressive position in Melanie Klein's work – and we know how much structural importance she gave to it – has the aim of avoiding definitive loss, which in Freud is postulated as an aporetic requirement for establishing the reality principle. Melanie Klein counts on a progressive conciliation of instinct and reality. Freud interposes a cut between them which will turn the lost objects 'which once brought satisfaction' into a kind of empty ensemble capable of gathering in all the work elaborated after this irremediable separation, thus providing an opportunity for interminable reparation. This reparation is not only affective, but conceptual, in the widest sense of the term. For, as Freud says in 'Negation' (1925a), the judgement as to the existence of something allows for a reconstitution fending against this loss:

> Thinking possesses the capacity to bring before the mind once more something that has once been perceived, by reproducing it as a presentation without the external object having still to be there.[16]

To put this another way, the re-presentation is a reproduction, a repetition of perceptual activity; likewise, I would add, word-presentation is a repetition (different, no doubt) of thing-presentation. Each of these operations introduces two other factors apart from repetition: interpretation and transformation (or distortion). Each repetition entails a new elaboration, a difference, due to the conjectural aspect of interpretation – and thus necessarily a distortion. Hence the importance of the transition from perceptual identity (the sphere of images) to thought identity (the sphere of language). Both re-find the object: the first by means of imaginary 'captation',[17] the second through the relations between the conditions of possibility for thinking about objects.

The transition from Freudian theory to Kleinian theory thus proves to be problematic. This is probably due to the fact that, in Freud, the introduction of the genetic model capable of accounting for operations correlative to the fundamental functioning of the unconscious infers, without always being explicit as to the modalities, a psychical apparatus which Melanie Klein does without. It is as though she expected the latter to emerge implicitly from the primitive mechanisms that she had just uncovered. Bion seems to have been aware of this. His hypothesis of an apparatus for thinking thoughts was an attempt to provide an answer. However, Bion's theoretical boldness does not shy away from the epistemological limits that Freud imposed on himself or which were imposed on him. For Bion, it is not the absent breast which is 'thought' in order to appease hunger; it is the 'no-breast' which is the first thought and which can subsequently become the object of thought processes. My own theoretical approach coincides with Bion's attempt, in his work, to articulate the works of Freud and Melanie Klein. The concept of negative hallucination, of which hallucinatory wish-fulfilment is the reverse side, allows us to evaluate the field of the inflections and variations of the relation lack-absence, but always by relating them to an *analogon* whose function of exclusion is the motive and motor of the renewed effects of structuring. The latter does not just displace the problem but opens it up to new registers.

Thus the work of thinking is a work of reconstruction: re-finding the object, repetition of the relational co-ordinates of experience, an imaginary non-memory that is found again but still subject to distortion, the search for a missing half, lost forever, which makes displacement necessary. The compulsion to repeat is a function of this irrevocable loss. From the breast to the mother's face, from the face to the mother as a whole person, from the mother to the wooden reel, from the wooden reel to the mirror, and from the mirror to identity. With his wooden reel the child thus re-plays, without respite, not only the mother's absence but also the disappearance of her face and the loss of the breast. A mother, Freud remarks, who had fed the child herself. In so doing he continually symbolises this loss. The disappearance of his image in the mirror shows that what is involved in this absence of himself where he constitutes a perception for the Other – quite apart from the imaginary captation by the image of the similar other in the mirror – is the relation between the perceived image, the perceiving ego, and the subject of the process considered independently of any form of perception. A relation is thus established between the continuity of identity in the mirror and the discontinuity which makes it possible to found the subject independently of any self-perception.

The passage from perceptual identity to thought-identity leads to two observations. First, this passage occurs in respect of the same object. It can therefore be said that thought-identity repeats the experience of perceptual identity. It is the same experience taken up again at another level and repeated. Secondly, perceptual identity and thought-identity presuppose that these operations are based on different properties: the plasticity of the sensible world of images that are compatible with continuity (transformation of a perceptive form into another closely related form through progressive distortions) – the (relatively) fixed nature of the intelligible world of words requiring discontinuity (opposition of phonemes).[18]

But what Freud omitted to say about this reunion is that it also involves a loss. The repetitions affecting the diverse kinds of signs never allow the primitive object to be found again as such, but only the co-ordinates making it possible to infer it deductively. Everything connoting the system of perceptual identity which aimed to assure itself of the object's presence, that is to say, all the sensuality which was its correlate, is lost. This sensuality will find refuge, partly, in what will mobilise phantasy, that is, the return of the pleasure principle at the heart of those domains where the sovereignty of the reality principle reigns – but only partly. It will invest itself in this new functional activity and will also no doubt change in nature as a result of its encounter with the new object on which it has an effect (thought-identity which not only makes it possible to recognise the object, but in its turn becomes an object of thought). The reduction in energy dealing with the 'small quantities' entails, in return, an investment of the secondary system whose level rises. An investment, moreover, which is itself capable – when the separation splitting it off from primary cathexes becomes too important – of being re-sensualised. The sexualisation of thought in obsessional patients is evidence of this. What stands in the way of this re-sexualisation is the way in which the serialisation of the work of thinking is constantly recommencing.[19] Initially, the obsessional attempts to stop this process by trying to slow down the displacement by focusing on trivial details. The failure of this procedure results in the sexual re-investment of thought-activity, countering the mummification of the displacement. Here, the obsessional poses, above all, the problem of the manner in which the response of the Other is thwarted at the level of thinking, as is indicated by the incorporation of phantasy into thought-activity. There is thus a dual inscription of the object of thought at the level of secondary processes: on the one hand, as an indefinite process of re-commencement, an empty ensemble deploying itself in multiplicity; and, on the other, as a conjunctive-disjunctive relation with the primary process via the copula of phantasy – the play of thought being instituted as means and end simultaneously.

On the contrary, with the schizophrenic, though the forces of destruction cannot destroy a hated reality (external or internal), they do at least still have the power to have a bearing on this reality, the individual confusing the way the Other looks at him with the process of destruction that he himself has initiated. The underlying phantasy of omnipotence sees itself transmuted in return; it ceases to become a phantasy and becomes a fact; and thoughts are submitted to the artifice of a concretisation which *compresses* instead of condensing, *fuses* instead of articulating 'things-in-themselves' (Bion). Everything suggests, then, that we should not start with this agglomeration of constituent structures, but with their differential deployment which will refer us to the work whose functioning, *a contrario*, may be seen in the psychotic process.

At this juncture, we must go back a few months to the autumn of 1924 when Freud wrote 'A Note upon the Mystic Writing-Pad'. I will not repeat the detailed description of the little device – just as detailed as that of the wooden reel game – the preciseness of which has impressed commentators.[20] Let me simply recall that it combines the advantages of unlimited receptive capacity (the slate) and the durability of the trace (the sheet of paper); to these Freud adds its capacity to receive multiple inscriptions. The activity of repetition, requiring successive re-inscriptions, is substituted here by their single inscription, which, at one stroke, gives diverse types of traces simultaneously. In one movement, the pointed stylus produces a triple conjoined trace, a model (preserved in the wax) and its two copies (one visible on the sheet of waxed paper, the other invisible on the layer of celluloid). Equally, one movement is all that is necessary to erase the two copies and to retain the model by means of an operation of separation-disjunction. This operation of inscription-erasure is reminiscent of the alternating phases of the wooden reel game. What was a rejection of the bad, the hostile, the foreign, here only affects what is perishable. Its trace in the wax endures. Repetition and time are connected. Discontinuity, necessary for repetition, is realised by means of the intermittent investment of the perceptual apparatus, which leads Freud to conclude that the discontinuous mode of functioning is the basis for the representation of time. What repetition contributes to this discontinuity which is necessary to its constitution is the reappearance successively of what was presented simultaneously.

This passage shows how this matter had continued to preoccupy Freud ever since Letter 52 cited earlier, in which he wrote:

Thus what is essentially new about my theory is the thesis that memory is present not once but several times over, that it is laid down in various kinds of indications.[21]

In 1896, as in 1925, we find identical affirmations: diverse kinds of indications are inscribed, diverse materials are used for recording inscriptions. In 1896 and 1925, respectively, the accent is placed on two contrasting notions: 'successiveness' in the letter to Fliess, and 'simultaneity' in the conception of the 'Mystic Writing-Pad'. This is explained by the fact that, in the former text, what is in question is the recurring effects of an inscription, whereas, in the second, it is the properties of the inscribing apparatus. In fact, one may wonder whether the conjunction of these two texts is not due to the fact that the properties of the system mainly comprise this material hetero- geneity of the various parts of the apparatus. The inscription is destined to repeat this heterogeneity in the form of a rearrangement and, above all, of a reinscription. Every later transcript inhibits the one before it and drains off the excitatory process available for a new transcription between the periods of reorganisation. We should be attentive to the fact that Freud intimated that repression might be the product of a failure of translation, a failure facilitated by the conditions of legibility of the traces, which depends on the material on which they have been recorded.

The structure of the mystic writing-pad implies, then, the material heterogeneity of the elements comprising it. Though Freud compares the different pieces of the *Wunderblock* to the different systems of which the psychical apparatus is comprised, it should nonetheless be noted that the three systems are made up of different materials. Wax is the 'substance' of the unconscious; the waxed sheet of paper that of the preconscious and the sheet of celluloid is the 'hardened', 'mortified' layer of the protective shield. Each layer has its specific properties connected with the material of which it is made, wax or resin, celluloid and, between the two, translucent waxed paper. Freud shows us, then, that the problem of writing depends not only on the surface and on discontinuity, but also on the material properties of the support which receives the inscriptions.

The psychical apparatus is a theoretical construction and no one is naive enough to believe that the mystic writing-pad corresponds to anything other than a sort of 'concern with representing' the concept. But it is not unimportant that Freud stresses the absence of uniformity in the texture of the parts of which it is comprised. If the destiny of the trace is a function of these successive re-inscriptions, it equally depends on the site on which it has just been inscribed.

Faced with this disparity between the surfaces of inscription, we may wonder if, rather than searching psychical life itself for the hypothetical unity which would make this disparity conceivable, it would not be more profitable to change cap and concentrate our investigation on the conditions under which the traces are inscribed in living matter.

Replication[22]

> With regard to the world, the act of generation appears
> to be the key to the mystery.
>
> Schopenhauer, 'The Metaphysics of Love',
> *The World as Will and Representation* (1886)

Molecular biology does not shy away from the complexity of facts, and its theories show a remarkable convergence of problems which cannot leave the psychoanalyst indifferent.[23] It seems to me that this implicit general problem is situated at the crossroads of three kinds of research:

1. The problem of hereditary transmission in reproduction: the study of the genetic code. That is to say, how is a common workplan perpetuated for the construction of a new organism in the act of generation, and what are the mechanisms which make it possible to fabricate an individual (undivided) from two others?
2. The problem of the transmission of the somatic programme; modalities for the elaboration of living matter in the construction of the organism and repairing the damage they can suffer: the study of protein synthesis.
3. The problem of the organic determination of the accumulation of individual experience: study of the mechanisms of storing information and its subsequent use. This last problem is still shrouded in mystery.

The interest for psychoanalytic theory of this field of research seems obvious. How, from a Freudian point of view, can a complete dissociation be made between the problem of the psychical consequences of the anatomical difference between the sexes and the most basic mechanisms of sexuality? Although the notion of sexuality still remains rather obscure, and its unity is much debated, it would seem that the genetic sexual identity and the sexual identity in which the individual has been raised represent the two extreme forms which are most decisive – given that a series of links, the role of which is extremely difficult to appreciate, is interposed between these limits. The nexus of questions that any psychoanalyst may be led to ask himself can be summarised as follows: what are the dialectical relations linking the adult's anatomical unisexuality with the psychical bisexuality discovered by Freud, taking into account the fact that anatomical unisexuality (the result of bisexual reproduction) leaves traces of the genetically unmarked sex in the human being, an animal capable of using language?

Envisaging bisexual reproduction entails making an implicit allusion to other forms of reproduction excluding man and vertebrates. The mechanisms of genetic transfer in bacteria indicate that the distinction made between growth and reproduction in higher multicellular organisms does not exist in such a clear-cut way in micro-organisms.[24] The operations involved (transformation, transduction and congutation) make it possible to assert that 'reproduction is correlative to growth'.[25] It is noteworthy, then, that the distinction between the germ cell and the soma becomes blurred, without however disappearing; and it comes as no surprise that it is the same systems which will intervene at the level of the transmission of the programme of protein synthesis.

This coincides with the remark I made on the generic role of memory. If I am not mistaken, the facts of molecular biology can be categorised as follows:[26]

1. *Fixed memory structures*
Fixedness is the precondition for the stability of the specific system which it is the task of these memory structures to transmit in an absolute manner. They are part of the genetic code and are entirely dependent on DNA. But this fixedness is counterbalanced by two properties:
   (a) the transmission only concerns half of the genetic heritage, which implies a separation followed by the genetic recombination with the other half coming from the reproducer of a different sex;
   (b) the aleatory character of recombination.

2. *Memory structures with a differentiated programme*
Under the dependence of ribonucleic acid (RNA), the production of which depends on DNA we have:
   (a) *non-neuronal cells,* whose programme is geared to the construction and repair of living matter through protein synthesis, a sort of renewable capital;

(b) *neuronal cells,* with a fixed capital, whose programme – as far as our present state of knowledge stands – seems only to concern psychical acquisitions.

Whatever the cellular differences may be, the fundamental composition of RNA, in the different tasks that are incumbent on it, is the same. Yet, from the psychical point of view, the study of conditioning shows that RNA plays a specific role in each experiment where it has been shown to be influential. RNA is thought to intervene in the facilitation of a particular instance of conditioning, but only of this instance. This fact, if it were definitively established, would confirm what psychoanalytic experience teaches us, that is, that singular experience is non-transmissible.[27] Primitive memory structures (hippocampus, fornix, mamillary bodies) are storage areas of RNA. I would just make the further point that this system is closely connected with rhinencephalic and hypothalamic structures which also play a fundamental role in the emotional life processes and sexuality.[28]

The situation of the nervous system in the human organism as it appears in this context elucidates the mechanisms of psychic structuring. Independently of what it may be able to pass on hereditarily (about which we know practically nothing at the present time) at the level of the germ cell and the soma, the nervous system has primarily to transmit its own acquisition. We are just beginning to notice, however, that the problematic relations between cerebral activity and the psyche, far from being resolved by the standardisation of these two fields, are such that they must be considered as being separated by a fundamental discontinuity. They become more intelligible when one goes back to the factors which themselves condition nervous activity. This means that the genetic code plays the role of a copula between sexuality and the phenomenon of memory. In its turn, the latter deploys itself at the various levels required to carry out its tasks, ranging from the constraints of the most strictly fixed deterministic aspects of heredity to the limits of the degree of play tolerated in elaborating psychical experiences.

At the end of chapter VI of *Beyond the Pleasure Principle,* Freud found he could go no further in his elaboration on the links between repetition and sexuality:

... science has so little to tell us about the origin of sexuality that we can liken the problem to a darkness into which not so much as a ray of a hypothesis has penetrated.[29]

The contradiction he came up against was the following: how can the idea of a compulsion to repeat (which he associates in his thinking with a reduction of excitation) be conciliated with the foundations of sexuality which consists in the fusion of a 'cell' which unites with another cell that both 'resembles it and differs from it'?

At this point we must provisionally suppress the coupure or cut he himself introduced between the sexual drive and sexuality, even if we come back to it later, if we are to avoid uprooting sexual life from its biological foundations. The purpose is not to amalgamate them, but to perceive more clearly the relationship of conjunction–disjunction connecting them.

We have learnt from molecular biology that, among the chromosome's constituents, only DNA represents the genetic material. This is comprised of polymeric molecules of which the monomeric molecules are deoxyribonucleotides composed of:

- phosphoric acid;
- a pentose: deoxyribose;
- purine base (adenine, guanine) or a pyrimidine base (cytosine or thymine),

thus giving four possible types of nucleotides. The specificity of these four bases is such that adenine is always associated with thymine and guanine with cytosine; it is simply the order in which they are placed on the molecule that can differ. The nucleotides are grouped in threes, forming a triplet, or codon.

By means of self-reproduction, DNA engenders a copy of itself at the level of the nucleus[30] and then produces RNA by a process of differentiation.[31] In the processes occurring in protein synthesis, a DNA copy of this kind serves as a necessary model for building a new model, that of RNA, both similar and different from DNA, which migrates towards the cytoplasm (ribosome) in the form of *messenger* RNA. The latter, which reproduces itself identically in the form of *transference* RNA, will transmit the programme for producing amino acids.[32] DNA holds the key to this by virtue of the play of correspondences existing between the position of the bases in the polypeptide chains and the situation of the amino acids in proteins.

What interests me here is the mechanism of self-reproduction inasmuch as it throws light on the concept of repetition. If, indeed, a chemical substance is capable of reproducing itself in an absolutely identical manner, we have here – particularly if what is involved is a fundamental mechanism underpinning the transmission of the most fixed heritage (that which operates at the level of the species) – a schema which can be a source of inspiration for this reflection. I am less concerned with the transition of one form of organisation to another than with examining the question at the level of the operations involved.

We are indebted to J.D. Watson and F.H.C. Crick for discovering the structure of nucleic acids in 1962.[33] They put forward a model of a double helix in which two helical strands are coiled around the same axis. Each semi-helix separates itself from the other by breaking off its hydrogen links and, through each polymeric chain, lays capture to the nucleotides present in the environment, while preserving the correspondence. Thus self-reproduction occurs by replacing two successive halves, each new half subsequently co-opting its complementary half, and so on.

According to J. Lamotte and P. L'Héritier:

> The hypothesis put forward by Watson and Clark has provided an elegant solution to a problem that has persisted for a long time without a satisfying solution. The self-reproduction of genetic material can, in any case, only be envisaged as a process of copying a parental structure. Now, if this process results from the interplay of steric correspondences between molecular configurations, it must give birth not to an identical replica of the model but to a complementary replica, to a sort of negative of the parental structure. This difficulty is removed if one considers this structure as being composed of two associated complementary parts. At the moment of self-reproduction, each serves as a matrix for reconstituting the other.[34]

On the one hand the findings reported here situate the understanding of sexuality well beyond the idea of the 'germ' cells of 1920, at a much more general level; and, on the other, they refer to a universal system of information. Finally, they create a relationship of conjunction–disjunction between the factors of a sexual order and those of a non-sexual order.

In fact, what holds our attention is the model thus constructed. The hesitation one feels due to the risk of being reproached for anthropomorphism must give way to the stimulation of thought alone. Rather than trying to know what such a model means, let us see what it says:

(a) Self-reproduction is a reproduction of what is identical. A copy of the original is required before any new operation of decoding can take place. A fine example of reading–writing!

(b) However, the reproduction of what is identical does not happen by means of a single operation of mere duplication. The original is divided in two and each of its halves is reconstituted through association with its complement. The latter, in its turn, will rid itself of the parental half with which it is coupled in order to create its exact replica. The identical is thus only attained through a double inverted twice.

(c) The copy of the original serves as a model for different tasks. The production of what is similar (RNA) (both identical and different) is based on a small difference, a negativisation[35] and a different locus of production in the activities in which the genetic code intervenes, without these being linked to sexual reproduction. The differential gap is then preserved by producing a copy of what is similar, which here constitutes another that is identical, whose role is to read the information inscribed on the copy from which it has come. Thus difference is inscribed between two identities. The first in order, subsequently, to produce difference, but involving a 'reproduction' in the mode of identity; the second in order to re-establish identity owing to the emergence of the new identity. On the other hand, identity is only constituted by splitting two complementary halves and by reuniting each half in turn. In other words, identity is assumed to be subordinate to an intra-differential mechanism (between two halves of DNA); its accomplishment being likely, in certain cases, to be pursued along an inter-differential mode (between DNA and RNA).

(d) The combinatory system functions in two ways: by placing the bases on the triplets or codons of the DNA chain and, randomly, through the process of *crossing-over* which occurs during the genetic recombination with another chromosome, itself separated by a difference (X or Y) governing the phenomena of human sexual reproduction. In addition, permutations occur between the order of the bases on the triplets and the situation of the amino acids in protein synthesis, depending on the information contained in the DNA. The substitutions and displacements are striking in this type of operation.

On the other hand, the combinatory system depends on genetic regulatory mechanisms having an inductive or inhibiting effect, whose intervention can be inferred both at the level of generation (inhibition of one or two chromosomes X or Y during fertilisation) and in cellular differentiation.

From the epistemological perspective, there is one very important thing that can be learnt from all this concerning the biological order, the implications of which could have a bearing on our thinking in the symbolic order. This is that the notion of unity needs to be entirely reconsidered. In the biological order, it is only apprehended via the mediation of two complementary halves. It is not only synchronic unity which is involved here, but also its diachronic correlate. For two stages are required for the substitution, successively, of each half of the missing replica before it is possible to find again a 'parental structure' that has provided for the replacement of the two terms of the dyad it constitutes. But when this moment is reached, it joins together two halves of a different 'age', one of whom is already, if not the parent, that is to say the progenitor, at least the elder of the two.

As for the genetic code and protein synthesis, there has been discussion of an alphabet, and then a grammar, which is less surprising than one might suppose, if one bears in mind the observations I have already made on the triple memory function of the germ cell, soma and psyche. Now language, even if it is insufficient for characterising human mutation, nonetheless marks it profoundly. Let us now turn our attention towards language, focusing first on its semantic aspects.

Replication is the act of doubling, twice over. Doubling means adding one thing to another of the same value, increasing the value by as much again, multiplying it by two. Here the effects of addition and multiplication coincide. What about concatenation? Does it proceed by a process of addition or multiplication? Herein lies the whole ambiguity of the double. It appears to be an addition, but is in fact a product; that is to say, it is the result of a multiplication[36] (sometimes with a slight difference).

Double and half are inseparable. Is the half not the particular proportion whose term it constitutes can be thought of both as unitary and as a necessary and sufficient complement of an equivalent with a view to forming another unity? From this point of view, the unity is not conceived as an indivisible minimum but, on the contrary, as needing to be posited in respect of its unitary (pseudo-half) other which reflects its missing equivalent. Rather, it is the virtuality of the trait which marks this union and this separation to which the traditional properties of unity would be transferred. The latter does not, however, pre-exist the potential combination, any more than it is identifiable when this combination occurs; for in order to identify it, we have to follow it along the path where its action is renewed through repetition. We must therefore give up the attempt to follow its course and direct our attention instead to the only representation by which it can be apprehended: the reflective process whose operations are governed by symmetry and inversion. Though the unity refers more to the system of operations than to their terms, which are unidentifiable in the series of transformations in which they are involved, difference can be established without ruining the system. An error of interpretation generates catastrophic aberrations; nevertheless, a minimal difference is required for the process to unfold.[37] It is as though the virtual differential trait governing symmetry and opposition[38] were duplicated by incarnating itself through the replacement of one of the terms whose necessary co-operation with its partner constituted the first difference. It is as though difference had to be included, so to speak, in the system, retained by the system when difference is materialised through substituting a term. The aim here is to be in a position to lend all its weight to the only expression of difference which results from situations occupied by the relations between the terms on the one hand, and by their complementary replica on the other.

The chief distinction here is that which separates the system and the terms. A difference between the terms does not affect the system in any decisive way that would ruin its functioning during the normal course of the process. The production of the double (inverse and symmetrical) is the gateway to difference to the extent that it can be considered as such without identity ceasing to apply to it. What we have, then, is an extreme point of tension in which the system is fully functioning, but also a point of possible rupture if difference is not contained within the limits assigned to it.

Let us now come back to replication. The verb *replier* means folding up again that which has been unfolded (*déplié*); but it also means putting back inside its cover that which has been deployed (*déployé-déplié*), exposed to view. The second sense reminds us that the fold is not unconnected with the relation between veiling and unveiling. If regression means to 'retreat', to 'fall back on', and if desire, as Freudian texts suggest, involves going back over traces, it is tempting to make connections here between the trace, the double and regression – all of which imply repetition. The relations between the compulsion to repeat and regression are complex. It would seem logical to say that regression is the manifestation whose categorial order is repetition. At the categorial level, this only concerns the fundamentally conservative role of the drives at the level of their manifestation. This implies an inverted process, so that one could almost say that as ontogenetic development normally occurs in an ineluctably progressive direction, regression is its complementary replica. This can only be said, however, if the compulsion to repeat, and not progression, is posited as the axe of reference. In this respect, Pasche is quite right to dissociate the compulsion to repeat from the death drive; and Laplanche and Pontalis seem to regard – if I read their line of thinking aright – the compulsion to repeat as the basis of fixation.

It is thus from the point where repetition occurs that we are carried forwards and backwards. At the moment when something new appears, repetition designates its relationship to what is central in the meaning, which it thereby signals in passing. Retro-gressively, repetition marks the moment – suggested more than clearly indicated – when what is repeated presupposes something that comes before that is contained by the binding which serves the progressive movement of serialisation. Repetition calls for its *analogons* to be linked up, both those whose return it fears as well as those it prefigures by anticipation. As much as by its content, it is by the constitution of the sequence that force and meaning, which have found that they are condemned to repeat, await their redistribution in the reticular ramification, creating possibilities for moving towards other operational theatres.

The Absent Cause[39] and Analogical Thinking

Freud found, then, that he was blocked in his endeavour to base his hypotheses on the scientific model of his time. This was at the time when he wrote:

... this function of the germ-cell is reinforced, or only made possible, if it coalesces with another cell similar to itself and yet differing from it.[40]

Having revealed the function played by detour in truth, he turned his attention towards myth, as used by philosophy. Freud drew on Plato's text with the sole purpose of finding support for his hypothesis concerning the need to restore an earlier state; but he only did so by sacrificing another major idea in this text, that is, the quest for complementarity, whether of the Same or of the Other. I cannot explore all the aspects of the Platonic myth here, yet Freud's blindness concerning the function of the cut (coupure) seems very strange indeed! It was in order to humble the pride of these primeval men that Zeus, 'after a good deal of reflection' eventually decided to cut them in two, and threatened to split them again if this first measure was not sufficient. But it was also important that this act remain present in the victim's mind: 'Man, having always before his eyes the sectioning he had suffered, would have better manners.' The inscription of this lack in human flesh would sharpen the infinite quest aimed at reconquering the lost unity with a view to restoring the primitive condition. Contemporary readings of the myth coincide with the scientific point of view:

When one of the halves died and the other survived, the survivor sought another mate, man or woman as we call them – being the section of entire men or women – and clung to that.[41]

It was only at a later stage, with the displacement of the sexual organs from the rear to the front, that the complementarity necessary for generation would allow for the union of sexual differences.[42] I do not think that the connection I am making, over Freud's head, between Plato, Watson and Crick is exaggerated.[43] It could be, though, that by distorting them through imaginative activity, understanding prefigures the constitutive figures from which it proceeds intuitively. As the compulsion to repeat inhabits the forms it engenders – forms it can only produce by introducing distortions and differences – there might be something to be gained from developing an approach based on analogy. For one would be wrong in thinking that I regard the model of molecular biology to be a final truth with an explicative value that makes its predecessors obsolete. Quite to the contrary, it constitutes additional proof that the idea of unity in psychical life, which psychoanalysis, before molecular biology, had severely undermined, must be regarded as both suspect and obfuscating.

After Freud, and in contradistinction to the genetic psychoanalysts – that is to say, those who draw inspiration from a historical conception of the psychological origins of development – Melanie Klein saw the value of this functional property of the dyad. Whereas they insisted stubbornly on remaining at the level of the mother and child alone, Melanie Klein understood that what structures the psychical organisation in the child's relationship to the lack of the mother is the good–bad breast dichotomy. This has to be referred – and here I am going beyond her own remarks – to the phantasy of the combined parent, the precursor or heir of the phantasy of the primal scene. The primal scene and primal unity are connected in so far as they are both the object, in the very way they are apprehended, of a double split: identification and desire alternate for both parents in the primal scene, and a split in the subject's unity through the mediation of the object's relation to the ego. However, this reconstitution of the primal unity in the relationship with the two parents (knowledge or ignorance of the distinction between the sexes has no importance here) works against separation. As it restricts its interest to the effects of what is observable, the genetic point of view completely overlooks the vocation of sexual destiny. To paraphrase Marjorie Brierley and Serge Lebovici, sexual destiny is invested before it is perceived – something all human beings know (except psychoanalysts, apparently). The realisation of this destiny comes about through adopting successive and simultaneous psychosexual positions alternately owing to the influence of libidinal vicissitudes (desire and identification). The Oedipus complex is the moment when 'what had been unfolded is folded up again', distributing separately, and in a contradictory manner, erotic and aggressive desires coupled with the double identification, masculine and feminine. Through the Oedipus complex, the subject[44] anticipates his function of generation. He is thus repeating here in advance. It is not that he foresees this by any means. It would be more exact to say that he actualises it in order to forget it. For who can maintain that the Oedipus complex occurs independently of sexual curiosity? But he does not only repeat 'in advance'; he also repeats through the summation of his relationship to pre-Oedipal objects[45] concerning which he does more than just draw up a balance sheet. He evaluates them by re-evaluating them, by refracting them through the spectre of castration. What is more, the repression of the Oedipus complex is upheld by disguising the Oedipal genital aims, appealing to their pregenital expression.

This process cannot escape being marked by the scansion of repetition-compulsion; but what justifies this is the role of the *coupure* or cut established this time between sexuality and the subject. It is at this point that psychoanalysis can affirm the rights it has acquired. And though memory is indeed an essential character-istic common to biological and psychological organisation, only psychical organisation seems to have had the power to constitute a memory based on 'forgetting', in the sense the Greeks gave to this term. For it is not enough to say that memory can also be anticipa-tory; what matters is the vicissitude of forgetting, which is different from the annihilation, the exclusion of what is perishable, repudiated and rejected. The fruitful complexity of psychical organ-isation does not reside in the effects of a pure combinatory system alone, but rather in its capacity – in which repression plays a major role – to transform what is undesirable into an absent cause.

Repression imposes silence only on the 'clamour' of life. The return of the repressed allows us to elucidate its function, which is that of keeping the tempestuousness of this excess of life secret. But reducing the undesirable to silence is not the same as working in silence; it is the contrary. It is as if this clamour that has to be reduced to silence could only refer us to the protest against silence which clamour represents.

In *Beyond the Pleasure Principle* Freud arrived at a conclusion that overturned his earlier hypotheses. The pleasure principle was no longer held to be the ultimate reference for explaining the func-tioning of the primary process. The activity of binding is what allows the pleasure principle to dominate subsequently, at a later stage, heralding the transfer of sovereignty to the reality principle. The 'beyond' of the pleasure principle is thus found in the direct antithesis between binding and the silence by which Freud charac-terises the activity of the death drive. To what extent can we do without this last concept introduced by Freud? Some claim that there is no need for it in clinical work. I am not so sure.

I am not thinking of the hypothetical suppositions we make in the face of deadly forms of behaviour, where it can always be said that the concept of the death drive compensates for our insufficien-cies. It is still necessary to explain the effects of a powerful force which hounds the psychical organisation into the most extreme forms of alienation. Concatenation is under attack here: no longer in the multiple aspects of its activity (psychical productivity, of which delusion can be considered as a subversion even if it should also be considered as a product), but in its binding structure, an effect of establishing links through the work of association.

In other words, it is no longer forgetting in the sense of subtraction (of the undesirable), that we are dealing with here, but of division at the level of what is held together. It is a subversion of the cut, which applies to the terms it disunites and reunites, but which is also cut off from itself, thus becoming the object of its own operation. The section no longer passes between the ego and sexuality, nor within the ego itself,[46] but within the structuring power of the cut. Here the absent cause is no longer perceived through its derived effects; it becomes an absence of cause. The picture is no longer the result of the arrangement of the connections which give shape to a structure; structure is now hidden in its connections, is weakened, and fails to acquire any shape. Thus the compulsion to repeat can only be evaluated from two angles: in so far as it preserves a cell of meaning, even if shaped by distortions; and, insofar as it is a process of binding, independent of the meaning it both carries and constitutes. In this second sense, what it repeats is the act of concatenation; for its acquisition, even if it is subject to mutation, is always under the threat of immanent destruction. This second aspect can appear when the fulfilment of the sexual destiny exceeds the possibilities of the concatenation which is its prerequisite.

> We have all experienced how the greatest pleasure attainable by us, that of the sexual act, is associated with a momentary extinction of a highly intensified excitation. The binding of an instinctual impulse would be a preliminary function designed to prepare the excitation for its final elimination in the pleasure of discharge.[47]

The trend toward discharge in the primary process is thus already a form of repetition in relation to this preparatory function. In this sense it is to be regarded as a challenge to the binding power of the impulse. Contrary to what might be suggested by a superficial reading of the text, the process does not concern the end of the operation (discharge), but its re-commencement. The movement of libidinal energy mobilised by the impulse (and also immobilised by the vectorisation which determines the direction it takes) returns beyond the involvement of the impulse in the new problem to be resolved, that is, of allowing the impulses to find expression in the bound or unbound state of the excitatory processes. It is as if the impulse had only fixed the portion that it was capable of taming for the sake of this momentary extinction. There is therefore legitimate reason to suppose that this excess of excitation, which is not fixed by the impulse, will intervene where binding or non-binding, as transformations of the properties of libidinal energy, will also neces sitate a transfer of functions on to another sphere of activity when the displacement occurs.

A plurality of meanings and modalities are condensed within the Freudian conception of displacement. Sometimes it is analogous either to a substitution or to the investment of a part which alone is accorded a value initially conferred on an ensemble; and sometimes it indicates a replacement, by covering over. All these possibilities concern not only the work carried out on the terms (representa-tions), but also the quantities (affect): energy is displaced or displaces the actualisation of the means of expression of the terms which are constitutive of meaning. The displacement involves the return both of the activity of binding and of what obliges it to transport this binding beyond the point at which it occurred. The pleasure–unpleasure principle, which governs the transformations of binding, points us even more surely to what seeks to repeat itself in its binding. It is only subject to the compulsion to repeat to the extent that the latter does not obey the pleasure principle.

> Our consciousness communicates to us feelings from within not only of pleasure and unpleasure but also that of a peculiar tension which in its turn can be either pleasurable or unpleasurable. Should the difference between these feelings enable us to distin-guish between bound and unbound processes of energy? or is the feeling of tension to be related to the absolute magnitude, or perhaps to the level, of the cathexis, while the pleasure and unpleasure series indicates a change in the magnitude of the cathexis within a given unit of time?[48]

These concluding remarks are extremely problematic. They contrast feelings and a certain tension, and then they speak of a 'feeling of tension' in which the pleasure–unpleasure series seems to have been calibrated by a given unit of time.

Freud is not thinking of an elsewhere or an outside the pleasure principle, but a beyond. What the compulsion to repeat creates is the capture of the absolute magnitude of the cathexis, before it is possible to speak of any psychical qualification as such. Repetition-compulsion is neither outside nor inside the pleasure principle. It involves capturing this tension in a sequence – the quality of pleasure and of unpleasure being the consequence of it. Up to this point in his work Freud had linked the couple pleasure–unpleasure to that of tension–relaxation. Foreshadowing what he was to acknowledge explicitly a few years later, in 1924, in 'The Economic Problem of Masochism' concerning their independence – albeit only relative – he took the initiative by granting a theoretical precedence to the fundamental postulate of the 'Project' in which the psychical apparatus has the task of getting rid of excess quantities. Linked up with this is the entire theory of the internal complication of the psychical apparatus, the secondary function of communication, the necessity of redirecting aims, the operation of displacement, the transformations of energy, and so on. Hence it is as if repetition-compulsion represented the dissociation of the couples unpleasure–pleasure and tension–relaxation. The theoretical function of repetition-compulsion is to make this mobilisation of tension visible and to indicate the transformations that are called for. Through binding, it saves quantity from annihilation, while resisting its flight into constant change that would eradicate the stability of binding. Change takes on meaning, then, by taking up a position *vis-à-vis* repetition.

The binding of the impulse has the effect of restraining the errant force. Here the force is endowed with a vector, established in a sequence. But, at the same time, owing to a phenomenon of internal resonance, this vector returns, retroactively, to the point from which it originated. If, by antinomy, it addresses itself to the shadow of the force constituted by the vector, the act of binding is reflected on the product of the binding along a recurrent path which doubles the direction taken by the force. This capacity of the result to reflect itself constitutes itself as a pro-position: position for and position towards. For and towards other bindings, insofar as the success of the act of binding is perhaps only due to the fact of abandoning the search for a complete and definitive solution, leaving in reserve the uncaptured force from which subsequent bindings will come.

Another consequence of the investment of binding by the pleasure principle will be that it will be partially forgotten. On the one hand binding identifies itself with the uncaptured force and, as it were, enters into an alliance with it; but, on the other, it disengages itself and appeals to other ties marked with the stamp of the transformations by means of which it will make its return. Here, repetition is only maintained with the purpose of deceiving repetition itself. The original binding not only results in other bindings, but has constituted the links of a different kind of binding: a virtual binding between the bindings. Forgetting is, in a way, the guarantee of this.

But one must be wary of oversimplifying things. Forgetting is not univocal. The latency it implies is open to contradictory vicissitudes. At the heart of forgetting itself, a new destiny takes shape. If, as forgetting recedes, memory has the opportunity of returning, via the distortions and disguises imposed, there is something radical in forgetting that is inherent to the power of forgetting. Here forgetting will be forgetful of itself as forgetting. The power of separation, which keeps forgetting apart, remains in obscurity, emitting no sign that gives the slightest indication of its presence as forgetting; unless, by expressing itself in this way, it denounces itself and is revealed as an absent cause. In my opinion, Freud was not saying anything different when, going against any form of scientific practice which requires evidence for what is advanced, he felt driven to say that the clamour of life comes from Eros and that the death drives work in silence.

It is possible to do without the death drive by reintegrating the characteristics that Freud gave it into the sexual drive. But this would be to attach little importance, except by rendering the sexual drive even more mythical still, to the separating power of the death drive. That this separation can still be of use to Eros does not alter in any way the root of the problem, which is to know what the sources of the activity of separation are. And one is justified in wondering whether, heuristically speaking, it is more advantageous to place the properties of separation and recombination at the heart of the unity of the sexual drive, or at the heart of the conflict between the latter and the ego. Or should Freud's conception be accepted? It seems to me that Freud remains more faithful to his thesis of the irreducible nature of the conflict by placing separation and recombination in two opposing fields.

There is undoubtedly a certain reticence, with regard to our habitual ways of thinking, about according force such a status. To speak of force is to speak of an aim, a goal. What Freud's thought gives us to understand, however, is something quite different. What force wants is nothing other than its own abolition, its separation from the background against which it emerges. It is through a lack that force manifests itself, but it only reveals the lack by trying to patch it up. What it encounters, accordingly, along its pathway, is not the absence of its object, but its non-object – that with which it seeks to merge through this non-existence. Any effort to imagine this non-existence (intra-uterine life, paradise lost, and so on) only circumscribes the hypothetical screening, or covering up of this non-existence. But the latter can only succeed in exhausting itself by finding a way out; and it is by looking for a way out that it maps out its trajectory. It is along this trajectory that it leads the object from a state of non-existence to another existence. The mediation leading there is the operation of binding carried out with the 'exit', as it were, in view, as if the latter had become the object of force. Through displacement, the lack at the origin of the expression of force is transferred to the external space by imagining another complementary and opposing binding. This gives substance to an absence of the object in which the object is invested by the force that has escaped binding and thus manifests itself as an absence of binding. There is an absence on one side of it, on account of the uncaptured force; and an absence beyond it, insofar as acknowledging binding also implies acknowledging the lack which is no longer situated at the level of force, but at the level of the response provided by binding to its request to be released. Here there is a possibility for a recombination which reactivates the processes of binding, calling the object into existence in the form of absence, as if to conserve its incompleteness for the binding of force. This lack stimulates a project of appropriation through fresh transformations when the vicissitude of loss occurs. In deploying itself from the point from which it emerges, force then re-invests the trace of absence, and binding is modelled on the configuration of the object. It is by means of this resurrection that the object is 'found'. However if, in its turn, it 'emerges' from absence, it is in order to enter a state of virtuality where, coming and going like force, the movements through which it manifests its own life show that it is possible for it to get lost in the process, succumbing to the action of repression which overcomes representation more easily than the power of instinctual activity. Desire makes the sacrifice of a full resurrection in order to save the emergence through which the released force, captured this time by the traces of the object, will remodel its replicas in new contexts. As the repetitions are solicited (repetition of bindings, repetition of the forms of the object, repetition of the transformations of the contexts in which the object participates, and repetition of the transformations of the bindings), they produce the reflection of their activity on itself, as if the progressive direction of the process was bound, contradictorily, to meet up with its point of departure by means of a counter-effectuation of its successive phases, which its very progression prohibits, offering in exchange the solution of simultaneity which splits the movement into act and scrutiny of the act.

Back to the Wooden Reel Game. A Second Reading

Becoming and Passing, a building and destroying, without any moral bias, in perpetual innocence, is in this world only the play of the artist and of the child. And similarly, just as the child and the artist play, the eternally living fire plays, builds up and destroys in innocence – and this game aeons play with themselves. Transforming themselves into water and earth, like a child, they pile up heaps of sand by the sea; they pile them up and demolish them; from time to time they recommence the game. A moment of satiety, then again desire seizes them, as desire compels the artist to create. Not wantonness, but the ever newly awakening impulse to play, calls into life other worlds. Children throw away their toys; but soon they start again in an innocent frame of mind. As soon, however, as children build, they connect, assemble and shape forms according to a law and an innate sense of order.

Nietzsche, 'Philosophy in the Tragic Age of the Greeks', 1872

The fact that Freud was stopped in his tracks by the ignorance of the science of his time regarding the origin of sexuality was what led me to inquire into the field of molecular biology. I have given particular attention to the relations which these studies have made it possible to establish between repetition and replication. It seems that in them structure is only able to ensure its permanence by virtue of the most rigorous repetition; however, this can only be achieved by reconstituting its missing half. It accepts difference on the condition that the latter is reincorporated by the repetition, the safeguarding of the system taking precedence over the emergence of the differential term introduced. It seems that, when one considers the plane of psychical activity, the properties of the system range from repetitive rigidity to the search for a minimum conservation of the intelligibility of a cell of meaning. This in no way detracts from the necessity for a determination that is as narrowly fixed as possible but offers replication the widest latitude of expression. In other words, it is as though difference, rather than being located between two replications, were making the most of its possibilities in the field of replication itself. This being the case, what matters is perhaps less the difference that repetition seems to reveal in the compulsion through which it manifests itself, than a broadening of the possibilities of replication within limits that are compatible with preserving the intelligibility of the cell of meaning which the system defends.

If every organisation presupposes an articulation, then the latter, while placing a limit on the displacements of the articulated fragments, is also an invitation to allow the articulation a certain amount of play. Now it may be that what is original in psychical activity is that this articulated displacement occurs as a result of operations of erasure and masking which, without altering it fundamentally, modify the replicative function that the products of replacement must fulfil.[49]

Difference and repetition converge in the myth of the incidence of twins and the double. According to the careful and patient analysis carried out by Otto Rank, the double in literary and mythological works is almost constantly the symmetrical and inverted half of its model. Less important than the qualities differentiating them is the opposition itself. Its effects of distribution are more important than what it separates.

The myth of the double involves an absolute split between separation and recombination, as if nature, mischievous or crafty, found itself reproached for having separated what should have been united; and as if recombination could only be carried out in death. What stands accused is parental sexuality which betrays itself through undivided generation owing to the fact that such a generation implied an undivided couple formed by two partners whose union excluded the subject. Though he mainly emphasised the importance of narcissism, Rank was not unfamiliar with the fundamental duality of life and death. He came very close to it when analysing the Devil's appearance to Ivan Karamazov:

The idea of the Devil has become the latest religious emanation of the fear of death. In assuming the form of anxiety, belief in the soul not only undergoes a transformation of meaning but also a displacement in time.

At first the Double is an identical ego (shadow, reflection), as befits a naïve belief in personal survival in the future. Later on, it also represents a former ego containing, along with the past, the individual's youth which he no longer wants to abandon but, on the contrary, to conserve or regain. And finally, the Double becomes an opposite ego, which, under its guise of the Devil, represents the perishable and mortal part which is detached from the present, actual personality, and repudiated.[50]

What we have, then, is an identical ego projected into the future, a former ego prolonging the past, and an opposite ego in the present. Rank draws our attention here to the role of the gap between history and structure for which equivalents can be found in all the fundamental knots of psychoanalytic theory.

It is such a gap that can be observed in the wooden reel game. When we infer that there is repetition of the loss of the breast but also – and already – identification with the Other who goes away, who has the power of going away and coming back, we are assuming that the game is the locus of these various figures of which Rank speaks. The child in the game is the one who silences his distress and his sadness, the one who avenges himself with the aid of the wooden reel – a solution that has much greater consequences than if he had given free rein to his anger. Having already adopted a position of renunciation, he foreshadows, quite apart from what the mother may mean for him, his own abandonment of her in conformity with the same taboo of incest, which, ultimately, is what her departure is connected with.[51] However, as I have pointed out, if such a game is possible, it is only because it is unconscious; it is because, at the level of the precursors of language, it is the wooden reel that appears and disappears: the wooden reel for the child, and the mother for Freud – that is to say, his daughter-mother. This detour via his favourite godson allowed Freud (who was himself his mother's favourite) to kill two birds with one stone; that is to say, to continue his self-analysis and to analyse his theory, rectifying it as a result. The Other, who is a necessary witness of the game – a position occupied by Freud – can perceive the meaning of it from where he is standing, through the product of what he has generated. In other words, from the point where his own childhood, which is escaping him, converges with this retrogressive movement. This retrogressive movement, however, is already present in the binding process of the game, which, as it is constituted, is self-reflecting. Just as its appearance on the world stage cuts the game off from the internal movement whereby it took shape, its emergence in reality brings about a new distribution of functions which puts the reflective position in a zone of extraterritoriality where the observer can position himself.

However, with this coming-and-going of the wooden reel, another game is being perpetuated, independently of all the games already played. I am referring to the libidinal activity of incorporating affirmation and expulsive negation (excorporating [added 1999]). And yet the entire game is already, in itself, a movement of the force towards the objects, ex-position; and in this sense it reiterates the movement of erasure-separation of the magic notepad. What we see being repeated, then, is how the act of binding expels everything that has escaped its control outside itself, as its missing half; and how this excluded half makes its return in the separation of absence. Finally, we see how absence is transmuted into forgetting by the present captivating effect of the game. This 'presence' of the game erases the historical dimension of the past, so that it is as if it had always been there, since the act of binding is a precondition for evoking anteriority. Unlike Lacan, I do not believe it is possible to limit ourselves to the effects of language alone, considered as an elevation of desire to a second power, by dissociating it from the other spheres of the game – the throwing away–pulling back and the seeing–not seeing of the wooden reel – in order to obtain this result.[52] For all the aspects of the game, in the widest sense of the word (libidinal activity, incorporating affirmation and rejecting negation, the appropriating inscription and the deleting erasure, the passage from the movement of externalisation to the return of internalisation, invisibility in the activity of throwing the wooden reel out of sight and then finding it again) are all connotations of speech emission which overwhelm it from all sides.

Furthermore, it has not been emphasised enough that the *o* and the *da* do not occupy equivalent positions in the game. First the 'o' of the German word *fort* [gone] is much more long-drawn-out. Freud writes it as 'o-o-o-o', as if speech accompanied or embraced the trajectory of the wooden reel, yet as if this prolongation alone absorbed the affect without allowing it to exist (was this disappointment, anger, resignation?); whereas the short *da* [there] is marked by unequivocal pleasure: an expression of joy. Furthermore, the o-o-o-o connotes absence, absence of the mother and an absence of explicit or decipherable affective expression; it raises a question, invites the interpretation that will be given *après coup*, in retrospect, based on the affect of joy expressed in the *da*. The single *da*, accompanied by an unquestionable satisfaction, denotes the presence of the wooden reel; it intensifies this presence and only speaks of it by linking up the joy that it causes with the contrasting phase of absence. Despite its reference to the contrary, one can call it a sign, whereas the *o* deserves to be called a symbol.

The wooden reel game expresses the act of symbolisation. It expresses it better, perhaps, than our current theories of culture where there is a difference between a traditional and modern conception of the symbol. As a tessera, that is, the encounter between two halves of the broken object,[53] the symbol has, by extension, included the reference to the relation between a sign and an absence which evokes it by means of another sign. Nowadays, the classical acceptation is often discredited. The looseness of the definition, having extended the 'arbitrary' aspect of the symbol to everything that rids itself of the presence of the sign, is partially denounced, because the link between the parts of the tessera proves to be both too tight and too loose, too close and too distant. The mediation of the symbol is too restricted by its link with its support – though, at the same time, and conversely, it is too open. The nebulous character of this relation (the result, perhaps, of the way it is used in the sacred) leaves in abeyance our preoccupation to understand how the symbol operates by means of the delimitation or closure which allows it to be identified. We have therefore come to prefer the rigour of a conception of the symbol linked to the independent relations between the terms of an ensemble. The operative limit posed by the terms is compensated by the multiplicity of combinations visible in the manner in which they are arranged.

The wooden reel game may help us to reflect further on the transition from symbolism to the order of the symbolic. On the one hand, the symbol (understood in a way that is close to the traditional conception) is posited in relation to an indicator as that which is not: the o-o-o-o as opposed to the *da*. Consequently, however, the status of absence changes. It was present in the indicator, but compared with its opposite, it lacks a limit to its dispersion. Not that it is an 'absence of absence' by virtue of the enigma it poses, but the absence of a grasp or hold on absence. The void it creates through the apparent affective neutrality of the phase of disappearance, in contrast with the obvious joy felt at its reappearance, only establishes its uncertainty by being linked to the indicator as its inverse and symmetrical form, requiring the two phases to be interrelated. Moreover, this would coincide with the modern conception of the symbol which takes into consideration the complete sequence. The symbol thus makes its return throughout the game as a whole (and not just in the phonematic opposition alone); the function of repetition is to scan the various phases and to draw attention to the way they are interconnected. Thus, while the limit set by the indicator can say nothing else about itself, its transposition to the whole game gives it the role of a replication inviting one to search for its missing half. At this point, it is the total situation of the game that is inscribed on two interpretative levels: either at the level of the indicator, that is, the relation between the disappearance–return of the wooden reel and the absence–presence of the mother; or at the level of the symbol considered as a system of virtualities, through the polysemy of one term in contrast to the monosemy of another, opposite it, which refers to the plurality of the *analogons* of the game, whether of a playful nature or not. Each of these becomes the keeper of the missing half constituted by the common locus of the others. The relationship between them can therefore only be grasped in the context of the process in which they all derive from each other and position themselves in relation to each other; that is to say, in the movement of passage in which each term can be seen as the result of the binding of its different, earlier moments. It is this binding that gives this movement the value of a replication concerning which the model has remained silent in respect of everything that binding has eclipsed through forgetting, repression, or denial.

Replication thus sets a limit to indefinite wandering, to the perpetual reverberation of the questions of polysemy. But its effect is not limited to this. The retroactive constitution of phantasy transmutes the relationship of opposition into one of splitting by maintaining it in the unconscious state.

The model described by Freud opens up new perspectives for symbolisation by introducing the notion of splitting. Splitting does not just separate or oppose, but makes two systems of thought which are not homogeneous, and are even contradictory, coexist side by side. It seems possible to interpret the wooden reel game in terms of a double instance of splitting: splitting (1) between the game and the phantasy it constitutes retrospectively; and, splitting (2) opposing a sign (*da*) and a symbol (o-o-o-o). In comparison with the sign, the symbol's field of symmetrical inversion is extended, by virtue of its connotative rather than denotative value, a polysemy which includes the analogies – whether playful or not – of the game. The connection between splitting (1) and splitting (2) gives the game its value of replication in relation to the *analogons* on the one hand and to phantasy on the other. The 'absence' of phantasy calls for a fresh replication through the interpretation of the game. This constitutes the replica of binding by means of which the game determines the absence of the object as its missing half. The complete function of the symbol has a double effect: there is an effect of drifting towards another space, and an effect of reflective creation in this new site. Although this effect of creation is striking for the one who experiences it or the one who witnesses it, owing to the insistent nature of repetition or the emergence of difference which it seems to inaugurate, in both cases what remains silent is the value of processual replication which emerges from this alternative.

The retroactive effect of creation is revealed through its opposite, repetition. The latter can allow difference to appear in the state in which it manifests itself – what will be disguised is the way in which binding was obliged to make use of difference in order to express itself as repetition. The insistent nature of repetition has the function of testifying in favour of the lack which is underlined by being reiterated. Repetition is the accomplishment of this process, as if the effective constitution of binding – in associations, dreams, phantasy, acts – were the necessary condition for its retrogressive reflection.

The paths thus opened up for the experience of pleasure – which always falls short of full satisfaction – anchor it by transforming the indeterminate nature of the 'lack to be satisfied' into the inverted or symmetrical figure (turning round against the self or into its opposite, displacement or projection) of the event of pleasure. The compulsion to repeat is beyond the pleasure principle insofar as the operations of separation and recombination transcend it. On the other hand, the only function of these operations in psychical activity is to serve it. And they serve it all the better in that what escapes it is reconstituted via phantasy.

Difference can be impressive in the form of this appearance of pleasure at the very place where the unpleasure of the lack was situated. But then why does pleasure repeat itself if it is only to assert mastery of unpleasure? Is it merely to celebrate its victory? Or is it to show how the ego's function of stopping unpleasure requires the drive and the circuit which binds the drive to its object to testify to what has eluded the object in this process of turning passive experience round into something active? It is also an indication of how the mechanism of repetition needs to be transposed to other operations in fields still to be explored. It is an indication, too, of how the displacement which has occurred in the direction of the exit area which binding has sealed off, must now take place within the terms united by binding, and through them. Binding ceases to be the bridge established towards the object but becomes the object of the modalities of displacement, replicating the original operation which governed its institution, thereby creating new categories of the object. Is the metonymy of psychical activity a condition for metaphor? Certainly, but can it not be said that this first binding of the impulse is already a metaphor for bodily organisation?

Difference and Repetition in the Oedipus Complex

The hypothesis I have put forward of the capacity of the impulse to be self-reflecting, concomitant with binding, gains even more credibility if one links it up with the fact that an impulse forms a pair either with a contrary impulse or with the contrary reaction which doubles the search for hoped-for satisfaction.[54] The onset of the Oedipal period allows for a deployment of this concentration of possibilities. Not only because the drives of love and hate fix themselves electively on to the two parental images, but because each image must accept, recessively, the feeling which has been attributed – in a dominant manner – to the other. This concurrence of desires is coupled with the concurrence of identifications (masculine and feminine) which themselves are presented as negations of desire, thus as a potential form of symmetrical inversion. It can be said, moreover, that each identification places itself in a position of 'scrutinising' the desire which it substitutes, even though this scrutiny is completely absorbed by the fact of the identification itself.

The different components of the Oedipal conflict, in its negative and positive aspects, will be recombined into a composite figure. What matters, though, is that the earlier network will become fixed, crystallised in a single scheme whose coherence will reside in the balance obtaining between the forces it comprises. Thus, though the Oedipus complex does not allow itself to be reduced completely to one of its aspects, either positive or negative, and though it cannot be embodied totally by either of them, the shape that it will take will have a decisive value. It is not important to know who decides and if someone decides. All that can be said is that the result has the force of decision. The Oedipus complex inaugurates the subject of repetition and the subject of difference.

He is the subject of repetition in that he has to relate himself to the process of generation. For it is via the object of generation, the penis, that the Oedipus complex is structured in castration. The organ of *jouissance* does not proceed from the organ of generation, as one would expect; but it is because the subject is faced with the threat of losing it that he sees himself as the product of generation in the relationship which unites him with his progenitors including this new complement, namely, the mutilation of that which defines his sexual identity. He thus places himself within the line of descendants; what is engendered is not generation postponed until later, but the relationship to generation. And this relationship to generation is grounded, by the meaning of castration, in the differential repetition of all the precursors of castration that prefigured it without revealing their meaning, which is apprehended retroactively. Earlier experiences of separation give their full meaning to difference. Firstly, primal difference which separates the infant from his mother through the loss of the breast. This difference is mutually agreed upon, forming the matrix of the instinctual renunciation which affects the child who is excluded from the mother's body, whereas the mother restores to the father what, for her, repairs, *a posteriori*, the non-fulfilment of the desire for a child given by one of her progenitors. Secondly, difference between the possession and non-possession of the products of one's own body, mediated by anality which gives 'the little thing detached from the body' in exchange for the pride taken in the illusory sacrifice without any other compensation than the mother's perishable and aleatory love. And finally, difference under the primacy of the phallus – the organ of *jouissance* 'not being where it should be' (Lacan). Freud attributes castration with playing the decisive role in the destruction of the Oedipus complex. But what he omitted to say was that castration is also the most powerful motor in structuring the Oedipus complex. For before crystal breaks, it first has to form. Castration is precisely what precipitates this inclusion *en masse* of the two aspects of the Oedipal configuration in the decision, before it emerges, no longer as a possibility that can be avoided, but as a threat (for the boy) or as a promise (through penis envy in the girl). The 'power' of castration as an event establishing the difference between the sexes at this 'fertile moment', under the primacy of the phallus, is to bring masculinity and femininity into the position of being complementary replicas for each other; and also to constitute the oppositions and alternations to which they can be subject in each case, owing to an internalisation of what was the mirror relationship – for experience shows that, in each sex, it is the sex of the Other that is rejected in oneself, even in a non exclusive manner. It is now that separation and recombination occur, bearing witness to the relations between sexual destiny and psychic destiny, associating repetition and difference.

Difference is duplicated in the Oedipus complex: castration has formed the pertinent characteristic of the difference between the sexes, and has gone back in time finding all its *analogons* developed in succession; but, in simultaneity it has recognised the difference between the generations. Attributing a place to the phallus does not make it any more available; it can only remain a coveted object whose powers exceed the capacity of whoever desires its appropriation.

These differences are repeated, then, between themselves. Can they all be included within a single difference of which they may be said to be manifestations? This single difference can only be the contrary of itself: generation whose sign, in the last analysis, is repetition. Generation requires the separation and recombination of difference in order for repetition to occur. Generation gives rise to a product which is the stock of a future generation; however, the begetters are themselves the products of the stock of their own begetters. This succession of three generations is punctuated at each phase by replication: the child often bears the grandparents' first name.

This, then, is how things are in psychical life, where each moment emerges from the one before it simply to constitute itself as a transcended-forgotten-repressed replica of the time prior to the moment posited as primal.

In *Moses and Monotheism* (1939), Freud assigns traumas with a double influence, positive and negative. Their positive effect is to bring the trauma into operation once again through memory, affect or action. These efforts constitute what we call fixation. The negative effects follow the opposite aim; they express themselves, on the contrary, through strategies of avoidance, inhibitions of all kinds.

> Fundamentally they are just as much fixations to the trauma as their opposites, except that they are fixations with a contrary purpose.[55]

In the last analysis, what unites them is their compulsive quality. But this coupling suggests, once again, the replicative nature of repetition. For the positive aspect implicitly calls for a potential inhibition, the trace of which must be discovered through reiteration, just as inhibition in the face of the obstacle designates a surplus over and above the fulfilment permitted by the lifting of inhibition.

Likewise, having pointed out how the manner in which repetition-compulsion is expressed is often felt to be uncanny, Freud then discovered that this uncanniness was related to what is most familiar to us; and further that a change of sign transforms the lascivious nostalgia for the mother's womb into fright at the sight of the female genital organs. The reversal into the contrary or the inversion of the value is not enough in itself – it is the mutual relationship between the terms that determines their intelligibility. It is also the fact that each term is apprehended separately, evoking the one that is absent; this allows a difference to be identified which cannot be isolated as such, but only in the relation of virtual complementarity which constantly has to be re-established in each situation that is affected by it in the process.

Groddeck was to speak of the compulsion to symbolise, thereby extending indefinitely the field opened up by Freud. And it is probable that we are not fully aware of the limits of the domain of symbolisation. Its different sectors should perhaps be thought of as playing a part in the relations of replication where there will always be room for the interpretative gap.

Through repeating, the subject recommences over and over again, for the more he makes his way through the forms he encounters, the more he forgets, as if the precondition for moving forwards lay in remaining unaware of what he has to accomplish. The more he forgets, the more he accentuates his difference and calls on repetition to help him eliminate this difference and institute a new difference. The bonus of difference resides, in the last analysis, in maintaining terms that are separate and distinct, which have been put together and reordered differently. Difference is limited by the extent of the gap. This is the economically and symbolically determined precondition of the process of an effective difference (that of the primary process and of interpretability).

The last function of repetition, in its relationship of conjunction and disjunction with difference, is probably to ensure this constant renewal by means of replication.

Theory is the replication of clinical work; but it is also the replication of a 'parental' theory whose posterity it extends. In this respect, my somewhat speculative remarks could be understood as the complementary replica of 'Beyond the Pleasure Principle'.[56]

4   Dead Time (1975)*

In 1895, apropos of the *proton pseudos*, Freud discovered the first hysterical lie (which, of course, is never the first) – a particular modality of the structuring of time which (in German) was called 'deferred action' (*après coup*)[1] in psychoanalytic theory. The trauma is not where it is expected it to be. There is no direct relationship with the moment when the event occurred (at least where psychical reality is involved); it is to be found in its evocation *a posteriori*. Before he had even discovered psychoanalysis, Freud was speaking to us about a time in latency. When, in a body that is transformed by puberty (with pre-sexuality undergoing the mutation which makes it accede to the sexual), the effect of some incident or other resonates with what might be called by analogy the pre-trauma or, rather, the pre-significant trauma, it is then that time, which had stopped, continues its course once again, but at quite another rhythm. The mere process of returning via unconscious thinking towards the past revives what happened earlier, and changes the pre-trauma into trauma. This process which, in the progressive direction, made a leap in time (latency), in the inverse, that is, retrogressive direction, seems to rediscover and appropriate everything that it had apparently ignored, with indifference, between the pre-trauma and trauma. Psychoanalysis, which started out from hysteria, strived for decades to fill the holes (of memory) that we encounter in the hysteric – namely, a leap from the psychic into the somatic (conversion); fragmented memory (amnesia); breaks in the continuity of behaviour (crisis); discourse in which elements that are indispensable for its intelligibility are lacking (gaps). The hysteric was the favoured subject of enigma and the psychoanalyst was more or less a detective. In fact, it was about something else: metaphor. What temporal metaphor was involved here?

'The patient suffers from reminiscences', says Freud. This statement was taken up again and given a much broader significance at the end of his work in 'Constructions in Analysis' (1937b). We are no longer dealing, then, with a trait that is the privilege of hysterics,

* First published as 'Le temps mort' in *Nouvelle Revue de psychanalyse*, 11, 1975, pp. 103–11.

since delusional subjects – but also those who are neither neurotic nor psychotic – are similar to them in this respect.

As a matter of fact, construction is not the prerogative of psycho-analysis either. It is already present in the formation of the symptom: hysterical paralysis or delusional system. It is present in the elabo-ration of the personal myth, i.e. the constructed version of the events of a life that can be obtained without difficulty from other people's accounts. Equally, it can be found in phantasy or in the screen memory. It is present in the dreams we have each night, concerning which there is a tendency to forget, now that their hidden meaning has been recognised, that their manifest content also has a role to play. The manifest content, a construction built by means of the pseudo-logic of secondary revision, has fascinating, hypnotising effects. The dream account is like the shining object wielded by the hypnotist in order to send to sleep the person who is about to sink into the suspensive sleep of hypnosis. By transform-ing what comes from within, as well as what comes from without, we are constantly constructing, that is, filling our psychic spaces. By the same token, in the external space, the world suffers in turn from these immense constructions, which has led the wittiest of our humorists[2] to demand that our empty spaces be protected.

The notion of the void or of emptiness is currently in fashion; or rather, it has come back into fashion. In culture, first of all, owing to the fascination for the Far East. Psychoanalysis is no longer the solution; better try the ashram. Dispossession makes us relive the promise of a new religious dawn just when Christianity is showing signs of running out of steam. Political ideologies have proved dis-appointing. There still remains the hope of Nirvana. Psychoanalysis itself is not exempt from this, having tried to fill the gaps of phantasy with Melanie Klein, or the gaps of the signifier with Lacan. In its turn, it is posing the question of the blank – the blank dream (B. Lewin), the blank relationship of the psychosomatists (P. Marty), the blank self (P. Giovacchini), blank psychosis (J.-L. Donnet and A. Green), negative capacity (W. Bion), the void (D. Winnicott). We are now realising, perhaps rather belatedly, that what lies between these terms is more important than the terms themselves. This remarkable re-evaluation of the structure of psychical activity has given rise to theories whose fruitfulness is indisputable and whose potential is far from exhausted.

This picture of things nonetheless has its shadow. It seems that it has been easier for these explorers of the great depths to formulate their ideas in terms of space rather than time. Analysts have surprisingly little to say about time, even though they are constantly involved with it (the length of sessions, the rhythms of treatment marked by its regular interruptions, the increased length of analyses). This is a surprising paradox, since the very object of analysis, 'predicting the past', is indeed the search for this lost time. 'Archaic' is one of the most hackneyed words in analysis. It is spoken about all the more lightly in that nothing is known about it. It is all the easier to construct a prehistory in that there is nothing to validate this hypothetical genesis. In order to avoid misunderstanding, let us say that the position of the 'here and now', which claims to be purely synchronic, and which was proposed as an alternative solution, is even less sustainable. The past cannot be eliminated. The problem of analytic time does not reside in pushing back the limits of a past that can be attested. A specifically analytic conception of time still has to be elaborated. The concept of 'Nachträglichkeit' (retroactive meaning) has provided one of its modalities. Plainly, it is not the only one. It has to be admitted that psychoanalysis had somewhat neglected it. Lacan reminded us of it at a time when the tendency to simplify the psychoanalytic conception of time had become widespread amongst analysts.

The theoretical status of time in the Freudian theory is caught in a contradiction. On the one hand, regression refers implicitly to the notion of development (of the libido, of the ego). By situating metapsychology in this context, one merely succeeds in transforming psychoanalysis into psychoanalytic psychology (of the ego); that is, in amputating the original contribution that psychoanalysis could make to the idea of time by reducing the desynchronised burgeoning of the discourse to the order of clock time. The genetic point of view leads, accordingly, to a search for the stages, the key moments of a linear development and maturation, however complex it may be. Sometimes a glance is even cast in the direction of Piaget.

On the other hand, the supporters of Freudian orthodoxy will always point out that the unconscious is unaware of time. They also underscore the role of repetition-compulsion, the label of unconscious phenomena. Against the ineluctable march of time, something is repeated, without the subject knowing it, or in spite of himself, which is fundamentally resistant to any possibility of being transcended. The paradigm for this is the fate neurosis, but one does not have to be afflicted by it to notice the periodic recurrence of these striking constellations which can sometimes be perceived in

the tiniest traits. It can be seen that the concept of *Nachträglichkeit*
lies between these two conceptions, obeying neither the principle
of a mere succession of events nor that of pure repetition.

As far as time is concerned, psychoanalysts have suffered from a
limitation which burdens the theory – namely, the solipsistic view of
the subject. For though Freud was at the origin of the epistemological
revolution which put the splitting of the subject in a regulating
position, denouncing the illusion of a unitary consciousness, he
nonetheless described a hypothetical child, developing in a quasi-
automatic way, with only a minimal attachment to the object
constituting it. This is probably due to the fact that the referent for
Freud was more the drive than the object – the latter being included
in the drive assembly.

Now, if one adopts the idea that there is a correspondence between
the splitting of the subject and an organisation as a couple (with the
object), the assumption can be made that time is itself split into a time
of the subject and a time of the Other; and, that a conflictual hetero-
chrony will link up these two polarities by the difference of potential
which separates them. Thus different times coexist simultaneously.

The analytic work distributed between these two protagonists
produces an effect of simultaneity at the acme of their encounter.

Hypothetically, one would have, on the one hand:

- the time of the drive tending towards discharge via action, a
  time of pure repetition which seems to reduce to zero the
  capacity to differ;
- the time of the unconscious which also tends towards
  discharge – psychic in this case – which only realises desire
  owing to the condensation of the different times, that is, due
  to the transformation of successiveness into simultaneity, with
  its corollary, the retroactive attribution of meaning to an earlier
  event. The unconscious is unaware of time;
- the time of the ego – a time of delay and of action to be
  differed;
- the time to come, subject to the injunctions of the superego and
  of the ego ideal both of which, as we know, have their source in
  the id, completing the circuit which links the agencies;

and, on the other hand,

- the time of the Other, made up of the same components, but
  regulated differently. The elements belonging to the drive and

to the unconscious do not act there openly. This time is dominated, on the contrary, by the present, vectorised by the future; but underlying it, there is an identification with temporal elements that are extremely resistant to development, to successiveness.

Between these two times, a separate place should perhaps be reserved for the time of phantasy, inasmuch as the latter is capable, by virtue of its composite formation, of desynchronising the natural order. It comprises an original timeless structure, due to the desire it expresses, which is rearranged temporally by the form of the narrative it constitutes. Freud compares it to mixed blood, which is imperceptible to the naked eye. The watch of phantasy is not on time. This time of phantasy is the time that regulates the exchanges between the child and the mother – when they are separated. The issue is no longer one of the child's phantasy alone, or of the mother's, but of the different nature of their phantasies. To each his own phantasy.

This asymmetric couple is in a state of chronic disequilibrium. It is the locus of transactional exchanges. The child only enters into contact with the object-mother by means of a progressive movement of identification which anticipates demand. The object-mother only enters into contact with the child by means of a retrogressive movement of identification with his desire, which echoes her own regressive desire. But the two efforts do not cancel each other out; difference persists, ensuring vectorisation towards the future. These exchanges are constraining; they force each of the two partners to emerge from their own temporality: the child, from his past pleasures and the mother from her future pleasures. From these transactions, a new time – less original than primal – can emerge in the discontinuous and joint relationship: transitional time.

This time will be outside-time; it is a potential time which, as Winnicott says, is established at the inaugural moment when separation from the object is initiated, transforming the separation into a potential reunion. And yet this time, outside-time, will be circumscribed at privileged moments, not only at the limit of the outside and the inside, but also between the waking and sleeping states: at the moment of going to sleep and at the moment of awakening, when transitional objects and phenomena are animated with an ephemeral life.

This transitional time may be contrasted with dead time, the chronic equivalent of empty space. Here the suspensive power of dis-investment is at work. For a moment, there is 'no more time'. The 'no more', in the augmentative sense, becomes the 'never again' of time. It is not the privilege of mystics or visionaries alone. Nor is it the exceptional time of moments of pre-mortal anxiety. The states that are indicative of its approach are boredom, a time of waiting from which nothing is expected, and a renunciation of the struggle. These affects foreshadow depression or follow it. It is true, moreover, that the world of depression is immobile, and that time, as the phe-nomenologists have described it, is frozen. States of melancholy without anxiety exist; they are cold and, above all, dominated by enormous inhibition. There are also melancholic states without guilt and without self-accusations; and there are others that are an enactment of death in a state of stupor. But something is at work there: mourning. What is terrible about mourning is that we know that one day we will have forgotten everything. This indeed is what hurts Marcel much more than the sorrow he experiences at having lost Albertine. This movement of disinvestment, which the ego effects between a destructive id and a hostile or conniving external reality, is experienced as a *fatum*. It is followed by an immediate re-organisation in which dead time is succeeded by the voice of a persecuting superego. The withdrawal is experienced as if a third object were chasing the subject from the scene. It is not me who is going away; I am not wanted here. I/they are expelling me. Dead time is a time of death, given or received.

These times are moments of crisis which disrupt the uniformity of everyday life. In other structures, as Winnicott has shown, the periodic recurrence of a fear of catastrophe can be related to something that has not occurred. The trauma, contrary to the meaning it acquires in Freud (sexual seduction) or in Ferenczi (the intrusion of adult sexuality, which speaks the language of passion, in infantile sexuality which only knows the language of tenderness), is, in these circumstances, a negative trauma, that is, a disappointed expectation. The hallucinatory wish-fulfilment has had no effect: nothing comes. Beyond a certain time, the possibilities of postponing the hoped-for satisfaction are exceeded. The object dies. Thereafter, whether it is present or absent, it will remain a dead object; that is to say, the patient from now on invests the absence, as an absence of hope. Though the absence oscillates between potential presence and potential loss, and though it is the expression of what is virtual, it will now undergo a change of status. Potential time changes into dead time. There will no longer be any room for a pause, a sigh, in the fabric of a life; but rather a long, uniform and unlimited continuity. This is what Bion called psychic death. This mortification of the psyche has the advantage of warding off unthinkable anxieties, the tortures of agony. Death is no longer dreaded since it has been caught in the net of life. There is no longer any need to mourn the object since the affect of mourning is dissolved in the course of everyday life.

In her fine book *In the Hands of the Living God*,[3] Marion Milner relates how, after nine years of conducting an analysis, she had the feeling that an essential piece was missing in her work with her patient. She finally managed, however, to gain access to it with the help of Suzanne's drawings. The circle opened up a door of discovery for her. The situation was less one of a fence than a hole; or, to put it in another way, less the ring than the space that it imprisons, protects or guards. The circle regarded as a hole refers just as much to a hole in knowledge as to a hole in bodily experience, or in affect. Something or someone is lacking,[4] 'leaving a blank, a void'. Always at pains to relate symbolism to bodily experience, she was tempted to see in the circle an emanation, an evocation of the empty mouth from which the nipple had been withdrawn. This coincides with the hypothesis of Maurice Bouvet who, in his work on depersonalisation, understood this phenomenon as being the result of a suspension of time following this sudden state of lack.

But in order to have access to the concept, the perspective needs broadening. Marion Milner writes:

Thus it was that I became increasingly interested in the idea that one aspect of the circle, when it was an empty one, could be to do with the urge to indeterminacy, a state which can be felt like being both everything and nothing; and that this must be taken into account as the necessary counterpart of the urge to be something, the urge to differentiate oneself out from the whole. I came to think also that it is perhaps not surprising that this state of no-differentiation should at times become identified with death, since it is a wiping-out of all images of the self, an achieved darkness that can feel like being nothing, a state which, to the busy purposive mind, can seem like death and therefore something to be constantly defended against.[5]

The concept of the death drive now becomes more intelligible than when it is understood in terms of the Freudian formulation of the 'return to the inorganic state'. On the other hand, however, Marion Milner argues that moments of psychic death are an integral part of the process which leads to a new birth. It is perhaps this dead time which will be necessary for establishing individuating discontinuity between the child and his mother. By the same token, it will be encountered in an almost imperceptible form not only in the blanks of the discourse, but also in its punctuation.

These psychopathological structures do not therefore sum up the figures of dead time. They do not sequester it within the networks of consumption. Everyone is familiar with this punctuation of time owing to certain events which institute a 'cut' (*coupure*), in the course of things, internal or external. What kind of situations mobilise such a disinvestment of time? Psychoanalytic experience shows that this system operates when different series coexist simultaneously in the event, thereby engendering a telescoping effect: phantasy and reality no doubt, but also the inside and the outside, the past and the present – represented by situations or objects – beyond the level of uncanniness, in the register of hostile fate. An emptiness is created when barriers collapse and limits are dissolved. We are in a state of shock, without any reaction or feeling. It is not only a place that is no longer inhabited; it is also a time that vanishes. It is this dead time which may make its return in what has already been seen, heard and recounted. This negative hallucination of time, which is motionless, at a standstill, creates the necessary space for the time of the screen-memory.

Psychoanalysis believed for a long time that analysing the screen-memory, dissecting it, would lead to the total lifting of infantile amnesia. Faced with the impossibility of achieving this result, this hope was displaced onto unconscious phantasy. And elsewhere, a synchronic combinatory system aims, in its turn to reduce time to its mathemes. Recently, Bion boldly recommended that analysts strive to adopt a state without memory or desire, the state of the unknowable at the source of what is knowable. Timelessness is the prerequisite for any idea of temporality. However, Bion says it would be a mistake to think that the analyst should aspire to an objectless state. Quite to the contrary, insofar as the asymptomatic curb tending towards it permits, it is a question of coinciding with the state of the object as numen, the thing-in-itself. The latter is a symbol of absolute truth without thought, for 'only the liar needs to be able to think'. In fact, it is an object without attribute, without difference. From this point of view, then, dead time is the infinite. The fascination for what is unlimited coincides with the fascination for eternity. Though one must strive for it, one can do no more than approach it. It is questionable whether this is the basic attitude that the analyst should strive to adopt. There can be no doubt that at certain moments *insight* only emerges from the suspension of time.

Psychoanalysis must resign itself to the impossibility of reconstructing *ad integrum* a period of time that has been lost forever. It is more likely that moments of dead time, traces of erased simultaneity, will remain without memory, punctuating the infinite succession of psychic events and the discourses we make about them.

5   The Model Child (1979)*

For Francis Romain

Objective Science or Interpretative Science?

Psychoanalysts today are divided as to which fundamental points of reference should determine future options. At this point in its history, the psychoanalytic movement is hesitating over which path to follow. Rather than reiterating these familiar divisions – whether it is quarrels between schools (the Kleinians, Lacanians, and so on) or differences of origin (doctors or laymen) – and listing the points of divergence over what should constitute the most privileged access to the unconscious, I think it would be more fruitful to try and delineate a more general theoretical opposition. The issue is to identify, amidst the mass of current knowledge, a fundamental discipline (in the sense in which 'fundamental sciences' and 'clinical sciences' are differentiated in medicine) which can serve as a paradigm for psychoanalytic theory. Psychoanalytic theory – which should itself be this fundamental science in relation to its applications (therapeutic or non-therapeutic) – has been handed down to us by Freud in a state of considerable ambiguity, open to a polysemy which it has not been possible to maintain as such. This is perhaps because Freud's successors have not been able to tolerate these uncertainties which, though they were fruitful for him, have become confusing for them. Thus all the different groups within the psychoanalytic movement, inspired by the theoretical leaders who have succeeded Freud, have become vehicles of epistemological implications constituting the basis of many debates.

At a time when questions are being raised about the identity of psychoanalysts, the best among them do not seem to agree with each other. This disagreement is not about what a psychoanalyst is – which can be defined by empirical or intuitive criteria – but about the territory on which a psychoanalyst can feel at home, or in his element, when it is not his own domain or field that is involved. Tell me who you haunt ... .[1] This question of the relations of proximity

* First published as 'L'enfant modèle' in *Nouvelle Revue de psychanalyse*, 19, 1979, pp. 27–49.

is not contingent; for it is in this context that the implicit aspect of the psychoanalyst's references becomes explicit. Naturally, there are psychoanalysts who are eager to protect their singularity and who will refuse to take part in the discussion on the basis that I am proposing here. Even if they profess to have no references outside psychoanalysis, these in fact become apparent in their very selection of concepts and the way they use them, in the value they place on this or that concept, or in the omission of another, as well as in the way they interpret them. This is inevitable, for psychoanalysis is evolving, changing. No one today can claim to be totally faithful to Freud; the epistemological horizon has been modified, *volens nolens*. We saw this in what was called in France the 'return to Freud'. Not only has there never really been a return to Freud – at best, a reminder of certain parameters of his thought – but, what is more, this return has merely served as a standard resulting in a way of thinking that is far-removed (it hardly needs stating that I am referring to Lacan's) from what can be learnt from a contemporary reading of Freud's work. Further, at the heart of the psychoanalytic movement, there is no group that does not openly acknowledge its filiation – still considered as the most legitimate – with Freud's thought. Everyone claims to further Freudian psychoanalysis, but no one agrees on the right way to proceed in order to realise this programme.

This is why it is necessary to go further and to look for the aporetic, imaginary referents which are never totally incarnated in the production of theory even though we can see their shadow in it. My purpose is simply to try and draw out orientations and not to circumscribe theoretical constellations which are immediately iden-tifiable in the discourse of psychoanalytic works. The distinction I am proposing here, with a view to making the theoretical issues intelligible, is between the objective sciences and the interpretative sciences. Psychoanalysts are agreed that the most fundamental quality of the psychoanalyst is the quest for truth; and this at a time when the concept of truth is being sorely challenged both by philosophy and science. The question is made more complicated by the fact that, though it was Freud himself who promulgated the value of the 'love of truth', he understood that this truth was a matter to be determined by science alone. Having the future of psychoanalysis at heart, he wanted to protect it from the twin influence of priests and doctors. Freud not only challenged the illusory function of religion, but also its dogmatism and its censuring of free thinking. We know that he had reason to complain about medicine, for nowhere else did he come up against such lively resistance to the unconscious, such blind ignorance of the libidinal body, and so many false certitudes concerning the subordination of the psyche to the brain. In short, psychoanalysis was viewed as being caught between the mystification of the soul and a reduction to neuronal machinery.

Freud's opinion has had a mixed following. Although psycho-analysis has not succumbed to the grip of religion – notwithstanding the rebellious attempts of a few priests – on the other hand, it has been appropriated by the medical body. The consequence of this has been that, in countries where medicine has become the only means of access to psychoanalysis, a certain idea of science has erected principles which it has sought to impose on psychoanalytic theory. I say a certain idea of science because scientists who are *at the outposts of science* often prove to be much more open, if not to psychoanaly-sis, at least to incertitude. This doubt leaves room for the possibility of psychoanalysis to have its place. And it is certainly no coincidence that these scientists, who are confronted with problems of an ethical order, are now crying out for help from specialists in the human sciences in order to resolve – in fact, to get rid of – the thorny questions by which they feel overwhelmed. Let us recall the example of Einstein who turned to Freud (who felt unable to help) for assistance in answering the concerns of the League of Nations about the means of preventing future wars.

This idea of science, which is in the process of becoming the dominant ideology in the most important group of the international psychoanalytic community, arouses reactions which allow us to recognise the other major pole of the discussion, that is, the hermeneutic pole.[2] At the extreme opposite of the pole represented by objectivist science, hermeneutics bases psychoanalytic progress on theoretical axes that are quite contrary to those guiding the 'scientists' of psychoanalysis. To the biological and physical parameters, they prefer cultural parameters and, in culture, they give pride of place to ideology, to mythical and religious productions (even when they do not profess any religious faith). To develop-mental psychology they prefer the teaching of History; to behavioural psychology they prefer semiology. Rather than adhering to 'scientistic' science, they espouse epistemological interpretation. So much so that the question is not one of observation – what can an analyst do in the analytic situation other than 'observe by listening' since, even if the eye hears, can the ear see? – but of

mediate, indirect observation. There is an anti-reductionist orie
tion here insofar as science deliberately chooses to adopt uns
position. Of course, all knowledge is reductive and it is the options
governing the reduction which need challenging more than the
principle of reduction itself. In fact, the choice of disciplines that are
opposed to the objectivist tendency in science is not guided by an
anti-scientific position. The orientation towards the examination of
culture, of symbolism or language, and their productions, is justified
in their eyes because men reveal what they are better in them, and
because the picture given by science reveals a schema without depth
or density in which all metaphorical thinking is absent.

That man is caught between the biological and the social orders
is obvious.[3] In adulthood, the interaction and intricacy of these two
factors creates such complex organisations that, in analysing them,
one can only observe the manner in which they are intertwined
dialectically, without being able to distinguish clearly what belongs
to each of the series in question. There is, accordingly, a great
temptation to think that, by going back to childhood, material will
emerge in which the separation of these factors is easier to discern.
Perhaps there is some truth in this. But one is still a victim of the
prejudice that it is necessary to proceed from the complex to the
simple in order to be able to elucidate, as things become progressively complicated, the obscure complexity of the point of departure.
The illusion, here, rests on an accumulation of errors of judgement:

1. Child studies are based on the idea that the complexity of the
   child is reducible, if not to simple elements, at least to elements
   that are more simple than in the adult.
2. It is assumed that they will make it possible to identify the
   elements of this simplicity *sui generis*, thereby avoiding adulto-
   centrism; the adult will thus cease to be a prisoner of his mental
   categories by discovering those specific to the child.
3. It is assumed that they will provide the key to adult categories
   which could then be understood as a product of the evolution of
   those of the child and be considered in their own right.
4. They are thought to have the advantage, insofar as the process
   of change in a child is intrinsically bound up with its status, of
   constructing the temporal genesis which will bridge the gap
   between the adult and the child and account for the complexity
   of the adult.

The child would thus have the privilege of making visible what, in the adult, is invisible, *because it is 'past'*. The purpose of studying the child is to discover the appropriate theoretical strategy which will allow us to determine the nature of the structure of the adult – although it is the adult who constructs the way we think about the structure of the child!

These prejudices are so obvious that it is unnecessary to spend time on criticising their naivety. The 'simplicity' of the child is deceptive; the identification of categories which make the child's being intelligible are always a product of adult reflection – it cannot be otherwise. Not only can adult categories not be understood by the so-called categories of the child, but the latter are always derived from the adult who, in the best of cases, that is to say, in psychoanalysis, has first of all made the journey, on the analytic couch, from the adult to the 'lost' child that he once was. Looking for the child directly would amount to denying that something has, first of all, to be repressed if we are to know what repression has to repress. The attempt to avoid this process is evidence of a *misrecognition* of the *misrecognition*[4] which thinks it is able to ruse with the unconscious by claiming to grasp in flight, as it were, what is going to be made unconscious just before it is repressed. This decoy is reflected in the postulate of the 'developmental' approach which, by multiplying the stages of investigation, hopes to re-establish a fallacious continuity, even though it lacks the theoretical means which would make it possible to understand the course and the meaning of the changes. Not to mention what, by definition, is left out of the investigation – always behavioural – namely, intrapsychic processes and, above all, the primary processes. Going back to the origins, as an explicative approach with the child as a guide, is simply another sexual theory which the adult adds to his conception of the subject. It is easy to see how these positions can be criticised. I can already hear the protests of those who will object that I am making a caricature of their thinking. But I am less concerned with representing faithfully what actually happens, or what is said about the issue, than with bringing out a latent aspect of the theory – which, in many cases, has already emerged from its latency and brightly claims to be the spokesman of scientific rigour.

However, the limitations that science imposes on itself may mean that it misses the essential psychic aspects of the human condition. And it was in the name of science that Chomsky stigmatised the behavioural sciences. Once psychology or sociology takes behaviour as its point of reference, it is condemned to a fundamental inadequacy. And when, in certain psychoanalytic circles, ego psychology is spoken of as an important stage in psychoanalysis – reference to Piaget being essential – one may wonder why psychoanalysis was involved in this business at all.[5] Critiques of psychology are also put forward by epistemologists. In an opportune article,[6] Canguilhem has pointed out the ideological dangers of the psychological approach. It is not only psychology that is in question, but all the disciplines which attach the prefix 'psycho' to their field: psycho-sociology, psycho-pedagogy, psycho-linguistics, psycho-physiology, and so on, inasmuch as they remain psychologies of consciousness.

The problem can be considered from quite another angle. It is said – but is it so obvious? – that, from birth to adolescence, the child is more dependent on a biological organisation which calls for a naturalist approach; however, this assertion needs correcting immediately and it is important to insist on the fact that the whole process of becoming an adult rests on factors of a cultural order, that is, factors arising from the relationship with parents and their substitutes insofar as they are profoundly culturally determined. Yet one still needs to understand how culture is transmitted: are we dealing with 'psychological' or 'sociological' influences? Alternatively, is the task of cultural adaptation achieved via symbolic mediations? It is here that hermeneutics has something to say, with the accent it places on speech, symbolism, myth (personal or collective, conscious or unconscious), rites (they still exist, especially rites of passage), tradition, history, customs, ideologies and, alas, nowadays, what is transmitted by the media. This whole domain comes within the scope of a science of interpretation.

In the past, history claimed to be scientific, deluding itself with Marxist economic theory. The 'new history' has realised – like Marxism moreover, and none too soon! – that social imagination has as much, if not more, importance than 'historical geography', demographics, class relations, the economy, and so on. The same can be said for the child: direct or longitudinal observation, the naturalistic approach and the appreciation of family relations will always be lacking the essential dimension – namely, the deduction of intrapsychic functioning which, alone, will be able to say, not how the child has experienced a given situation or event, but how he has internalised and interpreted his own human environment. This is the real science of the subject to which psychoanalysis can make a contribution. This is why my critique will spare the psycho-analysis of children – which is an application of psychoanalysis like any other, with its difference and its speciality – by distinguishing it from the work that psychoanalysts do with children which is necessary, but remains peripheral to psychoanalysis itself. This is on the condition, naturally, that child psychoanalysts renounce once and for all any claims that it is possible to reconstruct a 'realistic' view of the infant's mind.

The usefulness of the activities carried out by child psychoanalysts is not in question. What is questionable are the theoretical or practical inferences that they are tempted to draw on the basis of experience which they cannot help regarding as a special means of access to knowledge of the human mind.

The Child, the Norm and the Norm of Theory

Questions need to be asked about the political implications of these activities. Psychoanalysis is often reproached nowadays for being normative. Psychoanalysts who work in institutions – especially psychiatric institutions – are reproached even more for serving the ends of state ideology and power. Taking the defence of psychoanalysts who are trying to use their field of competence to relieve human suffering is worthwhile. The same is true for child psychoanalysts. But between the child and the adult there is a big difference. Even if the adult is subject to the constraints of society and power, he can always defend himself. This, moreover, is what he does. The child, on the other hand, is defenceless; or rather, he is nothing but defence. As he is incapable, owing to his condition, of modifying the reality surrounding him, he has no other option than to modify his psychic reality by setting up defences which mutilate him seriously. Winnicott's notion of the *false-self* expresses this situation. Far from seeing it as purely psychopathological, Winnicott recognised that the false-self is an inevitable product of education – Freud would have said, of civilisation – and that, to a certain degree, it is indispensable for civilised social relations. But he also acknowledges that this normal pressure becomes normative pressure, and that this pressure is applied by the mother who cannot accept her own impulses which she sees reflected in her child in alarmingly magnified proportions. The upshot is the false-self mutilating psychic reality. Where treatment is concerned, the question is reversed. It not only leads to an appreciation of the pathogenic

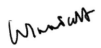

effects of this false-self, but raises the question of the extent to which therapeutic action can free the child from it. It is the ideal of the 'golden mean' which reigns in infantile psychopathology and the harmonising virtue of development, subject to cultural rules. Naturally, we are all, children as well as adults, subject to such rules; but, when we have children in our care, we make sure they are respected, whereas with adults, as the establishment of superego structures are more often an obstacle than a safeguard, the analyst does not have to worry about this – or he only has to do so when the superego has already undergone a pathological regression which is making the patient suffer in an unmistakable way.

The child follows, out of necessity, the channels that the adults have created for him; he obeys the rules that they have laid down; he introjects the knowledge that they have decided to teach him and he observes the code defined by the adult. Does he do so in his own interest? Or in the interest of the state which wants good citizens who are capable of realising the aims it has defined? And, if one wants to remain within psychoanalytic theory, without going beyond its limits, I would say that it is very difficult for the child to cut himself off from his parents' ideals, which he is always more or less expected to realise.[7]

What a black picture! Come on, we do not need to feel so sorry for them: childhood is still a green paradise! True enough. But why? Because the child has an extraordinary potential of vitality, a plasticity, an adaptability that the adult has often lost; and, because he faces up to the most tiresome vicissitudes with astonishing strength. Because, moreover, he is fired with a love of life[8] which is nourished by the love of the parents, brothers and sisters, substitute parents, and because through activity, play, and in the opportunity for having pleasure that the dullest events offer him, he finds immeasurable hope. The advantage of illusion is that the child 'stomachs things well'. But it is later, in adolescence, that he becomes aware that he has only been – for the most part – what the adults, and primarily his parents, have wanted him to be. He has to go through a difficult process of mourning, and then find the means to live in society while safeguarding his libidinal investments so as to be able to derive satisfaction from them within the limits of tolerable conflict. It is then that sublimations are put to the test.

These remarks necessarily lead on to the problem of adaptation – a problem that has been neglected by French psychoanalysis because it is overloaded with ideological resonances. In this respect, psychoanalysis is similar to Caesar's wife. But it is not by making American psychoanalysis a scapegoat that it will rid itself of the problem, any more than it will do so by denying its existence. The adaptive role of psychoanalysis must be considered with lucidity; for adaptation is not a norm, but a fact. Not being adapted is a form of adaptation, as is true of conformist over-adaptation. The real problem lies elsewhere. The adult can choose – insofar as his unconscious allows him to do so – not to adapt; the child cannot. For maladjusted children have never posed a real problem for society. Maladjusted adults, however, pose quite another problem, which prisons and social welfare institutions are unable to deal with. The adult's lack of adjustment can be positive; it can promote, within the context of 'a certain abnormality', as Joyce McDougall says, an original, creative way of functioning. It goes without saying that the artist is often not 'adapted' to society and the revolutionary militant even less so. The adult's lack of adjustment can be a factor of positive change; what is unadapted is often the precursor of what, tomorrow, will be another norm, which, when the moment comes, will in its turn have to be surpassed. The child's lack of adjustment is much more serious for him, and he pays a high price for it. It closes down more possibilities than it opens up, and gradually restricts his room for manoeuvre.

Hence the ambiguous situation of a child psychologist. Inasmuch as he is an 'educator', he will be acting in accord with the wishes of the state; to the extent that he is an analyst he will be trying to act in harmony with the subject's wishes; but, in this case, he will be obliged to take into account the wishes of the state which wants productive – and reproductive – citizens.

In both cases, there is a risk, under any regime, that child psychologists will only be able to form model children. The question that now arises is whether the child, who constitutes a model for the psychoanalyst, can escape the moulding of this child-model.

It might be objected that in practice things do not happen like that, and that all psychoanalysts assume a caring function by endeavouring to see to it that the child 'feels better', irrespective of any other consideration. To accuse the child psychoanalyst of being in league with the state would be to look for an unnecessary quarrel by casting suspicion on the specific aims of child psychoanalysts. This would once again involve adopting the themes of anarchistic thinking which cares little about suffering and thinks only of using it for its own ends. And it is true that we must avoid committing the same mistake as Reich who, in putting forward a more global theory of the parent–child relationship, qualified the first as an educator, overlooking the fact that the parent, first and foremost, is an object of desire and identification; and, that without the parent's love, the child will probably be unable to assure his progress in life. But this is the whole question. With the child, the adult is always caught in a cleft stick: he is inevitably an object of attachment, love, hate, and identification (that is, of alienation and individuation), and yet he is inevitably an educator. This being so, it is necessary, owing to the very fact of this complicated situation, to separate as much as possible child psychoanalysis – while emphasising its specific area of concern, which is the internal world of childhood – from all the other 'psychotherapeutic' approaches: family, educative, pedagogical, social, and so on.

This separation is not always made: some child psychoanalysts, with the best of intentions, move outside the scope of their specific analytic role even though nothing obliges them to do so. Furthermore, it is not enough. We also need to see, in the specific field of child psychoanalysis, what it is that participates in these tempting deviations of the psychoanalysis of extension. And it is at the level of theory that this vigilance needs to manifest itself. For practice, for its part, will always be solicited:[9] the child, like the psychotic, knows how to force the analyst to step outside the framework of the setting, using the vicissitudes of his condition as a weapon in the service of his defences which are no less demanding than those of the adult. What child psychoanalyst has never found himself at grips with a child who is manipulating his parents? What child will not use all the means at his disposal in order to multiply the number of people who are needed to take care of him: doctors, rehabilitation specialists, remedial teaching staff, etc., the number being designed to fragment, dilute and neutralise his treatment? What child will not play on his sense of guilt for using his parents' money to continue his treatment? These are all problems that are met with in the adult, too, but in a different way; and, they can be analysed because the analyst/analysand relationship is without a third party other than the absent third party, a symbolic reference.

It is in the domain of theory, then, against the unavoidable risks involved in practice, that the status of child psychoanalysis has to be defined. In child psychoanalysis a choice has to be made between childhood and psychoanalysis.[10] How, at the level of theory, is the wheat to be separated from the chaff in order to preserve psychoanalytic thinking? I now want to propose a hypothesis.

Everything in psychoanalytic theory that is inspired by a developmental conception of the psychical apparatus, everything that makes ontogenesis a principal reference, everything that sees childhood as a fundamental axe of the theory, everything that leans on this theoretical reference in order to intensify, by all available means, the longitudinal study of the child, everything that replaces the indirect approach of psychoanalysis by the systematic study of observable manifestations – not only direct observation, but the observation of the child in his family context, and, beyond that, in the set of structures which have dealings with him (pedagogical, judicial, hospital services, and so on) – pulls the child in the direction of psychology, pedagogy, relations with the law or medicine, and tends, ultimately, towards 'family planning'. I have the greatest respect for the work of psychologists, specialist teachers, specialists in child and juvenile delinquency, paediatricians and child psychiatrists. Their efforts are useful and necessary, whatever reservations one may have about certain directives that the state tries to give to organisms which come under its jurisdiction.[11] But it is important to realise that it will not be long before these disciplines impose their 'scientific' or pragmatic views on child psychoanalysis. Inspired by a concern for efficiency, or even evangelisation, child psychoanalysts run a considerable risk of being obliged to fall into line with the supporters of these other disciplines who always hope to be able to subdue psychoanalysis by 'assimilating' it.

So there needs to be a reversal of strategy. The only salvation for child psychoanalysis lies on the side of what in psychoanalysis is totally irreducible to the so-called 'realistic' or pseudo-scientific vision which informs the neighbouring disciplines. For the relations of proximity are seductive. They tend to make child psychoanalysts think that the related fields are all domains which can be penetrated by psychoanalytic thought, converting populations which are just waiting for the good word, whereas more often than not, what one witnesses – and sometimes in the best of cases – is a wild and loose use of psychoanalytic knowledge exploited by the new users with total impunity, and sometimes (guiltily) with incompetence, on defenceless children. We need to go further and challenge, at the heart of psychoanalysis itself, everything that claims to modify its theoretical axiology by making the child the privileged source of knowledge of the unconscious. For in no way does the child have priority as material for such a study.

The fact is, however, that today developmental th
dominates psychoanalytic theory more than any other approach.--
It can be a source of inspiration of the richest and most imaginative
contributions of Winnicott, the followers of Melanie Klein, or the
team of Serge Lebovici and René Diatkine. Or of the highly rigorous
observations of the group of the Hampstead Clinic in London, or
the centres of Yale or of New York – where the theories of Margaret
Mahler are elaborated. It can also, it has to be said, nourish theoretical conceptions which reflect a disturbing impoverishment of
psychoanalytic thought, the representatives of which situate
themselves on the side of a naive biologism based on a simplistic
psychologism which kills two birds with one stone: the child is the
norm of the theory which wants to produce future adults who
conform to the norm.

Ex post facto[13]

The unobservable in analysis – what I call the 'past' and the
'elsewhere' – has, when confronted with realistic thinking, only the
value of a void to be filled. The holes in the discourse, far from constituting a generative lack which gives rise to a new associative
process, must therefore be devoid of any theoretical function. They
are merely zones of obscurity on which it is necessary to shed light
very rapidly so as to evacuate the effects of imaginative stimulation
which could arise from them, and to bridle any thinking which
mistrusts a consciousness that only elucidates what it allows to come
to light, and to seal off at all costs this insult to reason which is the
unconscious. It is as if an unbearable danger existed of allowing the
lack to take effect, permitting it to engender a form of thinking
which denounces rationalisation. For this is always the risk involved
in privileging everything that belongs to observing consciousness.

Imagination, even theoretical, remains the 'lunatic' which has to
be driven out of the psychoanalytic 'abode'. What investigators of
the sensible – the visible, the audible, in a word, the observable –
seem not to have understood is that, although absence is the main
source of the analyst's imagination, even in its most audacious and
questionable approximations, it is subject to laws which allow it to
be given a value of intelligibility. In other words, it is not pure
unbridled thought. And, although it roams, this roaming itself
conceals a structure. This was true of Melanie Klein. Even though
one may think that she was mistaken – as Lacan can also be mistaken

– one is still obliged to recognise the extraordinary impulsion that each of them have given to psychoanalytic thought. This is how psychoanalytic thought advances. It makes, as it were, theoretical thrusts which are then rectified, redressed and refined by the work of successors who sometimes modify the basic ideas in the process (as Winnicott did with Melanie Klein and as she herself had done with Freud), finally arriving at a theoretical equilibrium in which the psychoanalytic thought of an epoch can be recognised. In other words, concepts are used as theoretical instruments for thinking about practice. The latter will in turn engender new concepts and so on ...

Nowadays, the richest theoretical work runs counter, in my opinion, to the developmental line of thinking. It is to be found at the opposite pole, on the side of communication, on the side of structures, inasmuch as these have holes in them, are never closed, and are marked by a fruitful disequilibrium. Everything pertaining to the concepts of lack and absence has a privileged position in it, for the function of this negativity is not to solicit desire to defend against this by looking for pieces which will finally make it possible to achieve a state of totalisation. On the contrary, lack and absence are places through which correspondences are established between open structures, by the effect of reverberation between the structures, whether these belong to the same temporality or to different temporalities. It is by virtue of absence that bridges are established between structure and history, and that repetition and retroactive meaning (*l'après coup*) become intelligible, as well as this Janus-like dimension of the human being who has the capacity to look forwards and backwards simultaneously. Though unable to see anything immediately, he arrives at an understanding *ex post facto* by means of 'veiled recurrence'.[14]

Representation

Precepts of defiance, calls for vigilance, or even an invitation to favour other theoretical axes are not enough. For if we want to avoid this 'infantilisation' of psychoanalysis, it is not enough simply to limit certain excesses. What is to be done with this child that Freud has left on our hands? Are we just to rule out with one stroke of the pen the inclusion of child analysts in the cohort of child psychologists? Should direct observation be banned? This would lead to an inevitable regression. It is better to propose another theoretical vision.

Everything that is already being done for the child should be pursued. Our habitual ways of thinking about the child should be re-examined. We need, perhaps, to finally get it into our heads that we never speak about the child. Because adults who speak about children still carry their own childhood within them, and psycho-analysis has taught us that this childhood never passes with time but remains intact in the adult. This child who is omnipresent in the adult, dictating his apparently objective views, is not the child-in-the-world, any more than he is the child-in-the-family. He is the internalised child; that is, the child internalises himself after he has introjected the parental imagos which are constitutive of his psychic reality. Psychoanalysis must give up the search for the child 'in himself', not because he is inaccessible, but because such a child is a fiction of the adult who claims his childhood is over. But the psy-choanalytic revolution has shown that the claim that childhood is a thing of the past is a myth. Infantile fixations exist which govern more or less massive regressions. But these fixations and these regres-sions are evidence, in those who suffer them, not so much of attachment to their childhood but of a rejection of it. The 'cure', when it occurs, does not consist in transcending this childhood but, on the contrary, in making it one's own by internalising it.

Consequently, psychoanalysis is not concerned with the repre-sentation of the child, that is, the attempt to reconstitute the world as it appears to him, or as it appeared to him in the past; but rather with childhood as a constitutive mode of representation. That is to say, childhood as representation, in the sense in which Schopen-hauer spoke of the 'world as representation'. As such, childhood comes within the sphere of representation, and the parameters governing its intelligibility have to be sought in the categories on which representation depends. It is, then, not because he is less subject to reality that the child interests us – on account of his presumed inferiority to the adult – but, on the contrary, because he is the most dazzling paradigm of a world that is solely an object of representation in which he only figures as the symbolic representa-tion of his parents' desire. From time immemorial, the child already has a childhood which is that of his parents, and which he must internalise in the difficult task of being adult.

This function of representation, which implies not only that something is represented, but that there are also representatives, leads necessarily to the double status of the representative: in the child's eyes the parents are representatives, just as he himself is in theirs. And his major task is to represent; that is, to represent for others, and to represent for himself. It now becomes understandable how everything in the investigation of the child which partakes of the sensible can only, at best, play the role that is played by the day's residues in the constitution of the dream. Just as the dream work can only be constructed retrospectively, childhood can only be talked about in the past. And this past is without any discernible origin.

The best use, then, that can be made of everything that we learn about the child is to dream about it. Everything that we learn from childhood is essential for psychoanalytic theory, but this reflection is only worthwhile inasmuch as it makes us think, and what it provides in terms of food for our theoretical stimulation will always depend on the preconceptions of whoever has devoted himself to its study. In other words, of whoever has not been afraid, in the child's presence, to listen to him while allowing his own inner child to speak.

Today, some psychoanalysts have understood the need to overcome their objectivist prejudices. The counter-transference, which was regarded for a long time with suspicion, has become an indispensable instrument of psychoanalytic elaboration. Interpretation has shed its rational limitations and opened itself up to the paradoxical dimension. Because there is a temptation to objectivise the child, the latter lends himself to the machination which silences the subject in him. For he is the subject of representation which, by definition, escapes direct apprehension by the senses. Even though the descriptions of the analyst who attempts to give an account of his experience can never lay claim to objectivity, the temptation of objectivisation is so strong that he sees in what he reports the evidence, the very proof, of his theory. Which naturally only convinces those who are already convinced in advance, but who need to come up with proof for others.

We have to choose between the sensible and appearances on the one hand, and the imaginable and the deducible on the other; even though this distinction is already conceptually out of date to the extent that the 'purely' sensible no longer exists. Let us say that one has to choose between the limitations imposed by objectivisation and the inevitable 'supplement' of the basic heuristic hypothesis. The first approach, which claims to be rigorous, is, at most, silent in its wish not to infer anything; in any case, if it is coherent with itself, it must relinquish all hope of understanding anything about psychic representation. The second attitude, which takes representation as an object, openly accepts that it is conjectural, as is, by definition, representation. For the specificity of representation is precisely that it is not subject to the limiting exigencies of reality; however, it possesses the essential quality of making the possible happen through psychic activity alone. It is, therefore, conjectural in its essence, as will be, necessarily, the theory that gives an account of it.

When psychoanalytic reflection and its theoretical aims are so defined, psychoanalysis can no longer be suspected of adaptive purposes or normative obedience. As its domain is that of the organisation of the intrapsychic world, inasmuch as the latter is not the reflection of reality but of the study of the power of reality to transform itself into an infinite number of possible worlds, it can no longer be reproached for showing solidarity with those who fabricate reality. Not as it is 'really', but as this conception allows them to impose it on others. Let me add that childhood is not the only, nor the privileged, locus of infinite possibilities. Childhood does not have the power to transform reality into the possible. Fiction is not its prerogative; far from it. Fiction governs the world in its length and breadth, gives shape to the past, constructs history from it, commands future objectives, and orients the vision of the present.

Freeing the child of the responsibility for fiction implies ceasing to make him responsible for all our troubles[15] and ceasing to require him to live out the fiction which is in us. It also means returning to the unconscious in both its timeless and atopical aspects. Finally, it means accepting that there is no view of the human being that is not adultomorphic and anthropomorphic. And that the human being can never silence the dream of the child who dreams in man, who himself dreams of the child who is in man, and so on. He is never finished with representing.

Which Model for Psychoanalysis?

There is nothing to date which contradicts the validity of the Freudian model. Though the application of the data constituting the model can be called into question, its general structure remains valid. In the history of Freudian theory, identifying the powerful moments and the turning-point they represent, is much more important than, so to speak, making a longitudinal study – *à la* Jones – of the life and work of Sigmund Freud. If value is not placed on these moments of 'interpretative rupture', nothing is intelligible; just as nothing is intelligible in the direct observation of the child without the body of theoretical hypotheses which elucidate the findings that emerge from it. In order to be able to apprehend the relations between basic hypotheses and observational findings in psychoanalysis the psychoanalytic reference itself, namely, the unconscious, has to be applied to them. To put it differently, both the corpus of theoretical hypotheses – the analyst's 'sexual theories' – and the psychic functioning of the analyst-observer are unconscious. Their conscious formulation always occurs retroactively. It is indeed this retroactivity which is functioning in the analyst-theoretician when he endeavours to render conscious what is unconscious in the Freudian theory. For it is first necessary to know it thoroughly – from A to Z – in order to be able to identify, understand and integrate *a posteriori* what the powerful moments of the interpretative rupture are, and what they signify. Naturally, this treatment of Freud's work can be continued in post-Freudian theory, but in a different relation, where the first plays the role of what is repressed by the second. Thus the quasi-general adoption of a developmental point of view is the sign of an interpretative rupture with Freud regarding his legacy to us of that which was unthinkable before him and barely conceptualised by him. By choosing the theoretical axes that are the easiest to assimilate (the developmental point of view), post-Freudian theoreticians have simply followed the path of the theoretical pleasure principle by avoiding the unpleasure of having to think the unthinkable.

Fortunately, even within this general orientation, the repressed content of Freudian theory is making its disguised return in the current preoccupations: namely, in the work of Bion, Winnicott and Lacan. It is paradoxically in the work of these innovators that we again come across the repressed content of what Freud was unable to think. 'Developmental' psychoanalysis has not theorised 'the child in Freud's work'; it has simply made a naive hagiography of it. So much so that it is not in the opposition to the child-model that this return of the repressed is manifested, but in the emergence of another theoretical status assigned to childhood by these authors. For – and it needs stating – in all three, the child is there. Even in Lacan, whose first contribution to psychoanalytic theory was the concept of the mirror stage, a subject that was to be a constant point of reference throughout his subsequent work. Chasing shadows, he abandoned the *infans* for the signifier; however, he was obliged to return to it in the later stages of his work with *lalangue*, which it would not be improper to break down into *lallations* – language of

desire for/of the mother, even if this is in the Name of the Father.
There must surely be other viable solutions than this matricide to
which the Lacanian problematic of the phallus leads us.

The work of Bion, explicitly, and Winnicott, implicitly, is derived
from Melanie Klein. And it is with her that there lies an ambiguity
– no less so than with Anna Freud – concerning the status of the
child. No one more than Melanie Klein has attributed the child with
a categorial structure of thought, by describing a baby who, though
absolutely mythical, sometimes has a ring of truth about it for adults
who are in search of their tragic childhood. And no one more than
she persisted in holding the paradoxical position of wanting at any
price to legitimise this mythical child as the real child, by claiming
to be able to date chronologically the order of the schizo-paranoid,
depressive and Oedipal positions. Though she attempted to think
about what Freud had been unable to conceive, she sought to deny
the parricide she was carrying out unintentionally. By offering this
reference to chronology, from which Freud never freed himself, she
was trying not to cut herself off from the elements of realism which
still persist in Freudian thought.

Bion and Winnicott, each in their own way, modify the Kleinian
model. But they do not do so in the name of chronological realism.
Bion is careful not to give his 'grid' a temporal framework, and
Winnicott, even though he still conserves a conception of time that
is rather linear, does not give any very precise time markers. He is
not averse to observation, but, if I may say so, this is very indirect,
is practised randomly or is solicited by the occasional singularity of events.

How does he proceed? In his article 'The Observation of Infants in
a Set Situation' (1941), Winnicott's point of view is much less characteristic of 'direct observers' than of Freud watching his grandson
playing with the wooden reel. Moreover, between the two studies
there are obvious anastomoses. Although the description is
meticulous in its detail, the psychoanalyst's identification with the
baby largely makes up for the very ordinary character of the facts
described. It is noteworthy that Winnicott does not adopt the
position of a passive observer, standing back from the situation, but
participates in it by trying to get the child to take the spatula into his
mouth. The child is not observed in isolation, but jointly with her
mother. The same remarks may be made concerning another study
on 'the string' concerning the metapsychological conclusions that
Winnicott draws from it. It is even more true of the study of one of
the most common forms of child behaviour, the choice and election

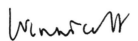

Winnicott

of the transitional object, a crucial observation (like the experience of the same name) for describing a group of transitional phenomena occurring in a field whose heuristic value opens the way for a theory of symbolism and the cultural area of experience. We owe the creation of these new concepts to Winnicott's liberty, to his willingness to get involved in the situation, to the calculated risk of introducing his own unconscious through the squiggle game.

Nevertheless, Winnicott only ascribes a limited value to the squiggle game. He uses it to establish contact, playing on the encounter between the infant's preconscious and the analyst's preconscious. The key moment in the therapeutic consultation is where the child is able to relate a dream which, this time, says something about the unconscious. Asking the child to relate his dream and to talk about it would have been experienced as intrusive without preliminary stages. This apparently incidental position adopted by Winnicott is extremely important for the implicit distinction he makes between the squiggle game and the dream. The squiggle game is a 'crossed' game and reciprocal game of spontaneous and immediate projections involving a minimum of psychic work. The dream is quite the opposite.

Absence only acquires meaning by being a time of psychic elaboration. It is the working time of the unconscious. In order to become familiar with this work – retrospectively – it is necessary to wait for the projection, or the reprojection of unconscious formations.

Bion and Winnicott both understand the child in relation to the adult – based on the analysis of psychotics, in Bion's case, and borderline patients in Winnicott's. The child provides the retrospective theory of the adult's psychopathology.[16]

In order for analytic influence to be possible, Freud writes in his introduction to Aichorn's book, Wayward Youth, very precise conditions are necessary which can be summed up by the expression 'analytic situation'. It requires the development of certain psychic structures and a particular attitude towards the analyst. When these structures are lacking – as in the case of children – 'something other than analysis must be used'. What prevents the child from being placed in an 'analytic situation' is the absence of the development of certain psychic structures. This means in fact that it is their emergence which allows one to gain a better understanding of the state in which the psychic structures are in germ – and not the contrary. Freud does not adopt the approach of going from the simple to the complex, but thinks that it is by analysing the complex that one can see the hidden complexity of what appears in a state of pseudo-simplicity. It is as the ego comes into being that one is able to infer, retrospectively, 'where the id was' and not the contrary.

All this poses the problem of construction in analysis. Though we have learnt, since Serge Viderman, to call into question the validity of our reconstructions, thinking of them rather as retrospective constructions,[17] this does not invalidate the value of our theories. For the question is, 'What do we claim to construct?' This necessarily leads on to a discussion whose terms were defined by Anna Freud: is the real child constructed (or reconstructed) by psychoanalysis? My answer to this is an unambiguous no. However, in turn, I would say that the role of psychoanalysis is not to reconstruct the real child but rather the mythical child, the mythical childhood of a real child who is the object of child psychology. I shall distinguish, then, between the true child of psychoanalysis – in the sense in which Freud speaks of historical truth – and the real child of psychology. Beyond them, the child of material truth can be nothing other than a combination of the real child of psychology and the true child of psychoanalysis.

It is not only psychoanalysis that speaks of the true child. Myths have much to say about him, and novels too. Who does not sense that there is more truth in Marcel Proust's account of the goodnight kiss than in the mass of direct observations that claim to be scientific? Further, who cannot see that there is greater proximity between the infantile universe of Winnicott and that of Proust than between Winnicott's thought and Spitz's, for example?[18]

When Winnicott tries to think about the child, he can only resort to paradox, which makes him a sort of Lewis Caroll of psychoanalysis. And when Bion, in turn, gives us his conception of the child, he grants the child attributes which stem from philosophy, modern mathematics and logical thinking. This is quite different from the digestive tube dear to the paediatricians, even when endowed with an elementary, so-called sensory-motor intelligence (Piaget).

Whatever we do, the model of the child in psychoanalysis will always remain more within the order of the indispensable myth of ontogeny than of ontogenesis. And it is just as well that this is the case, so that one cannot apply to child psychoanalysts the anecdote of the man who was looking for his key under the street lamp – when in fact he had lost it on the opposite pavement – because, at least, there he could see more clearly!

With respect to the child, it is necessary to repeat Freud's inaugural act. Starting from the clinical material of neuroses, he discovered the unconscious in broad daylight. For the benefit of Fliess, who was a reticent 'scientist', he gathered together the theoretical elements which made it possible to account for the totality of the visible; this was the 'Project' and its failure. Freud then understood that he was trying to see things too clearly. So he decided to shut himself away in the nocturnal world of dreams, his own dreams, from which he returned each morning after his descent into hell.

He analysed the dream after having dreamed it, after having been the hero, the spectator in it, blind to what he was doing there. Indirectly he came back to the dream via the memory that he had kept of it – which was no longer the dream itself but the dream remembered. He took it to pieces, looked for the day's residues, the latent thoughts, and, with the help of associations, set about reconstituting the dream work which enabled him to discover what was absent in the dream; namely, the infantile wish reactivated by being transferred onto a present scene. In this way he came across the wishful fantasy behind the dream.

With the dream model, we can construct a more general model which includes childhood. This model comprises several phases and is discontinuous.

(a) Something is organised: the complex of perceptions and phantasies. It can be seen that I bracket perception and phantasy together in simultaneity, one masking the other. This ensemble is organised. There is a meaning; this meaning is conscious, the unconscious meaning of the phantasy being hidden, but active.

(b) The work of the negative undoes this organisation. Here all the modes of negativity described by Freud under the category of repression have their place; but today we distinguish between repression, denial, disavowal and foreclosure. The list is not exhaustive; the field remains open for further investigation.

(c) The effect of this work of the negative[19] is to constitute another positivity; that of the repressed-unconscious which is a structured organisation, but diversely structured according to the prevalent mode of the negativity at work (repression, denial, disavowal, and so on).

(d) The unconscious organisation makes its return to the organised complex with which we began – which is already no longer the same since time has passed. There is now a struggle to keep it in an unconscious state. When the breakthrough has occurred after being disguised, the meaning of what is organised becomes disorganised to make way, retrospectively, for the meaning that modifies the events that follow. A conflict now erupts between the organisation of the ego and the organisation of the unconscious which points to the absence of organisation in the drives, the compromises of which find their expression in a variety of clinical situations.

I am well aware that I am simply reiterating classical findings, but I am doing so in order to stress this consistent hard core of Freud's theory which is his basic model for dreams just as it is for phantasy, symptoms, transference and the child. For this model continues to function throughout the whole of life. This means that the diachronic view has to be subordinated to the structural perspective. An open structure that is modified in certain circumstances by the aleatory nature of things, but which remains unchanged as far as its constitution is concerned. For the unconscious is constitutional, that is, it is there from the beginning. For reasons of schematisation, I have excluded the role of the object from this description. Introducing it would only complicate the schema, but above all in one sense: namely, that the Other possesses the same structure, at a different level of functioning.

When, at a later stage – the last stage in the constitution of the theory – Freud got to grips with infantile sexuality, he did not observe it (or did not only observe it); he constructed at the same time the hypotheses of the unobservable: anaclisis, for example, which cannot be deduced from any observation, but which can be constructed by thinking. And, above all, he introduced the essential discontinuity of a human sexuality which has been present since the origins – repressed or rendered latent, then re-emerging in full flower. Life-death (apparent) and rebirth. It is this model that we need to have in mind for the child-model in order to avoid turning the child into a model child. A lovely child, as say his parents whose love will constitute for him the essential element of survival. If he is to live and not simply survive, he will have to cease being this model child and to know the proscribed nature of the outcome of this love. He will have to know the object in hate and transform this primordial 'hainamoration'[20] (Lacan) in order to be able to invest elsewhere, not only in other objects but in other object-relationships. Herein lies the whole difficulty for man of being.

6 Memory

A. REMEMBERING:
EFFECT OF MEMORY OR TEMPORALITY AT WORK?[1]
(1990)[*]

The process of remembering and the moment of recognition, of understanding (*prise de conscience*) are considered as two distinct psychic events, although in the early days of psychoanalysis the remembering of repressed memories coincided with this moment of understanding or awareness. The more time passed, the more it became necessary to distinguish the two phases in this process. My hypothesis is as follows: relatively speaking, psychoanalysis is not very concerned with remembering; its real object is temporality. A non-psychoanalytic example, taken from Proust, will help us to understand this: the *Recherche* is identified, for anyone who is at all familiar with it, with the fabulous description, found at the beginning of the work, of the impressions aroused by the madeleine of Combray dipped in tea or tisane.

'A little time in the pure state ...'

As I was re-reading this extremely rich episode of the *Recherche*, I noticed something that is not usually remarked upon. The miraculous recollection stimulated by the madeleine follows the evocation of bedtime scenes in which little Marcel is sent to bed at seven o'clock in the evening. These scenes in themselves sum up 'all Combray' in the narrator's memory, owing to their affective significance. In fact, before the memories liberated by the madeleine emerged, all this, he says, was in reality 'all dead' for him. For death, as a result of forgetting or the end of life, is the key to the work. Just as each bedtime is an agony, each night is an entombment for little Marcel. The movement of memory of recollecting the madeleine, which we are all familiar with, is a resurrection due to an accidental, unforeseen and unpredictable coincidence.

[*] First published as 'La remémoration: effet de mémoire ou temporalité à L'oeuvre' in *Nouvelle Revue de psychanalyse*, LIX, 1990, pp. 947–72.

In the richness of the resurrected impressions, none is more powerful than this sensation of invulnerability, of indestructibility, of the deep happiness of the Ego 'having the same effect which love has'.[2] Love and life have triumphed over the burying involved in forgetting, a sign of death. Forgetting, loss of the memory – mental sleep – the loss of the mother. Is this a rediscovery or a search for truth? More the latter, I think. It was a titanic psychical work until the moment when the memory of Aunt Léonie was recaptured. A psychoanalyst cannot avoid detecting displacements here. Aunt Léonie takes the place of the mother and the madeleine dipped in the tea serves as a screen for the nourishing breast. A degree of discretion is advisable here; for men of letters would not approve of this 'reduction'.

Memories are what persist beyond the death of individuals 'amid the ruins of all the rest'. Proust's memory is undoubtedly affective but it is above all associative. This will become clearer presently. For though the Japanese flowers make us imagine the whole of Combray contained within the savour emerging from the little piece of madeleine[3] after it has been dipped in Aunt Léonie's tea or tisane, it is not until the end of *Le temps retrouvé* (*Time Regained*) that we – and equally the narrator – will really know what it is that he wants to say. For the time being, let us simply note that when the 'drama of getting undressed' is evoked, foreshadowing the loss of the mother, and this psychic demise which is feared each night to the point of awaking the child in the middle of it, this 'all Combray' of despair will be replaced by the 'all Combray' of happiness which puts the spice back into his life.

It is, of course, quite improper of me to cite this bit of anthology in isolation. By the author's own confession, its meaning remains to be discovered, and this will only become clear at the end of the work in *Time Regained*. For it is here that the associative process goes beyond the initial framework and allows connections to be made between the piece of madeleine evoking Combray; the unevenness of the paving-stones in the Guermantes hotel courtyard, which were reminiscent of those of the baptistery of St Mark's in Venice; the noise of a spoon touching a plate, resonating with the noise of a railwayman's hammer striking the wheel of a train; and the starched linen napkin in the library, where the narrator is made to wait, with which he wipes his lips after eating some pastries and drinking some orange juice, calling to mind the Grand Hotel in Balbec. Triggered initially by absorbing a drink which takes the narrator's mind back to childhood, the different stages in the associative process will end with another pleasure of nourishment, completing its course with the silent allusion to young girls in flower, idle musings whose roving nature belies their internal logic. Here childhood is no longer isolated; it is linked up with later episodes which, when taken together, acquire meaning. And it is by setting things in perspective in this way that the moment of understanding, of awareness, emerges, needless to say, retrospectively.

All these moments of happiness are wrenched from time and no longer obey it. In other words, voluntary memory is powerless to evoke them, whereas association makes them come out of their sepulture and emerge from the kingdom of shadows. What Proust tells us, in fact, concerning this involuntary remembering, is that it counts for less in terms of memory than in terms of what it signifies about time. For, as far as association is concerned, each instant offers us many opportunities for associating a present impression with another from the past with which it belongs. The selection that links them together inserts each one of them into a chain. In isolation, their significance is limited, and even misleading. When they are set alongside each other and compared, they show what they have in common and indicate implicitly what they represent for the unconscious – the word is used by Proust. It is necessary to be graced with a permeable state of mind if the memory is to be revived. And it is by situating oneself outside time (Proust speaks of the extra-temporal, like the unconscious in Freud) that present and past coincide, in the real sense of the word. It is, then, in this singular property of emergence which helps him elude death, that the unforeseeable occurs.

Remembering has the virtue of allaying anxiety about death and gives one a feeling of immortality, associated with the happiness that is procured from enjoying things. If sexual pleasure is said to be a 'little death', the pleasure of remembering is in fact that of a timelessness synonymous with eternity. It is not the past that returns, but 'something that, common both to the past and to the present, is much more essential than either of them'.[4] In order to manifest itself, imagination, which is our means of enjoying beauty, requires absence. In the case we are considering, imagination transcends this condition and activates itself, making the present and its buried double, the past, echo each other. The human being thus obtains – for a moment as brief as a flash of lightening – 'what normally he never apprehends: a fragment of time in the pure state'.[5] That the latter is incarnated via the senses even more than via the imagination helps us to recognise its undeclared familiarity with sensuality, rather than with sensibility.

Owing to its associative form, remembering is not just a process of recovering what has been forgotten; it is a process of creation. But it is because the upheaval which causes this creative process is too intense that the narrator's enjoyment risks turning into raptures (yet another syncope comparable to the interruption of life), that it is rare, transient, evanescent. This relation to Time is the project of the *Recherche*. To Time, and not to memory. Time is not just the basis of Proust's elaboration: the whole work is a process of becoming conscious of time that is all the more pressing in that, sooner or later, forgetting will always impose itself. It is with this fundamental revelation that the *Recherche* closes. The unconscious, Proust says, is 'the interior book of unknown symbols'; it is not so much refound as it is called on to manifest itself through an act of creation which, based on what I have called the uncreateable,[6] is also a relation to Time.

One morning when he was at the Duchess's home, the narrator, seeing the Duc of Guermantes getting up from his chair, suddenly became conscious of men,

> as occupying so considerable a place, compared with the restricted place which is reserved for them in space, a place on the contrary prolonged past measure, for simultaneously, like giants plunged into the years, they touch the distant epochs through which they have lived, between which so many days have come to range themselves – in Time.[7]

To say that is to acknowledge that a man's old age is not just the time that has passed in his life, that is to say, the whole journey from birth to death traversed by his body deploying itself, before shrinking and, finally, fading away; it is also the accumulation in him, through memory, not only of what he has personally known, experienced, and stored up, but also of his relationships with others, his contemporaries, ascendants and descendants. This chain of lives establishes a link between his ancestors and those who follow in his line – a line which gives anyone who is conscious of it the sense of being something more than just remains! Being is time, because being, in its relation to the other who grafts himself onto its being, enriches itself from the other's life, either by the way in which it imagines itself proceeding from it, or by placing itself in the position of a donor or interlocutor, in order to survive itself. In a certain way, if our children are our memory, our memories are also like beings to whom we give life and which survive the effective presence existing between us and them and them and us.

I will refrain here from making the commentary which I would very much like to have developed on this work, which sometimes speaks of itself as if it had not been written, as if it still remained to be written, and simply say instead how writing, or the trace which makes it possible to hold back Time or to create its own temporality, can also erase itself. I will go straight to the point by asserting that this moment of consciousness is nothing other than consciousness of Time.

Remembering and Insight[8] in Freud

Right up to the end of his work, Freud never abandoned his early intuitions concerning the aim of analysis, that is, of lifting infantile amnesia in order to get rid of the anachronisms of psychic life:

> It is familiar ground that the work of analysis aims at inducing the patient to give up the repressions (using the word in the widest sense) belonging to his early development and to replace them by reactions of a sort that would correspond to a psychically mature condition. With this purpose in view he must be brought to recollect certain experiences and the affective impulses called up by them which he has for the time being forgotten. ... What we are in search of is a picture of the patient's forgotten years that shall be alike trustworthy and in all essential respects complete.[9]

Analogous statements – allowing for a few variations – can already be found without difficulty in the *Studies on Hysteria* (1895), and in any case in *Three Essays on Sexuality* (1905).

There is a logical sequence in Freud's mind, which goes something like this:

- symptom = return of the repressed, a compromise between desire and defence, which is related to:
- repression = counter-investment so as to avoid unpleasure, which is related to:

- repressed = a reserve of unconscious ideas and affects, which is related to:
- the recollection of experiences which were probably repressed.

It follows that: analytic material = dream memories, dream work, incidental ideas related to repressed experiences, suppressed affective impulses, signs of the repetition of affects, acting out, and, finally, the transference relationship; which is related to,

- resistance as the repetition of repression; which is related to,
- interpretation (or construction); which is related to,
- the lifting repression and insight; which is related to,
- reactions connected with psychical maturity = cure = end of analysis.

This series of propositions is, as you can see, underpinned by what is an apparently self-evident logic. Even a superficial examination would show, however, that this is only intelligible to the extent that certain conditions are fulfilled. For instance, that the symptom, in all cases, and not just in neurosis, is a compromise between desire and defence; that what is said about repression can be extended to the case of splitting, of denial, etc; that interpretation is regularly accompanied by the lifting of repression, and, finally, that psychical 'maturity' is established once this has happened. Though this logic was clearly called into question by Freud's successors, he himself became increasingly doubtful about it as his thinking evolved and as he was able to reap the fruit of his experience.

This schema which I have put together as a guide needs modifying in certain respects. In 'Remembering, Repeating, and Working-Through' (1914a), Freud already knew that if the aim was still to fill the gaps of memory, it was necessary to add that memory is not easy to define, psychoanalytically speaking, since the amnesia observed in analysis cannot be likened with forgetting. This is what the patient leads us to understand when he states: 'I didn't (ever) think of that.' Such a declaration links, in an indissoluble way, amnesia and negation, or in more contemporary language, amnesia and a work of the negative.

Towards the end of an analysis there is often a sense of disappointment. The analysand has not recovered his memory as much as he had expected to. What is more, the memories that have come back to him often turn out to be screen-memories. As such, and inasmuch as the memories are supposed to refer to real historical events, they demonstrate that it is as well to place little faith in them. On the other hand, they give an indication of the incessant transforming power of the mind which makes use of everything, not only for the purpose of disguising, but also for signifying through the disguise. For the screen-memory is more revealing than an ordinary memory. Freud recognised its power to contain everything essential in infantile life. The function of the screen-memory has given rise to widely differing commentaries. What appears initially is the existence, at the very heart of remembering, of a persistence of repression which hinders access to the clear, unambiguous evocation of a past event. If the forgetting is lifted, it is not in order to give access to a resurrection of the past history reappearing in a naked simplicity which shows how it persists intact in the psyche. On the contrary, this recovered memory reveals that the juxtaposition of elements belonging to different periods, while preserving the signifying capacity of the psyche, not only presents it in a distorted way – which will be noticeable in certain cases – but turns the mnemic production itself into a rampart against what apparently has to remain inaccessible, thereby making way for the idea that meaningfulness has to pay a tribute to the unacceptable and renounce the entirety or neutrality of meaning as it is concealed by the past.

In parallel to this, remembering cannot easily accommodate itself to the status of being the double of a buried reality. And we know – since Jung – how much capital has been made in the epistemological discussion of the foundations of psychoanalysis from the fundamental uncertainty surrounding what is 're-found' in psychoanalysis, implying that it is possible to reconstruct a reality conserved in a state which would be the equivalent, on a psychic level, of deep-freezing on a physical level. But Freud had himself announced, had he not, that our reflection on the relation to the past was insufficient. For it is not the memory, nor even the screen-memory, which solicits the work of the psyche. What the hysteric suffers from is reminiscences. Reminiscence is not remembering. It is difficult, moreover, to know what it is, for Plato is of little help to us here. We would certainly be going astray if we were to regard it as nothing but an attenuated form of remembering. And though it is tempting to consider it in terms of the greater or lesser degree of consciousness that accompanies it, in so doing one misses its principal dimension which, in such a context, is the possibility of causing suffering.

Which means, more broadly, the possibility of shaking the psychical apparatus, of assailing it, questioning it, not only in a way that is rather obscure and sometimes painful, but above all in a mysterious way, as the souls of the dead would do – their ghosts wishing to remind the living of some unpunished deed or some unpaid debt. For it is often their exceptional vividness, their power of occupying the psychic stage at the expense of any other consideration, which can take on a quasi-hallucinatory character and astonish us with these mnemic manifestations. In reality, Freud never abandoned this point of view, even when in the middle of his work he was asking himself questions about the *déjà vu*, the *déjà entendu*, as haunted forms of memory which owed less and less to memory.

The possibility that there is a distinction between memories (more or less filtered by screens) and phantasies has been cast in doubt. In such cases one is justified in wondering if, in analysis, there exist memories which are not screen-memories and if screen-memories can be completely distinguished from the phantasies with which they are regarded as being in absolute opposition. Nonetheless, Freud insisted on maintaining this opposition for, in his view, phantasies are 'purely internal' acts, whereas memories (screen or not) refer to an exteriority, that is, to the dimension of events. In fact, it will be understood that all the suspicions cast on memories cannot lead us to conclude that it is useless to refer to them, for memories are representatives of a category which refers to reality. In this respect, it is necessary to distinguish between the reference to reality, even if we have no means of affirming with certainty what it is, and our capacity to provide the proof (and not the test) of the reality of a psychic event which remains highly conjectural. In other words, reality is an inescapable aporia. Being familiar with the experience on which it is constructed is the first indispensable step for anyone who wants to examine it. But instead of being content to simply rely on it, anyone who examines it will cast doubt over the manner in which we feel involved in it. We have no choice but to make a deduction about the nature of what it is; but, in its turn, this deduction can only take place at its core.

'Repeating, Remembering and Working-Through' ruins the classical conception of the memory in many respects. Later, in 'Constructions in Analysis', we feel a bit doubtful when Freud states that a sense of familiarity in the analysand with the analyst's interpretation is enough to protect him against the absence of memory. Suggestion is not far off, and heaven only knows how much Freud mistrusted it. But the most fundamental acquisition of this text is that it established the existence of an amnesic memory, that is, of remembering in the form of non-mnemic events.[10] This is repetition, where the repeated act is a substitute for remembering. What are the consequences of this for treatment? Although the memory function of acting out extends the field of remembering, it makes *insight* more difficult. But, once again, one cannot overlook the gain made at the expense of psychic functioning. We already knew that the memory could, in fact, only be a montage or a collage of memories from different periods; we acknowledged that the demarcation between memory and phantasy was open to doubt. Up to that point we still remained within the internal world, within the limits of the psychical domain; but now memory was extended also to the act, while excluding its function of remembering, its significance and its content. It will be seen that, at each step, the extension of the domain of memory is in fact a recognition of the resources of resistance as well the indisputable contradiction of a rejection of the appearance of reality at the very heart of that which grounds us in it and obliges us to return to it.

Remembering or Resistance, Psyche is above all Transformation

Can the compulsion to repeat be considered as another form of memory? For Freud, the answer was yes, on the condition that the domain of the remembered be extended to phylogenesis; for, according to him, the instinctual drives were once acts in the history of the species. He considered their transformation into the state of drives as the result of a process of internalisation. For me, repetition is certainly a form of memory, and thus a characteristic of life; though its ontogenetic transformation poses complex problems which modify its meaning. Henceforth, however, remembering, which Freud referred to later on in 'Constructions in Analysis', depends on the interpretation of material which is by no means only confined to memories, as we have seen. In the article just cited, Freud explains the passage from the state of remembering to that of action (as a substitute for memory) in terms of the intensity of the transference or by its hostile colouring. Everything depends, then, on a quantitative factor affecting the transference, which increases the resistance. This indication refers implicitly to mental functioning. For it can be said that such transferences, marked by the compulsion to repeat, consist less in evoking the past mnesically (and psychically), than in actualising it. Let me mention in passing that Arthur Valenstein has described 'affectualisation' as a mode of actualising the transference. This exaggeration is simply the reinforcement of the normal state of things, since Freud recognises that he must treat the patient's illness 'not as an event of the past but as a present-day force'.[11] Hence, instead of the patient gaining insight as expected, his symptoms may be aggravated, though hopefully only on a temporary basis. At this point Freud insists on a new factor. He appeals to the patient to find the courage to direct his attention to his symptoms. Insight is far from guaranteed as a result of remembering alone.

The conclusion Freud draws from all this is of the utmost interest. After commenting on the disturbances in the transference which, as he says somewhat lightly, can result in 'passing disasters', and the attitude required of the doctor who must endeavour to keep events in the psychical sphere, Freud concludes, in the spirit of Winnicott before his time: 'the transference thus creates a sort of intermediate region between illness and real life, through which the transition from the one to the other is made'.[12] More precisely still, the *Standard Edition* was to qualify this sphere as a *playground*, whereas the French translation was an 'arena' which makes one think more of circus games or bullfighting.

The question has shifted and now becomes one of the relations between remembering, repetition, and transference as a playground for working-through. In other words, insight does not depend on remembering but on the quality of the transference. The elaboration of resistances is the heir of abreaction.

Remembering and Transference without Insight

The article on which we have been reflecting dates from 1914, the year in which the treatment of Serguei Constantinovitch Pankejeff, alias 'the Russian', alias the Wolf Man – the parade horse of psychoanalysis, to use Michel Schneider's expression – was concluded. No other case shows more dramatically that insight is not a product of remembering. For was it not in this text that Freud pushed furthest the exploration of the 'primal era'? How should we read today the passage written by Freud in 1918:

In this case history, it is necessary once again to note that one had the impression that with the mastery of the scene with Grouscha, the first experience which he was actually able to remember without supposition or intervention from me, the task of the cure had been fulfilled. From then on, there were no further resistances; we just needed to collect and recompose.[13]

There is reason to doubt this, in view of what happened after, based not only on the accounts of later analysts but also on the patient's memories as he was writing his own story or answering the questions of the journalist Karin Obholzer.[14] How much insight can the Wolf Man be credited with when one sees him shutting himself in a double bind and trapping Freud with his paradoxes? For it was he himself who regarded Freud with scorn when the latter started to doubt the reality of the primitive scene and suggested that it should perhaps be interpreted as a retroactive phantasy. And yet he also told Karin Obholzer that he could not believe in such a scene, which, moreover, 'was not in his dream'. This is proof that he never acquired insight into the nature of psychoanalysis, in spite of Freud's elucidation of his infantile neurosis and of memories going back to the age of eighteen months. Shortly before his death, Serguei Pankejeff believed only in the transference; a position, moreover, that many of us would agree with. Unfortunately, this was what he said about it: 'Either there is no transference, and in that case the treatment is useless. Or the transference occurs, but then you run the risk of putting yourself in the hands of others, of no longer deciding for yourself.'[15] This takes us back to the era of suggestion! Let us not forget that it was on this subject that the famous *Verwerfung* was written (which Lacan named 'foreclosure' and Laplanche now translates as 'rejection'). In other words, the most complete remembering is not worth much if repression takes the form of rejection. Memories return, for sure, but this is less a lifting of repression than a return of memories – a return affected by a form of splitting which removes all their power of conviction. The transference itself is caught in the same logical impasse. This is what I have called, apropos of the Wolf Man, the 'bilogic': 'The drives are split between themselves, and are globally split from the object on the one hand and from the intellect on the other. The intellect inherits bisexuality and ambivalence; hence the bilogic.'[16] Basically, from this moment on, Freud understood that both the lifting of amnesia and recognition through a purely intellectual acceptance of the repressed were not sufficient to create *insight*. To put it another way, the recovery from amnesia and of the repressed is dependent on categories of judgement which transcend the straightforward opposition between Yes and No; it requires a felt conviction and an object-investment of the analyst, though this should be moderate and should not prevent one from thinking for oneself.

In 'Remembering, Repeating and Working-Through', acting out was explained by the intensity of the transference. In the case of the Wolf Man, the failure can be attributed to a transference blocked in a mode of functioning based on parasitic dependence. This new domain of psychopathology, first noticed by Freud – think of the last chapter of *The Ego and the Id*, 'The Ego's Dependent Relations' – then uncovered by Ferenczi, and fully developed by Winnicott, seems to relativise the value of remembering considerably. The transference is caught here in the actualisation. Thus, when Winnicott says that in such cases the analyst does not represent the mother, but *is* the mother, he is not only alluding to the vitiation of symbolisation; his remark also touches upon temporality. For it is not rare to hear the analysand react in the following way to an interpretation by the analyst: 'This has nothing to do with my childhood or my parents; it only concerns my relationship with you and nothing else. You are avoiding me by referring me back to my past.' This is confirmed, much too superficially, by the partisans of the technique of the here-and-now. What is inferred here is the non-existence of the transference which assumes the mask of a transference resistance. But to deny the transference is to deny the relations between what is repeated and what is repressed; it is to deny the reference to history and its foreclosure by exalting the present, the absolute novelty of which is only defended with a view to carrying out an absolute neutralisation of the past.

Permanent Amnesia

The case of the Wolf Man inaugurated, as we know, the psycho-analysis of borderline cases. It has become the case of reference for a whole sector of the analytic population. The latter, however, are far from gratifying us with a memory comparable to the Russian's, allowing us to describe an infantile neurosis which is as enlighten-ing as that of the Wolf Man. Here I should like to pose a somewhat irreverent question: the light which radiates from the exposition of the case – do we owe it to Serguei Pankejeff or to Sigmund Freud? In his memoirs, moreover, the former at times imitates perfectly the latter's style, to such an extent that one would say that certain passages were written by Freud. And they contain almost nothing about his analysis with him![17]

What is perhaps most striking in the borderline structures we come up against, is the absence of childhood memories. Litza Guttieres-Green has even described a syndrome of painful amnesia in which pain impedes recollection and takes the place of what cannot be remembered.[18] Her work opens up a discussion on the significance of the black hole frequently mentioned by these patients. Very often the analysis gets going after the evocation of a certain stock of memories, recalled in a typical context. These constitute a precious mnemic reserve, without the slightest significance being drawn from their evocation. Neither is there any link which makes it possible to understand their selection, their connections, and their storage. It is often the case that, for some length of time, the analysis of the transference consists in referring the material of the here-and-now to one of the elements of this stock. Sometimes a new interpretation, arising from the transference, will make it possible to envisage a new version of the memory by making use of mediators. Accordingly, a recent dream will refer back to an old dream which has been linked up with a memory or a phantasy.

What is more, while in one session links are forged (Bion) which make the present and past intelligible, leading to an affect of recognition (in the two senses of the term), with the analyst keeping a favourable impression of the work that has been achieved, the following session sees the illusion that analytic work has been accomplished collapse like a house of cards. And yet, during the preceding session the impression of insight was clear. Not only due to the patient's acceptance of what the analyst had advanced, but also because of the generation of the patient's associations – the touchstone, according to the Freud of 'Constructions in Analysis', of the exactness of the interpretation. It seems as if the interruption of the analytic relation at the end of the session has more reality than the session itself; or, that for the patient, the session seems like an illusion once the analyst's presence can no longer receive, welcome, drain, distribute, orient, allocate and give meaning to what is happening. Freud compared the reconquest of territory invaded by the id to the drying up of the Zuyderzee; one could also compare it with Penelope's endless weaving of her piece of cloth.

Remembering is related to infantile amnesia. But insufficient attention is paid to the fact that often the amnesia concerns more or less recent events. These may be events of adult life by which one has been deeply affected and which were often very traumatic and, precisely because of that, forgotten. Sometimes it is very recent events that are not mentioned spontaneously in the session. They can, however, be found again through the associations alluding to them unconsciously. The interpretation of the associative derivatives which serve as a screen brings them back to the surface. Is repression involved? To some extent, probably, but the dominant impression is that these events, or rather the memory of them, are not only located behind the associations but remain inaccessible, as if they had broken off all the semantic links which give them meaning. One might, then, speak of a permanent amnesia in the sense that Trotsky spoke of the permanent revolution. But do not both expressions basically cover the same idea? For Trotsky, the past always tends to reconstitute itself; hence the permanent effort to prevent its re-installation. Is it not somewhat the same thing for the patients in question? But in both cases there is the same thought: there is nothing to be gained from preserving these old-fashioned ideas.

Thus irrespective of the fact the Wolf Man came to Freud with a rich harvest of ideas (direct or indirect), or that certain patients can only offer the analyst the desert of their memory, the success or lack of success of the treatment cannot depend on remembering alone. It is more likely that memory or remembering are just the signs of the functioning of temporality as a support for historical truth.

I am thinking of certain patients who affirm during long periods that they cannot remember anything from their previous session. (We do not actually ask them, but they never forget to tell us.) It is often the same ones who claim to be prone to a certain deafness in listening to interpretations, as if to challenge their analyst's approach, which makes them inaccessible. What the analyst notices is the dangerous character of insight. It is as if this signified the loss of illusions, the imminence of a sanction, the danger of a rejection or abandonment. The analyst is provoked, his efforts destroyed – which does not prevent a feeling of profound gratitude for the intense psychic effort he makes in persevering in his attempts to give meaning to what unfolds in the analytic exchange.

For the dominant impression that these patients have in uttering their discourse is that it is deprived of significance, and that the only significance that can be drawn from it is the necessity of convincing the analyst that there is scarcely any causal temporality at work, nor any link between antecedents and consequences, between causes and effects and, ultimately, between subject and object.

Listening to the material of such patients who have often suffered serious traumas and survived them, leaves the analyst with a strange impression. The session seems to unfold in a present that is very heavy, but not very significant; for one does not understand what causes the anxiety or the distressing affects which they are speaking about. It lacks meaning, just as it lacks representations. By dint, however, of bringing these affects back into the transference and linking them up with the available reserve of representations and memories, one ends up by obtaining details which throw light on the current circumstances that are awaking old injuries. Behind the complaint about destructive anxieties, one can surmise the existence of rage, fury, impotence, envy, and the desire to destroy everything – which are all returns of past affects that a few, rare, screen-memories have sometimes made it possible to link up with a childhood context. Nonetheless, the suppression of any allusion to the recent triggering causes is designed to maintain the isolation from the past which has led to catastrophic reactions. Sometimes it is the connection that the patient made in the past between certain traumatic events, perhaps caused by quite independent reasons, and certain prohibited or violent desires, which leads him to maintain, or even reinforce, the isolation of memories. Moreover, any reactivation of desire carries with it the threat of disorganisation which is warded off by a defensive strategy aimed at rendering such a desire impossible or making it depend on material conditions which do not allow it to be realised. The constructions that the analyst can make meet with the inevitable response: 'I can't remember.' Just as the transference interpretations on what is happening in the here-and-now of the session provoke the ritual comment 'I don't understand.' Everything seems to be assembled under the heading of 'I don't know.' The cell 'I ... don't' indicates one of the particularly malign forms of the work of the negative of which amnesia is simply the most superficial level. The transferential quality of what is happening is all the more remarkable in that the subject is extremely regular in attending his sessions. It is not here that we will witness a phobic flight into absenteeism. The analyst has to experience the same sense of chaos or incomprehensibility that the subject experienced in the past.

It seems to me, in fact, that these structures, which have not only been subject to the amnesic treatment of the defences but a genuine diachronic disorganisation, are still linked to alienating maternal fixations in which the subject has the impression that he has lived to serve the needs of the mother more than his own, with little hope that she will be able to respond to his needs and expectations of her. Nonetheless, these reproaches with regard to the maternal imago coexist with a quasi-delusional love for her that is genuinely sacrificial; although, at the same time, the subject devalues the paternal law or, rather, the split with maternal fixation. For the girl, the father will appear to be no more than the mother's pale stooge, more or less indistinguishable from her. For the boy, the father's words will arouse ambivalence, or even be totally devalued, as they are by the mother. This will lead, as a consequence of the opposition manifested towards the father, to the need to provoke the intervention of a symbolic paternal authority: the boss at work, the policeman, tax inspector, and so on.

This situation, which will lead more than one to lose hope, needs to be counterbalanced by the constancy of the interpretative attitude and an unshakeable faith in the positive effect of analytic understanding, even when the patient does everything he can to make one think the analysis is useless.

For, with the help of the analysis, one witnesses, after a long period of time, remarkable modifications:

(a) a relative disinvestment of maternal omnipotence, with the appearance of a more 'human' and more credible imago;

(b) a new investment of paternal authority, the paternal transference being modified by the quest for the help that the analyst can provide by giving meaning to what is happening in the patient's psyche, which is preferable to acting out, which is harmful for the ego;

(c) the resurgence of memories of a more clearly Oedipal nature, marked by an awareness of desires for transgression and the appearance of guilt feelings, calling for self-punishment and not for a real external sanction. The reconstitution of memory goes hand in hand with a movement towards the Oedipal organisation and the latter gives a temporal meaning to that which had been deprived of it. As a result, remembering assigns the subject with a place in the succession of generations and a gender in relation to the difference between the sexes. This then permits him to have access to a type of historical causality represented by his affiliation with the maternal and paternal lines of inheritance whose crossed effects are present in him.

Under these conditions, the treatment takes on a new significance. The separations (at the end of each session, or when there are short or long interruptions for holidays) break the continuity of the process. These 'interrupters' stop the flow of the analysis and become breakers of meaning which work against the retention and storage of the events of the analysis in the form of transferential memory. Only affects and acts can take their place in a disguised manner, without the subject being aware of their function of remembering. These findings seem to confirm my hypothesis that psychoanalysis has little to do with remembering and everything to do with temporality, in respect of which remembering is simply the intercessor and indicator of the relations between psychic causality and historicity.

It is usually maintained that it is destructivity that prevents associativity. One still has to determine, though, what triggers the destructivity. In order to understand this, the patient's counter-associative strategy needs to be resisted with an associative counter-transference, directed towards the substitutes for association which are often expressed in the form of painful affects.

Of course, it is important not to confuse temporality with historical chronology or a developmental perspective. It is something quite different. Temporality is the precondition for insight. While the absence of remembering does not facilitate insight, its presence does not suffice to make it emerge. Remembering reflects the effective functioning of temporality, but the latter is acquired by a deployment which depends less on the sequential ordering of memories than their historical significance in relation to generational differences. To put this more clearly, what stands out in the relation between remembering and temporality is the relation between temporality and causality.

Insight consists, then, in the internal vision – the introvision – of what, in the adult, speaks the language of a child to another who is an adult, and towards whom one's desires, unconscious desires of love or hate, can under no circumstances be realised, owing to the limitations imposed by the context of childhood. To have insight is to recognise these desires and the repetition of the impossibility of realising them; it means recognising in the transference what has already been lived and what is radically new. It also means analysing the various functions of memory, screen-memory, phantasy, and acting out as an impossibility of realising desire on account of the transference. Temporality, then, is indeed linked to the transference; it is the eternal recurrence of a time that is never past which will be put back into its orbit by the analysis. Every analysand will be able to identify with the line from Hamlet: 'Time is out of joint.'

Pseudo-insight

So far I have not distinguished between insight in the treatment, following interpretation, and its definition *stricto sensu*; namely, the internal vision obtained by the analysand, from himself, by himself, and for himself. Such an occurrence comes about as a result of a process of internalisation. The question arises as to whether all insight does not depend on a depressive, or at least nostalgic, movement? After all, what forces me to see more clearly into myself but the failure of my defences and the persistence of my suffering? Here I am at one with Melanie Klein who holds, I think, that insight is closely linked to the depressive position. And yet ... It is true that, though the depressive movement facilitates insight, true insight contributes to freeing oneself from it. It is here, perhaps, that pleasure comes into it – the pleasure of seeing into oneself clearly. It will be understood that its precondition is to maintain the capacity for pleasure – the depression in question obviously cannot be of a melancholic nature.

The case of melancholy is very instructive, both for insight as well as for remembering. In effect, insight is always retrospective: 'I understand now what I have done, what I have been, who I was, what it is in me that continues to be and to behave as in the past.' While this meaning is structured retrospectively, this retrospection is the very essence of 'binocular vision' which puts the present and past into focus in order to accommodate the future. The melancholic claims his true self has been revealed thanks to the crisis he is going through and which is accompanied by unexpected recollections! 'I am an impenitent criminal because, when I was seven years old, I stole some cakes from the baker's after school.' A Kleinian would say this was probably a displaced attempt to make reparation for the theft of babies from the inside of the mother's breast, resulting in their starvation. On the contrary, the revelation of the delusion contains a sense of extra-lucidity in the nature of *outsight*, as was the case with the female patient, an antique dealer with a large shop window, who claimed that she had been photographed by the Israeli secret service because of an adventure she had not even had with a citizen of that country, and that they had put together a montage of pornographic photos in order to discredit her. The *outsight* had the value of a counter-investment of her unconscious homosexuality which soon appeared in her delusion. The projection, which was literal here, saved her from displaced guilt feelings. Nevertheless, her delusional belief drove her to suicide.

The fact remains that the case of the self-accusing melancholic is a troubling one. In 'Mourning and Melancholia' (1917), Freud wrote:

> Indeed, we must at once confirm some of his statements without reservation. He really is as lacking in interest and as incapable of love and achievement as he says. [Freud interprets this as a consequence of the work of mourning.] He also seems to us justified in certain other self-accusations; it is merely that he has a keener eye for the truth than other people who are not melancholic. When in his heightened self-criticism he describes himself as petty, egoistic, dishonest, lacking in independence, one whose sole aim has been to hide the weaknesses of his own nature, it may be, so far as we know, that he has come pretty near to understanding himself; we only wonder why a man has to be ill before he can be accessible to a truth of this kind. For there can be no doubt that if anyone holds and expresses to others an opinion of himself such as this (an opinion which Hamlet held both of himself and of everyone else,[19]) he is ill, whether he is speaking the truth or whether he is being more or less unfair to himself.[20]

In other words, what is unhealthy is to let such ideas into consciousness, and to express them out loud to someone, whether it is oneself or others. Whether this is true or false, it goes against the conventions of civilised behaviour which, Winnicott tells us, implies the false-self that is indispensable for any form of civilised social life. In this case, the presence of a witness excites the desire for exhibitionist satisfaction – a counterpoint to the voyeuristic satisfaction of insight. One can also think that the ego, having lost the object and identifying itself with it, kills two birds with one stone. Criticism of the object is a form of self-criticism and, as the object is no longer invested, this boils down to a kind of self-knowledge. The paradox of self-knowledge in melancholia is that the ego can do nothing with it, since it is identified with the lost object, and because this self-knowledge proves to be nothing but a sham, its discourse being addressed, in fact, to the object. The ego can therefore not make any use of anything it says about itself, for an obscure consciousness makes it clear that it is the object that is being addressed. In other words, it escapes the revelation of what it is because there is a *quiproquo*, a case of mistaken identity. This screen ego only has existence as a substitute and intermediary for the object, these very terms being inadequate because the ego, identified with the object, has no distance which would allow for the interposition of any kind of mediation.

Another version of the paradox of the actor is that what the melancholic says concerns the role he is playing and not himself. But he is an actor who has no existence except when he is playing his role; he is not a character looking for an author, but a role in need of an interpreter.

Thus the self-knowledge of the melancholic, which in itself is exact, has the same result as ignorance of oneself, since this knowledge is not addressed to its real object, but to the object's stand-in. This is why, when the subject recovers, the ego acts as if nothing had been said about it, since what had been said was addressed to the object which was liquidated when the process of mourning was over. To come back to a more direct clinical approach, what needs pointing out is that the loss of the object becomes the condition for gaining access to self-knowledge, as if investing the object depended on self-knowledge: 'I am like this not because it is really me, but because my love for you makes me like this – I even sacrifice all my self-love for my love for you. Nothing must be visible for you except the love I have for you (which will also save me from myself).' This is to reckon without the hate which is its shadow.

The transference is paradoxical in that it contains both a repetition of love and a demand for self-knowledge which should show its true face. The solution of getting rid of the witness is impossible except through excluding the transference object by means of a narcissistic organisation. What other benefit can the subject reap than self-knowledge of a self-depreciating kind? The only thing that remains to be invested is a naked ego, which is what subsists in the case of loss. Why not self-satisfaction? It exists *a minima*, in the form of telling oneself that, because one is 'conscious', one is superior to those who are deluding themselves. Lucidity is the consolation that self-esteem grants itself when love is betrayed by the experience of abandonment or loss, even when the ego's own criticism of itself is pitiless. But is this anything other than a form of self-love?

This is not *insight*. Insight appears when the desire to be loved by the object takes the shape of being conscious both that one is separated from it, and of the prohibition which marks it, when the subject has renounced the satisfaction of Oedipal desires. Nonetheless, the narcissistic wound of insight entails an immediate repression. It is not like the stroke of a sword through water; a modification of the investment of external objects often follows as well as an acceptance of the analyst's different investments which puts an end to any pretension of being his unique object.

Insight, however, remains linked to the superego. The relations between them are, in fact, complex. Although for Freud the superego is the result of the division of the ego, that is, the part which splits off from the rest – I do not say 'dissociates' itself – observing the other, it is an agent of internal surveillance that is supposed to notice even that to which the ego remains blind, as can be seen from the example of obsessional neurosis. But, on the other hand, since there is a question of blindness, the blind Tiresias, who knows, dissuades Oedipus (who is sighted and does not know that he will later become blind himself) who does not know, though he would like to know, from continuing his search, and invites him to turn away from this frightful internal vision which is awaiting him. 'Perhaps King Oedipus has one eye too many', writes Hölderlin, underlining the pain of recognising what is. When the eyes of the sighted person open, they will leave him no other choice but to close them again immediately, with his own hand, forever.

In fact, sight is the very material from which the unconscious is woven. The detour via speech shows this. 'I can see' is a synonym for 'I can hear', 'I can understand', 'I can grasp ...', where the scopophilic instinct, turned round upon itself, comes into play. Insight, then, implies a relation to object- or thing-representation, a relation to representation, and a relation to the object. But reflection, in all senses of the term – reflection of the mirror and meditation on oneself – cannot be tolerated for very long and Hamlet had such difficulty in tolerating himself that his desire for self-destruction found no other outlet than that of inducing Ophelia to commit suicide in his place. How, then, can insight be tolerated during treatment?

The Time of Insight

When, after several years of analysis, a patient makes us the gift of a session, in the course of which what the analyst has long been waiting for finally happens – that is to say, when the patient is capable of demonstrating a certain lucidity concerning the meaning of his symptoms, his behaviour, his way of being, and his feelings toward the analyst; and when he shows he is capable of detecting what is hidden behind the productions of his unconscious, that is, behind his dreams, phantasies, memories and bungled actions; and when his discourse literally reflects on itself, revealing its secret intentions; and when, finally, he sees what is being reproduced and repeated in the transference, causing whatever had resisted understanding of what was happening in him to cede its ground – the analyst thinks that such a moment is so decisive that he is justified in expecting that the patient will soon recover and imagines that he can glimpse the harbour of the analytic crossing.

In the next session, this propitious encounter is no more than a half-erased memory. Admittedly, things are not as they were before; but here we are again, back in familiar territory, with the old habits still well-entrenched. Is this to say that nothing has happened? That would be false. Does it mean that nothing more will happen? That would not be right either. If it lasted, this moment of grace in which the subject becomes conscious of how he functions could be generative of depression. On the contrary, even after a long period of analytic work, insight never takes the form of eureka, in spite of so-called mutative interpretations.

So what are we to think of insight? After challenging the role of remembering, now it is insight itself I am calling into question! In fact, just as I regard remembering as a sign of psychic functioning that is necessary, but not sufficient, to provoke insight, similarly I consider insight to be a necessary, but insufficient function for resolving the analysis. As for its beneficial role, it is inseparable from its destiny. For the whole question is, what will become of insight? In fact, insight will prove itself fruitful retrospectively when modifications in the form of the transference occur. In other words, once *insight* has occurred, the transference object is then perceived as a projected representative of a psychic function, that of transformation, seen from the armchair. In short, insight is an externalised function in the analyst, equivalent to the internalised function in the analysand, which produces interpretative transformations of his own discourse in the light of his psychic reality. The analyst's interpretative capacity is the inverted echo of what is at work silently in the analysand's mind. The moment of awareness (*prise de conscience*) here becomes reflection, a reflecting mirror of the image, which is itself reflected by another mirror. Reflexivity.

Representation and Association

There is still a need to understand this moment and why analysis is possible. By stressing the role of transformations, which are as many distortions, we discover that interpretations are not corrections of experiences or distorted memories. For no linear narration can show what 'transformation' is transformation of – in other words, what has been transformed, from what, and why. It is solely the breaking up of the narrative continuity which makes repetitions, underlinings, parentheses, inverted commas, the very syntax of unconscious desire, appear in the associative discourse. Without associativity, the discourse has every chance of being circular or tautological. No discourse is less likely to lead to insight than that which I have called narrative-recitative – the speciality of narcissistic subjects. The example of Proust shows that, without knowing about psychoanalysis, he had understood this through experience, being closer to the inventor of psychoanalysis than to the inventor of introspection, Bergson, with whom he has so often been compared. What still needs to be explained is the associative phenomenon itself, its nature, and its origins. In order to do this, it will be necessary to refer to the preconscious. I would like to say more about this.

In the comments I made on Alain Gibeault's paper on symbolisation,[21] I cited the passage from Freud's work on aphasia where he defends the idea that, in the psyche, representation cannot be separated from association. To be more exact, one should not think of representation as being located in one place (the brain), and of what is associated with it as being located in another. Representation and association operate together. And one can even doubt the possibility of an isolated, static, pure representation that would not be automatically caught up in an associative network. A representation without association can only be the product of an arrest in the psychical process, that is of a resistance.

Now, if one assumes that the associative network has been built up and is continually enriched over the course of time, associative representation is necessarily a temporal knot. Nevertheless, owing to the non-existence of time in the unconscious, the temporal knot, like the screen-memory, groups together elements belonging to different temporal experiences. Moreover, the absence of any reference to the passage of time makes of these temporal knots forms of pure present (even if they are referred to in the past), and thus, as Proust says, they are moments of extra-temporality or 'pure time'. But this 'pure' time is also a negation of continuity.

Another Temporality

How does analysis operate in these structures where memory is deficient? In order to understand this, we need to stand back for a moment. As early as the *Studies in Hysteria*, Freud remarked, almost apologetically, that his case histories read like novels. But he was speaking here as a reader of the nineteenth-century novel. Would we say, in turn, that our case histories read like the 'nouveau roman'? The latter has broken, has it not, with the ordered temporal organisation of the narrative, characteristic of its ancestor? The answer will contain nuances. Let us say that, even when the neurotic agrees to respect the fundamental rule, his discourse is still governed by an organised narrative making it possible to follow the meanings when free association seems to be progressing in a disorderly fashion. In fact, the discontinuity of the analysand's discourse – who often apologises for jumping from one subject to another, even though this is exactly what is expected of him – has its continuity re-established by the analyst's mind. The latter remains available and capable of linking up the multiplicity of themes presented by the analysand, weaving a thread which succeeds in holding together the pearl necklace of his patient's apparently disconnected discourse. The blanks in the discourse, the absence of conjunctive elements, the lack of logical connections is not too disturbing for the analyst who is still able to re-establish the meaning of the sequence according to the hypothetical unconscious logic. Interpretation is calibrated in a way that is quite close to the patient's discourse – as if manifest content and latent content still entertained relations of compatibility. I have defined these relations in terms of the 'generativity' of the analysand's discursive production, and I have attributed the regulation of this production to useful distance and efficacious distance. In other words, the patient's memory is under guarantee.

This is not the case, one senses, with structures where amnesia is widespread. The lack of intelligibility goes hand in hand with the massive quantity of memories and their weak value as organisers of the narrative. Free association has become so loose that the discourse becomes unintelligible. The relations within the discursive development are not 'readable' to the listener. Hitherto, I have been discussing the lack of temporal organisation. But it would be wrong to think that the trouble lies solely in the extreme looseness of the links, as if the blanks in the narrative organisation had taken up an excessive amount of room, invading the chain of the discourse to the point of 'eating' the tissue, like moths devouring the stitching of a knitted woollen jumper.

This is just a facade. Indeed, I think, and numerous sessions suggest that this is the case, that the discourse of the 'amnesic' analysand consists of over-condensed elements which are in fact linked to each other by apparently incomprehensible ties. It is this signifying over-condensation, however, which allows one to understand that the lack of temporal organisation stems from a shortage of mechanisms of decondensation, as if the words were obliged to tighten their texture, to gather up closely connected meanings and to unite on the basis of ties which no longer have anything to do with preconscious logic.

In neurosis, conscious and preconscious logic coexist peacefully. Elsewhere, in addition to being surveyed excessively – the superego keeps watch – the explosive quality of the discourse entails measures designed to restrict meanings, as if it was necessary to prevent the words from breathing, from linking up with phantasy, or from airing the discourse by letting it unfold with ease. Given that memory cannot be relied on, as there is a lack of deeply embedded roots in the language of memories, and since any loosening of linguistic links seems to entail the risk of provoking a haemorrhage of the thing-representations which are contained, with great difficulty, by the words, the forms of the discourse are condensed in the compactness of anxiety, threatening to unleash themselves at any moment. In order to grasp their mysterious intelligibility, the analyst must abandon his relationship to preconscious-conscious logic – which is based on a memory which has meaning – and instead listen to the traumatic resonance of the words in order to link up their signifiers with a more unconscious logic, in the proximity of the id which is supposedly devoid of any logic, that is, which is closer to instinctual functioning. It is evidence that elaboration is impossible. It is in this way that the subject can be helped to reveal his mode of functioning – that which is hidden behind the amnesia and which has become the last line of defence against a nameless anxiety. That is to say, an anxiety which is without language and which knows no other discourse than that of the mad act or of injuring the sick body, or both at the same time.

The analyst, then, listens to this discourse, taking it apart, before putting it together again differently – but not by decoding meaning, which is always somewhat derisory in these circumstances – in order to deliver the phantasy imprisoned in the shell of words. In so doing, he discovers another way of writing history. This way of carrying one's history about with one, that is to say, without memories to remind one of its high points and to confine it within the frontiers of the past, thus without clear limits between the past and the present, but with a potential for acting out or hallucination, is a way of making one understand that actualising repetition is a means of assuring oneself that one is still completely there, still present, and that the past has neither died nor disappeared. It is as though consigning limits to this past, keeping it in the reserve of memories, were just as dangerous as when a mother is obliged to leave her sick baby at the hospital: in so doing, she accepts to lose sight of it and to put its fate in the hands of strangers, that is, in fact, to resign herself already to regarding it as dead. The amnesic patient teaches us, then, that his amnesia is another way of living the present. But, if the analysis continues to be invested, it is because there is a secret hope of living differently. And it is up to the analyst to show that he is capable of discovering what lies hidden in a history that has been constituted but which can also be constituted in terms of a different type of historicity; and which is always a potential cause of anxiety owing to its constant re-actualisation. Certainly, everything is still there. But this re-actualisation revives the dangers of the past which have never been transcended. Hence the need for acrobatic thinking from the analyst if he is to be able to perceive the actuality of this past in the immediacy of the present. It is at this price that the tamponing of the unconscious derivatives is constituted, so that the clash between preconscious and unconscious is mediated. It is thus extremely surprising for the analyst to hear the analysand getting back in touch with very early memories which he had lost all hope of seeing return to the surface.

In the analysis of borderline cases, where skimming (le 'feuilletage', P. Marty) does not make it possible, when there is a return of the repressed, to formulate a coherent interpretation of the meaning of the material, meaning is constructed when the reverberated signifiers of a temporally ramified set of issues are superimposed within the same session. The problem, then, is no longer one of identifying one meaning by means of interpretation, but of arriving, after a process of interpretation, at a 'constellation of meanings' which reveals the resonances of several key situations (separation from the mother, separation of faeces from the body – a sense of intrusion, of forced extraction, denial of hate and breaking off of contact, guilt and shame, intolerable passivity, omnipotent reactive activity, impotence projected onto others – adopting the position of a victim and being unaware of espousing a retaliative attitude, the condensation of phantasies, each of which is linked to very different periods of development and history, and so on).

It is here, indeed, that the *raison d'être* of transference lies. It is not so much repetition which matters as this temporal avidity, always in search for a possible re-actualisation and an unlimited meaningful deployment, since we know that analysis does not have an exclusive monopoly on transference, but simply endeavours to create the best conditions for analysing it.

Remembering and insight are 'pure time' and they are also outside time; as past repetition and absolute present, they can only be appreciated in relation to the transference understood as a temporalising potentiality, in a permanent quest for re-actualisation. But the transfer itself has to be appreciated for its value as a playground, as Freud and Winnicott said. That is to say, it is necessary, from time to time, to put oneself into touch, as it were. We were on the field of action, involved in the game, caught up in the conflict between the opposing teams, sometimes playing with our hands, sometimes with our feet, alternating kicks, scrums and tries, whether converted or not. And now we have been replaced by someone else, and are watching the game from the substitute bench from where we have a different view of the game; just as those who were not playing in the game, but were among the substitutes, could not directly experience the game as it was being played on the field, because they were at a distance. Here we have a playful version of Heisenberg's uncertainty principle.

There is no insight in isolation. There is a vision in perpetual accommodation, seen from within, from without, binocular or monocular, just as there is circulation between the inside, the outside, the past, the present, the ego and the object. Nothing in analytic communication can be subsumed under the heading of the One. If unity there is, then it is variable, moving, oscillating, and precarious. It is a theoretical result much more than an immediate finding.

But, if associativity is the specific characteristic of temporality, on the basis of what referents can the associations be decoded? In other words, on what basis does insight function? When structuralism was at its height, the debate of ideas opposed structure and history.[22] The partisans of structure were quick to point out that history could scarcely be deciphered without referring to a structure. The debate is too vast to be given any more than a passing mention here. If memory refers to history, and history to time, how are we to understand time? I can only answer this question by resorting, like Freud, to the hypothesis of primal phantasies. They do not always carry conviction with psychoanalysts, owing to their phylogenetic presuppositions. For my part, I shall propose a provisional strategy which consists in accepting their organising value while suspending judgement as to their origin. However, to this structuring matrix of the unconscious, I shall add a grid of conscious origin which encounters the former, each of them giving shape to the other. This conscious grid would be constituted by the key influential events of each human life from a cyclical perspective; that is, the series can be started at any point of the cycle. Let us adopt the simplest series, although it is never presented to us in this order as it has to be conceptualised, and thinking requires a certain degree of development.

The issue here is not to identify the ages or milestones along the trajectory of an existence, but to mark the significant and powerful moments in the continuum of a life which are the equivalent of symbolic matrices, marking events. Such events are birth, the Oedipus complex and the primitive scene, family separation accomplished by society, adolescence, beginning active life through the choice of a profession or companion, procreation and parenting, maturity leading to the beginning of decline, becoming grandparents, and finally death. The moment when understanding occurs is always related to the elements of this conscious grid, structured by the grid of primal phantasies. It allows one to situate oneself in the personal, family, and social history by discovering oneself in it as a subject.

I will conclude with an example which I have already had occasion to refer to elsewhere. You will know how much Freud admired *Don Quixote*, which he encouraged Martha to read during their long engagement. Who did he recognise in the hidalgo? The death of Don Quixote is for me one of the finest passages in world literature. On his deathbed, having called for the priest and a few friends, he said:

You must congratulate me, my good sirs, because I am no longer Don Quixote de la Mancha but Alonso Quixano, for whom my way of life earned me the nickname of 'the Good'. I am now the enemy of Amadis of Gaul and the whole infinite horde of his descendants; now all those profane histories of knight-errantry are odious to me; now I acknowledge my folly and the peril in which I was placed by reading them; now, by God's mercy, having at long last learned my lesson, I abominate them all.[23]

What is amusing is that on hearing this, the hidalgo's friends were certain, initially, that Don Quixote was in the grips of some new madness, before they finally believed him.

We are pursued, then, by madness until our deathbed and it is in only this final extremity that we are prepared to recognise it. We are led to do so because, as Don Quixote says, 'a man must not trifle with his soul'. And it is then that we open our eyes sufficiently to be able to say, 'I was mad and now I am sane.'[24]

B. TIME AND MEMORY (1990)[*]

Psychoanalysis was born in and out of the medicine of the end of the nineteenth century. In the medical tradition that preceded it, history was practically absent. Illness was understood as an attack or disturbance occurring at a given moment without any relation to the prior condition of the patient, which should not be confused with the idea of susceptibility. The only aspect of time that was taken into consideration was the course of the illness. However, parallel to this practice, global conceptions had developed in which temporality was in the foreground. In psychiatry, from which Freud came, Morel's theory of degeneration conceived of illness as the outcome of a *phylum* which had existed for several generations. Nearer to him, and belonging to the same spirit of modernity, the ideas of Hughlings Jackson, which Freud boldly espoused in his interpretation of aphasia (1891), presented a physiopathological conception of the disorganisations of the nervous system based on time. Finally, beyond that, the general framework of thought was provided in biology by Darwin, and in philosophy by Herbert Spencer. While it is certain that this was not the only source of inspiration for Freudian theory, it was not in contradiction with others.[25] The historicising vein which runs right through Freud's conceptions is original in that it is, in fact, a precipitate of the biological history of man, the last bud of the species, and of his cultural history transformed by the

---

[*] First published as 'Temps et mémoire' in *Nouvelle Revue de psychanalyse*, 41, 1990, pp. 179–206.

process of civilisation. The combined effects of both give birth to a psychic causality traversed by temporality, which in turn makes it necessary to clarify the role of structures – products that are fixed and presented as such – originating from a phylogenesis recapitulated by ontogenesis. In their turn, these structures will be put to the test of experience, which will sometimes be governed by their intervention and sometimes will have 'revealed' them, as it were, causing them to pass from a state of latency to one of manifestation.

This brief introduction shows to what extent the notion of temporality in Freud is a knot containing the threads of several discourses. For beyond the relations between the normal and the pathological (to be brief, let us say dreaming and hysteria), Freud's conception of psychic causality – and how could the idea of causality be considered independently of its links with temporality? – from the theory of reminiscence to that of phylogenetic schemes, is an original creation. It is a result of the combined effects of the organisation of a psychical apparatus that is independent – yet inconceivable without it – of the nervous system of man, understood as the outcome of animal evolution and the transmission of a history – a memorable sediment of a cultural chain of events. Both are subject, in the continuity of their development, to powerful moments – symbolising and symbolised? – which are all marks of intelligibility whose meaning cannot be easily identified, however, owing to the heterogeneity of the 'worlds' thus brought into relationship with each other. Here, I shall only be considering the problem of memory.

Memory and Psyche

A point on which Freud's position did not vary was that psychoanalytic treatment should have the goal of lifting infantile amnesia. Though the goal has remained constant, the content of the proposition has not remained immutable. In his correspondence with Fliess he had already observed that remembering always comes up against a limit – that is to say, the primitive scenes[26] cannot be recalled. He had learnt from long years of practice that there was no point in trying to break down the resistances: the patient would never completely recover his memory of the earliest years. Not – something Freud had never hoped for, and which no one had ever believed possible – the recollection of the totality of childhood memories, but, at least, of fragments whose recombination would make it possible to form a 'picture of the patient's forgotten years that shall be alike trustworthy and in all essential respects complete'.[27] Of course, because this has proved to be impossible to achieve, we are justified in wondering if Freud's construction – or the picture he himself forms of how the essential elements are arranged – is not open to doubt. Two arguments may be called upon to answer this doubt. On the one hand, no other 'picture' proposes a more convincing conception of what is essential in the child's past, the effects of which are still noticeable in the adult's present life; and, on the other, even if remembering does not take place, it does not mean that memory is absent from the manifestations which seem to owe their existence only to the present of the time when they are evoked. Three separate questions are thus involved here: the first concerns the reconsideration of the mnemic function, in respect of which significant steps forward were made as a result of Freud's reflections; the second is that of the relevance of his reference to manifest memory as the basis of psychic causality; and the final question concerns the reference to the sexual as a kingpin of the link between psyche and memory, as the corner stone of development in its most ordinary forms as well as in its most innovative creations.

Concerning the first point, there seems to be evidence that what was initially called the 'memory system' (by contrast with the 'perceptual system') is still operative in psychical activity, in spite of the persistence of amnesia, on the condition that we broaden the spectrum. This is indeed the lesson to be learnt from 'Remembering, Repeating and Working-Through'. Defending the idea that the patient repeats instead of remembering, Freud is led, in fact, to argue that, by repeating certain acts, he remembers without knowing it. This psychic short-circuit which puts the sphere of the drive in direct relationship with that of action – which does not mean to say, however, that acting out is the direct expression of the drive – led Freud to pass from the domain of the accidental (even if it is considered as a defence) to the structural. Acting out, understood as a going to the limit, was to become the illustration of a basic characteristic of the drive: the compulsion to repeat which is always the mark of a failure in psychic elaboration. For if one of the arguments advanced for inferring its existence is based on the repetitive dreams of traumatic neurosis, it is because they are 'beyond the pleasure principle'; and so it cannot be claimed that they still remain within the context of wish-fulfilment. Freud was led to believe that such dreams represented forms of psychic disqualification. They are, then, the closest approximation we have to raw instinctual functioning. The real meaning, then, of mnemic functioning now emerges. Faced with the repetitive functioning of the drive as blind memory attached to the human equivalent of animal instinct, the psyche does not just reproduce by discharging; it 'holds back'. Under this guise, retention goes hand in hand with restraint: the psyche becomes the net that is interposed between the body and reality against the inclination to relaxation (the inversion of 'restraint') via discharge. The reticulated grid which constitutes it distributes the energies, divides them up, concentrates them in certain knots, opens up passages, facilitates deviations, determines orientations, and so on. This is because the creation of a network cannot be dissociated from establishing meaning; and because, in return, establishing meaning goes together with the quest for mastery which enables the subject to stand back and get an overview of things.

This was in fact Freud's idea: lifting infantile amnesia was not limited to removing a sense of tension – catharsis had demonstrated the highly partial and temporary character of the relief it brought – but, owing to the discovery of the determining causes of amnesia, it made it possible to master disturbing memories. Gaining access to the psychic level means, then, recognising the inherent paradox of this condition. On the one hand, psychic phenomena justify the hope of gaining control as a result of being liberated from the instinctual level. It is because the phenomena under consideration are freed from the automatic nature of repetition-compulsion that they are offered a way out – that of no longer being subject to the fate whereby they are only liberated via discharge. The psyche only becomes 'controllable' because it is no longer automatically discharged. On the other hand, the complex network that is supposed to overcome its roamings can, owing to the subtle balances which govern its functioning, offer as many possibilities for 'evasion' which sometimes thwart the purpose of the arrangement. Thus amnesia is at once an obligation, in order to make the psychical apparatus capable of continually receiving new impressions, while permitting it not to encumber itself with the presence of the traces of earlier experiences; a necessity, in order to select, among the traces of past inscriptions, those which, either in part or in total, will become part of the schematic picture which makes it possible to give meaning to what is registered; a safeguard, in order to avoid the unpleasure connected with certain disagreeable evocations (which cannot be accepted by the subject or by the other whose love he wishes to preserve, depending on the idea he has of his demands); and, finally, an accident, when the desire to have certain of these traces at his disposition encounters an impossibility or a resistance.

It can be seen how 'mnesia', at least in analysis, cannot be dissociated from the aspect of the system 'psy' connected with meaning. Whether the latter is a meaning that is inscribed and laid down, awaiting its later accomplishment, or whether it reveals an after effect, what matters as far as psychoanalytic memory is concerned is the organising function of the psyche, not just in terms of the relations between consigning to memory and remembering, but also in terms of the couple amnesia-remembering. For it is recognised that it is preferable and normal that repression should have taken place, and in an efficient way, so that an underground process of elaboration can continue unconsciously; and, so that the derivatives of memory appear in the later products of the evolution, even if they are sometimes unconscious of their origin in memory, in order that the psychical apparatus is capable, in return for the necessary transformations, of granting itself whatever satisfactions are possible. An example here is the object-choice of adult sexuality.

We are obviously some distance away here from the traditional conceptions of memory which imply the notions of the inscription of information, its conservation (accompanied or not by a change of state), the mobilisation of traces and the evocation of memories. The major novelty, which was not only contemporaneous with the discovery of psychoanalysis but also with the subjective experience of writers, philosophers, and psychiatrists, was the idea of involuntary memory, reminiscence, ecmnesia. This enriched the traditional ideas, not so much because it contested an over-intellectual vision of memory, but because memory depended on internal forces whose effects it suffered more than it seemed to control them. The unearthing of forgotten memories seemed to increase the potential number of factors determining a given form of behaviour or of a programmed action. It added to the long list of reasons invoked to support the validity of an undertaking, an opinion, or an argument. The assistance of memory backed up the resolutions of consciousness. With involuntary memory the tendency was reversed: consciousness was no more than the cork floating on the water's surface, itself agitated by the movements which have their origin in the unconscious depths. But, before Freud, we were a long way from discovering the system governing the currents which had initiated these movements. Hence the idea, which is in contradiction with the relations between memory and time, that we are all amnesic in respect of our childhood and that the unconscious is ignorant of time. Time is at once lost and immobile; it has vanished, yet is never past. Hence the idea, too, that ultimately, nothing is less appropriate than memory for making us understand what time is. But conversely, we cannot understand psychic causality without taking time into account. In fact, the genesis of psychic causality depends largely on the mutual effects of two subjects which are both necessary to each other if such causality is to occur, separated by a large interval of time, that of a generation. The causality I am referring to here cannot be separated from the internalisation of this relation, seen from the angle of this interval, one of the consequences of which will be reduction, and sometimes reproduction.

Historical Reality and Mnemic Objects

Modern epistemology and science have contested the traditional schema: inscription, storage, re-evocation. There was a refusal to accept any longer that what is not considered as present can be regarded as known or even knowable as the past. It is a position that is as strong as it is debatable, for the next stage of such a thesis is probably to know whether what is regarded as present can justifiably claim to be known. It has also been shown very convincingly that what presented itself as memory depended on the perceptual organisation of the moment and the context.[28] These are in effect wise rectifications of the schematic simplifications which constitute the basis of our reflections, often without our knowing it.

The category of memory cannot, however, be suppressed anymore than it is possible to conceive of the idea of a psychical apparatus obstructed by all the mnemic traces which it is incapable of getting rid of (Borges has described this sad condition in *Funes, the Memorious*, 1941). Conversely, one cannot imagine a psyche perpetually living in the present. And it is here that one must doubt the reliability of a memory which regards itself as being sufficient proof of what it advances, a claim that raises many questions about illusion, the confusion between phantasy and memory, memories as screen structures, and so on. It would appear, then, that apart from these obvious adaptive purposes – which Freud calls the 'exigencies of life' – the reference to memory is based on the invocation of a reality that is not circumscribed by the present, but is grounded in a meaningful, i.e. historical continuity. It is not important here to

know whether history (with a capital or small h) has a meaning or
not; what matters is to acknowledge the necessity of it having a
meaning for consciousness, as a response to the challenges coming
from the unconscious with respect both to continuity and the
coherence of this meaning. One should not be too hasty in underlining the illusory character of this historical reality, since a
psychoanalytic treatment does not lead to the conclusion that
history is incoherent or non-existent, but rather to the discovery of
another kind of historical coherence than the one in which we
believed before the analysis; the earlier point of view needs, however,
to be maintained so that comparison is possible. The advantage of
the operation is not simply one of replacing a history that was only
approximately or fallaciously coherent by another which is just
slightly more coherent; to this needs to be added the recognition of
what, in such a psychical apparatus, calls for this historical ordering.
The issue, above all, is one of establishing a reality (even if only to
contest it), of grasping the historical dimension and its contradiction
with other dimensions of the psyche (the urgency of desire, uncontrollable repetitions, and the presence of the past in the present, and
so on); and finally, of approaching a conception of psychic causality
which always has to find its way between the seductions of rationalisations and the dogmas of doctrinal reification.

From a psychoanalytic point of view, these operations are at the
root of the experience which makes the analytic process an actualisation for an other (*un autre*), both through the diversity and
heterogeneity of the mnemic formations, and in relation to the non-
mnemic formations of retrospection as a double of actualising
introspection and of the dependence on restricting factors unconnected with history.

The originality of the psychoanalytic position calls for the
mnemic objects to be categorised since they cannot be defined solely
by their qualification with respect to explicit memory. There is thus
a need to distinguish between:

(a) *memories designated as such*: conscious, recovered through psy-
     choanalysis, including screen-memories, more or less mixed up
     with phantasies, and so on;
(b) *mnemic derivatives*, as contextual elements at the periphery of
     the content of the memories (such as those Freud evoked in
     'Constructions in Analysis'), dreams, delusional states, halluci-
     nations, and so on;

(c) *amnesic memory*, the compulsion to repeat, depersonalised or somatic states, and so on. They differ from the above by the intense nature of the actualisation, the reference situating these phenomena less on the side of memory than as equivalents of it which are often connoted with a hallucinatory quality that is far removed from figurative nature of representation. Here priority is accorded to the maximal expression of a minimal meaning, recourse to representability being sacrificed to a function which is more akin to the signal than the signifier. It is thanks to this creation of meaning at the limits of non-sense that a minimum of intrapsychic circulation is maintained, having broken its links (unlike the signifying function) with the intersubjective face of communication and its intrapsychic face with oneself. They are more 'for oneself' than 'for others'.

The correlates of anxiety strive here to save a threatened autonomy whose links with references to castration are severed. For what is involved, above all, is conflicts to do with separation (feared or desired), intrusion (rejected or wished-for), ascendancy (through captation or solicitation), negativism (paralysing or aimed at impeding the *jouissance* of the other) based on an obsession with dis-appropriation (possessive dispossession). In short, this non-memory, which is not so much unaware of its mnemic origin as it desperately attempts to deny it, is constructed on a subjective position that is too de-narcissicised to be able to accept that this psyche could address itself to another that is historically anterior to it.

In this last category of mnemic objects, amnesia, far from being defined in relation to childhood, involves the present of the trans-ference relationship. That is, it presents itself essentially as an agnosia of the actualisation of the transference. The more the quality of repetition is accentuated, the less such analysands need to make use of the help of the analyst's interpretations in order to recognise, beyond their repetitive quality, the transferential nature of psychic phenomena (that is to say, these are history emerging from its actu-alisation – with the inevitable distortions which change them – re-edited by the setting), and the more they are lived as a pure, self-sufficient present.

This conception of mnemic objects is derived from Freud's last observations, which he sets out in 'Constructions and Analysis'. Though it is generally recognised that this text can be considered as a codicil to the chapter on psychoanalytic therapy of Freud's testament, 'Analysis Terminable and Interminable' (1937a), it is not without consequence that its theme once again concerns infantile amnesia. And though the inventor of psychoanalysis is prepared, without making any concessions on the rigorous nature of the psychoanalytic experience, to advance the idea that construction is the equivalent of remembering, this should be interpreted not so much as a sign that he was making the best of a bad situation as a significant advance in understanding the problem of the subject's relations with his past. Far from resigning himself to the impossibility of lifting infantile amnesia – an affirmation already present in the letters to Fliess (probably reinforced by the fact that it still proved to be valid after forty years of psychoanalytic practice), he undertook a final revision of the relations formed by the mnemic deposits (whether repressed or available, still totally unconscious or having entered the preconscious), entrusted with the task, not only of remembering but, above all, of understanding the significance of what has been forgotten through the *Durcharbeiten* (working-through), in the actualisation of the transference. Although psychoanalysis was still in its very early days, Freud had understood that memory and psyche could not be dissociated from each other; and, further, that memory was based on a multiple system of traces which were re-inscribed periodically, being 're-translated' in the light of new circumstances.[29] The heuristic value of the metaphor was greeted so favourably that little thought was given to the question of how such a conception was compatible with one of an unconscious that is unaware of the passage of time. Indeed this is one of the signs that Freud's theories can only be elucidating, and elucidated, by means of a dialectical mode of thought which attempts to confront its apparent contradictions. It is also precisely because he denied this, claiming that they were entirely understandable by means of analytic reasoning alone, that Freud gives rise to diverse and mutually conflicting interpretations, some of which are based on his explicit formulations (analytic), and others unearthing their implicit meaning, assumed to be buried or unrecognised by the inventor of this new way of thinking. There is no solution, in fact, to this theoretical quarrel except to defend its demonstration without presenting a picture of Freud's thought that is supposedly illuminated by another mode of thought that is foreign to it, and whose similarity with his own he denied (even if this rejection is a matter of interpretation[30]). If one wishes to defend an implicit vision which transcends its explicit content, without falling prey to a hermeneutic arbitrariness which can always easily be opposed by another interpretation, another attitude needs to be adopted, that is, one that inserts, between the implicit and the explicit, the implications of the contradictions of what is explicit.

It then becomes necessary to infer that the new registrations of earlier systems of traces are carried out not, as direct intuition would suggest, to introduce change, but in order to avoid it. A recent re-transcription of events already registered – and which, consequently, constitutes a mould of the past (and not simply the image of a lost copy) – absorbs, so to speak, what is new, better than by annulling it. For simply annulling it runs the risk, faced with the force of the present, of seeing the network constituted by the traces of the past succumb or collapse. On the contrary, if absorption is preferred to rejection, then the novelty will be better accommodated and the change noted. Its rejuvenating effects will be taken into account even more for having been adopted by the norms of the existing system, which thus preserves itself from the threat of disappearance represented by what is new. For this system is a depository not only of the past but of the pre-forming organisation of the present. What I mean is that it orients the form of the present according to the pre-formations left by the past which integrate this present in the mesh of an unconscious grid constituted by the heritage of this past which is without any real mnemic character proper. Thus the existing system sees the novelty as a contribution of fresh investments capable of consolidating it by seeming to assimilate it before making the disturbing aspects of such a novelty disappear. This is partly what Freud means when he stresses the conservative nature of the drives. What Freud's vision does not embrace is the protective character of the re-transcriptions. The more things change, the more things remain the same. Nevertheless, the benefit of the operation lies elsewhere. It brings into view the cornerstone of the new mode of thinking: repression. What is more, it is a dynamic repression which does not act just once, but repeats its effects periodically. Hence the re-transcriptions.

The significance, then, of the theorisation should now be clear. Memory is no longer just an affair of conservation or of forgetting, of fidelity or distortion; it becomes, above all, evidence, from the psychic point of view, of an organisation and not just adaptation. The 'meaning' of such an organisation is that it stages the conflict between veiling and unveiling, while preserving a self-image, strengthening the sources of pleasure and possibilities of satisfaction.

Thus adaptation emerges as the common factor at both the biological level as well as at the psychic level. Non-memory must include at the highest level what, at the precedent level, seems to be merely a weakness, that is, forgetting as a lack of adaptation. At the psychic level, forgetting is integrated as requirements change. It is not just a question of arming life to cope better with the tasks it has to face; it is the subject's relations with himself and the other which is in question; and it is then that forgetting sometimes becomes more useful than harmful. On this last point, the references to the letters to Fliess, or even to the 'Project' are not enough to make us recognise that we are dealing here with what is necessarily explicit. But the fact is, at that time, the explicit aspects of Freud's theory of memory contained no references to the amnesic memory which he was to postulate subsequently.[31] And it is indeed the fate of such a theory of memory that it is unable to understand the necessity of forgetting through repression initially, except, I would say, in relation to propriety and civility, which only goes half way to explaining it. The tragic vision of the unconscious in Freud's work, the deterministic character of his conceptual edifice, would only come to light when the idea of the unconscious itself was replaced by the hypothesis of the non-mediated effects of the drive. That is to say, when the unconscious was no longer considered as the ultimate staging post of a non-memorisable memory, as this role now fell to the compulsion to repeat, considered as the fundamental characteristic of the functioning of all drive activity – the death drive representing the absolute accomplishment of this amnesic and amnesia-producing repetition. To Freud's mind, the drive itself was, was it not, the memory, internalised by the species, of old acts transformed by phylogenesis?

I can imagine someone saying to me here: 'Really, you are quite incorrigible. We started out with the most ordinary phenomena of psychic life such as memory, forgetting, and reminiscence, which, as it were, weave together the relations of life, in its most familiar aspects, and psychoanalysis. It turns out that the second is connected with the first, linking up the living experience of existence, its resonances with knowledge and culture, and its vicissitudes in illness which bear ferments that enable one to believe in the possibility of being cured and of returning to our common destiny. And here you are dragging us into the most questionable speculations which are prejudicial to what you are supposed to represent in the way of recourse and hope.'

How else can one answer this except by saying that one would have to have lost the memory of one hundred years of psychoanalytic experience not to see that these ideas, introduced in 1920, are the product of it? And while, of course, they are no longer totally convincing, in my opinion, no satisfying alternatives have been forthcoming for at least fifty years. Currently, it is psychoanalytic theory itself which seems, in relation to Freud, to be carrying out a vast operation of forgetting under the pretext that what is forgotten is obsolescent anyway.

Retrogression and Novelty: the Narration of an Event

One of the most inevitable and the most naive effects of the desire to make advances in the psychoanalytic theory of memory was to gather together the observations of a systematic 'follow-up' of the child. The assumption was that if one was in a position to witness the unfolding of events in infantile life and the observable psychic transformations, one would have a better idea of what one was talking about. Kris' article, 'The Recovery of Childhood Memories in Psychoanalysis' (1956), was a classic at a certain period. It has since been supplanted by the painstaking studies of American investigators who considered that their psychoanalytic 'training', or their membership of official psychoanalytic institutions, provided sufficient justification for their ideas to be integrated within the doctrinal corpus, or even to be presented as indisputable evidence of the need to reform the theory. I have already criticised these illusions sufficiently, from Spitz to Mahler to Stern,[32] however much they have received the stamp of recognition from many of my colleagues – especially in North America – to feel justified in returning to arguments which, it has to be admitted, have not always succeeded in diverting psychoanalysts from the attraction exerted by psychological studies, circulating under the psychoanalytic flag, on account of the extraordinary simplification they offer concerning the solutions for complex problems.

I am now, therefore, going to relate a sequence from the life of a little girl (which I witnessed periodically), in order to give some idea of what is overlooked by approaches based on observation.

A young mother, who was the daughter of a psychoanalyst, and in psychotherapy, was pregnant for the second time by her own choice. This had been kept secret up till then, owing to an earlier attempt to have a baby which had ended in a miscarriage in the early stages, a few months before. When she was two and a half months pregnant and felt unable to give adequate attention to her twenty-month-old daughter, owing to her condition, she was worried (not unreasonably) about the situation. Especially as (and this was one of my own reflections which had apparently occurred to no one else) her reticence to go on carrying her child – due to the previous interruption – was reminiscent of a situation experienced six months before the previous pregnancy, i.e. when the little girl was about one year old. As the mother had had an operation on her foot, she was using crutches, and so was unable to continue carrying her child. She was worried, therefore, about the effect, not of her temporary incapacity, but of the way this necessarily changed the relationship she had with her child who could not understand why her mother was unable to carry her for several weeks. Having already begun, for practical reasons, to inform those nearest to her, the mother thought that she ought to be the first to tell her daughter before the latter learnt of it inadvertently from the staff at the day nursery she was attending happily. So she said to her daughter, 'You know, we're going to have a baby.' The child cried out, 'Baby, baby', looking around her as if in the hope of finding one of her playmates who was addressed by her own family in this way, and who had stayed in her parents' home for a while. The mother then added, 'The baby's here', pointing to her tummy which, of course, at two and a half months, showed no noticeable change. The daughter then went and got one of her dolls and placed it against her mother's tummy. Then, about an hour after, according to the mother, the little girl was found hiding in a cupboard, sucking her thumb, which she usually no longer did. The mother called out to her nicely, 'What are you doing there?' and made her come out of the cupboard. The child then asked for her dummy, which she no longer used at all, substituting it for her thumb. She kept it all day; even during mealtimes, and only withdrew it momentarily to be able to take food into her mouth, keeping it in her mouth between two mouthfuls, even while masticating. The following day, she continued to keep the dummy in her mouth and started playing in the cupboard again, but this time she asked her mother to accompany her and to shut herself in the cupboard with her.

I shall break off the narration of this event at this point, for it is a sufficient basis in itself for posing a certain number of questions. I assure the reader that its consequences during the rest of the pregnancy and after the birth were no less rich in meaning and bear

witness to an ongoing activity of symbolisation and memory. This
account was composed partly on the basis of what the child's grandmother – herself a psychoanalyst – told me about it, and was
completed by what I learnt from her own daughter's account. As I
have said, it evoked associations in me (concerning the operation
on the foot) which had not been mentioned. The grandmother
pointed out to me, moreover, that her daughter was now the same
age as she had been when she was pregnant with this same daughter,
and that her twenty-month-old granddaughter was the same age as
her daughter was when she herself was expecting her third child.
These mnemic, amnesic reverberations cannot be considered independently of the event; however, they can only be deduced and
never inferred directly from the event, even if they bear heavily on
its significance.

A case of this kind raises numerous questions. If one gives it even
a modicum of serious thought, one will see that it is impossible to
distinguish between:

(a)   what should be attributed to an unconscious memory, mani-
      festing itself here via the connections which may be supposed
      to exist between the mother's discourse, the induced fantasies,
      and the 'memory' of the child's relation to the mother's breast
      and womb, which cannot be objectivised by any particular
      limit;

(b)   what can only be interpreted on the basis of phantasy, the only
      framework being the present of the actual circumstances
      without any relation to the past;

(c)   what is to be understood as an inextricable mixture of the two
      preceding cases, and which should be attributed to a process of
      symbolisation which could have two different effects: the first
      being that of binding the psychic events considered from a
      synchronic point of view (owing to their factuality); and, the
      second being the effects of the past spilling over into the
      present, depending on a temporality which manifests itself both
      before and after the present which solicits it;

(d)   what refers to inscriptions, both of the past and the present,
      mobilised by phantasised expectation. This virtual registration
      can only be inscribed by reactivating the structures of meaning
      which make it 'thinkable' and which, in order to do this, nec-
      essarily link up with the system of inscriptions of the other. The
      latter implies the reference – which, here, is not only inferred

but also attested – of a balance between inscriptions that are evoked and revived, or only implicitly activated; or, reduced to silence in spite of being activated. It is this whole system that enters into resonance with the activation of the constellation memory-phantasy (or phantasy-memory) which is doubly inductive of the system's past and future harmonics.

Apart from memory and phantasy, we also need to take account, in symbolically productive communication, of an agent with open possibilities: allusion, a vehicle of latent transformations, which dominates time. It alone transcends it, uniting the different modes of conjugation and presiding over the operation which transforms the present into actualisation – namely, the time of the manifestation which, for consciousness, corresponds to the present, becomes, for the other systems, that which can be actualised in the various forms of memory (projected into the past) or of a phantasised wish (anticipated in the future). The categories of past-present-future consciousness, which give time its specificity, make of it a continuous thread whose successive phases cannot be delimited, so that they become indiscernible. The timelessness of the unconscious finds it has an accomplice here which lends a hand in negating time which passes and drifts inexorably towards death. During the course of events, however, the repercussions which the systems of signs have on each other is not limited to the mutual reflection of these systems, but entails the inclusion of the system of signs of the other system. The reverberations, repetitions, acts of remembering, actualisations, reminiscences and revivals are no less punctuated by the difference between the generations (and, consequently, by that of the sexes), supplying, by means of this basic discontinuity, the complement of temporal continuity, upholding the illusion of an immobile time which the unconscious is assumed to have the power to stop so that desire never sees the potentiality of its realisation suspended.

Although, in life, such a vision of temporality is imagined more than it is perceived, notwithstanding the occasions when one becomes momentarily aware of it, it is in analysis, and more specifically, through analysing the transference, that the extent of the aim of such an insurrection against the extinction of childhood causes (in the legal sense) can be apprehended. Analysis appeals against this.

In other words, amnesia – which is evidence of conflict – is also the most efficient agent against becoming conscious of this conflict, insofar as it becomes amnesia not only of what is to be forgotten but of the fact that there is material to be forgotten.

The Situation of Primal Phantasies

In another study on memory,[33] I have shown how, throughout Freud's work, remembering functioned as a lure of psychoanalysis. What is ironical is that it was the original case which was supposed to bring into broad daylight the primal event – that is, the primal scene in the case of the Wolf Man – which unfortunately constituted the clearest evidence that the solution to the problem of gaining understanding did not lie there, since no one more than Serguei Pankejeff, alias the Russian, as Freud called him, proved more resistant to understanding psychic causality as it had been revolutionised by psychoanalysis.

The question of remembering has been somewhat overshadowed by two tendencies in contemporary psychoanalysis. If, as we have just seen, it has, so to speak, been outflanked by the study of the constitution of memories in the examination of development, a hiatus nonetheless subsisted between the problematic issue of remembering in the treatment of adults and the developmental study of memorisation. Another tendency has seen in the fact of infantile amnesia a false problem. Radicalising Freud's views, Melanie Klein and her followers considered, in spite of the apologia of the 'here and now' of transference interpretations, that everything in analysis concerned remembering, but the remembering of archaic phantasies or primitive anxieties. Or, as Melanie Klein said, of 'memories in feelings', meaning by that that the formulation in imaginary terms of her theoretical themes simply reflected the need to translate into adult language (in order to make oneself understood, thereby killing two birds with one stone, by one's analysands and one's colleagues) affects that otherwise would remain incommunicable. Kleinian analysis as a whole, then, can be considered as an analysis of the remembering of fundamental psychic processes, which have to be given verbal content in order to give them a meaning which cannot be reproached with being abstract but which, in reality, seeks to put into words primitive, preverbal forms of mental life from the past, which have been revived by the neurosis and the transference.

This approach can claim to be consistent with the continuity of Freudian thought, except on one point, albeit an important one. Let us leave to one side the extension given here to the value, in terms of memory, of almost all the phenomena that appear in the field of the transference. The fact that Freud circumscribes more the field of mnemic objects does not constitute a cause for disagreement. Where Freud and Melanie Klein diverge, without there being any possibility of compromise, is on the issue of the models of reference. For Klein purely and simply erases (and she is certainly not the only one) the cornerstone of Freud's theoretical development: the primal phantasies. The swamping of the field of mnemic objects owing to the introduction of the compulsion to repeat as an expression of drive functioning accounted, partly at least, for amnesia. If memories – belonging unquestionably to the psychic system – do not reveal themselves so often and are not so completely available, it is probably because of repression. But why is repression so rigorous towards psychic phenomena which, moreover, belong to the past? The compulsion to repeat comprises, in fact, a *powerful capacity for actualisation* – both in the sense of making present and of manifesting itself in an acted (or active) form – which is always likely to rekindle the embers in the hearth of the unconscious. The extension of the sphere of influence of the drives, the inextinguishable force of the instinctual impulses which, in the second topography, take over from the unconscious wishes of the first as the basis of psychic activity, is such that, at this level, where the unconscious communicates with the id, any distinction between memory, phantasy, desire, impulse and acting out is precarious. There is a risk that each of these elements may break through the partitions which, alone, the bound state of consciousness can only maintain with difficulty.

This can be seen in one aspect of the contemporary clinical manifestations of non-neurotic analysands. With surprise, the analyst notices that the question of amnesia goes beyond the scope of childhood. Later events (traumatic, it is true) can be subject to total amnesia for several years before being reactivated by analysis. What is more, amnesia affects the very way in which the psychoanalytic process unfolds; for the analysand seems to feel bound to refer to it in each session without any particular sense of trauma that is noticeable ('I've forgotten everything that was said last time ...'). It is difficult to know if he is complaining of a real infirmity, if he is glorifying in his capacity for invalidating the process, or alternatively, if he is warning the analyst that whatever he says will be destroyed as soon as he has said it so as to discourage any subsequent attempts at interpretation. Fortunately, what he is asking for unconsciously is not to be believed. But, for him, the duty to preserve his state of amnesia, which in fact maintains his sense of guilt, is like a request for amnesty so as not to carry out the murder of his past. It was this infiltration of the theory by forces acting at the limits of sense (and thus of non-sense) – which Freud felt obliged to recognise, along with the instinctual memory of the compulsion to repeat – which compelled him, by way of compensation, I would say, to counterbalance this modification by resorting to primal phantasies, understood as timeless psychic structures which classify experiences and give direction to temporality. A little more force in order to give meaning more weight on the one hand, and a little more meaning to express the force on the other.

The question of primal phantasies embarrasses the psychoanalyst. If, owing to the context in which Freud situated the notion – that is, their phylogenetic nature – he decided to do without them so as not to be suspected of giving precedence to his presuppositions over the scientific views of his day, he would still have to demonstrate that by formulating as precise a conception as possible of ontogenesis with original temporal mechanisms (*après coup*, reorganisations of mnemic traces, and so on), one can account just as well for what Lacan had once called the key signifiers, a denomination more in keeping with current tastes than these primordial phantasies attached to a mysterious and hypothetical primal category. It still remains to be explained how the singularity and variety of individual vicissitudes make it possible to identify, in a quasi-general manner (to refrain from saying universal), certain organising formations relating to the difference between the sexes and generations, separation and reunion, and sexuality and destructiveness, which seem to constitute both semantic crossroads, by means of which they communicate with each other, and knots which are interconnecting and have a bearing on the course of psychic events. These are what I have called symbolic matrices.

The strictly ontogenetic vision stands in contrast to the archetypal conception dear to Jung who regards the particularities of the specific history of any individual as a matter of contingency, so as to drown the quest for the categorial in generalities, invoking the emanation of a sort of transcendental spirit whose pre-traced course cannot not be affected by the vicissitudes of a trajectory whose chance mishaps do not modify the general plan. It is sometimes said that, in this respect, there is only a bare thread separating Freud and Jung. This seems to me to be minimising their differences. Jung, believing in superhuman spiritual powers, necessarily restricts the significance of human time which has no other function than to incarnate the effect of these transcendental powers, overlooking epochs and territories. For Freud, on the contrary, it is as though individual temporal experience – obeying the rather vague general schema of all forms of evolution marked by the phases of existence – gave birth, as and when its deployment brought it into contact with more complex situations, to forms that refer to the determining factors which govern their course and alone make them intelligible. They are not apprehensible *a priori* by an individual, any more than they are given. They are formed and enriched through the effectivity of the revelations of the body and of the partners convoked in order to realise their potentialities, organising ensembles whose functioning will give birth to these organising structures which do not so much govern time as they make it emerge from processes without which it would not be possible to conceive of it. What makes this interpretation less abstract than it seems initially is that, according to Henri Atlan, this self-organisation, which is difficult to conceive of as such, becomes much more intelligible when one sees it as resulting from heterochronic temporal structures, as the intergenerational relation – an *a priori* of all development – necessarily implies. Primal phantasies (there being a prescription against asking any questions as to their origin) are assumed to have a comparable status to the pre-forms of language which can never be acquired if they are not activated by the incitement to speak in response to being spoken to at a specific stage in development. The efficacy of this incitement is very limited, both before and after this precise period of external activation. The foregoing helps us to understand how contemporary ideas on memory relativise considerably traditional ideas on storage and the use of mnemic stocks for the benefit of current and contextual elements. This means that establishing meaning takes precedence over the simplifying vision of the recollection of memories. And furthermore, as I have intimated, the problem of hoarding and expenditure (involuntary and voluntary) cannot be involved when forgetting concerns a recent event and the impossibility of recalling it. Everything suggests, on the contrary, that memory is in fact based on a phenomenon of perceptual anticipation. In other words, it is the mobilisation of a current configuration which is linked up, without adequate precautions being taken (that is, without a 'buffer formation') with events which do not succeed in 'entering a state of

latency' and whose presence poses a threat at the gates of consciousness. These events, which are, so to speak, in a raw state, are
then in danger of becoming charged with a potentialisation which
one cannot simply describe as affective; and one can only give an
idea of it by referring to the instinctual impulses. The latter seem to
be invested with an explosive charge which has to be defused by a
so-called act of forgetting. What happens, in fact, is that the present
is disconnected from contextual elements with which it enters into
a relation – the latter being insufficiently mediated, and thus feared.
Forgetting functions here as a mask for unconscious recognition
which, as soon as it has taken place, has to negate itself in order to
save psychic functioning as well as the object which is the addressee.

The question becomes one of the acceptability of the intelligible
– that is, of the agreed and agreeable forms whereby the isolated or
grouped elements can acquire meaning for a psychic organisation,
without endangering its fundamental parameters: the subject, the
object, and the transference. This is why, in certain cases, it is the
task of the transference-object to accomplish the impossible work of
self-revelation expected from an analysis when its bearings are more
assured. Interpretation, in the cases we are considering here, ceases
to be a question of simply elucidating an unconscious which is
hesitating between irrupting into consciousness and remaining in a
state of repression. It becomes a test of temporality, taking upon itself
the task of confronting the risk posed by the end of time. It is clear,
then, that the issue is less one of lifting infantile amnesia than of
authorising childhood to constitute itself as a fictional memory.

Successiveness and Sequentiality

The consideration of a time T2, which can only be posited in relation
to an earlier time T1, has the consequence for the psyche that, when
T2 is in a position of conceiving a hypothetical T3, T1 is no longer
the same as it was before the occurrence of T2. T3 only has
importance as a figure of temporal generation, which gives it the
power of having had a retroactive effect on its antecedents, even
those with which it has no direct link, like T1. Consequently, T1 has
changed not only owing to the passage of time distancing it from
its initial state, but owing to a 'return of time' which, with the
appearance of T3, attributes this event with the effect of having
modified T1, not only from a distance but also backwards. Thus it is
not the closest antecedent which necessarily finds itself most

affected by the change that has occurred with the appearance of T3. What is more, the closest antecedent T2 can absorb the effect of T3, making it flow back towards its own antecedent whose 'resistance' is weakened by the distancing of the zone of investment which has moved from the space T2–T3. Though T1 is no longer conceived in the same manner, the conception we have of the most distant term can also be modified, depending on the modification of the effects of radiance which occur upstream and which will be concerned by the return from T2 to T1. Radiance, diffusion, distribution, fragmentation can only bring into play limited aspects of T2 towards T1 or T3. In the long run, the effects of propagation from T2 towards the terms of the series which go beyond T3 change our understanding of T3 if something of the relation that exists between the terms is not maintained.

We are thus led to posit the relation T0-T1 as primal time. This is not to say that T0 would have the value of an absolute standard, itself an origin without antecedents; but rather that it plays the role of a conventional point of reference which 'holds' the series, without being represented as such, in the manner of T1, T2, T3, and so on. It is however more than a pure convention, since it is endowed with a generative potential (of which it is itself the product) which will be necessary for posing the question of the nature of T.

The question that emerges here, then, is the position of any given T, for it involves the legitimacy of segmentation: there is nothing in psychic time whose properties can be compared, for example, with those of whole numbers. One can understand, then, that the possession of defined units is not indispensable for a conception of psychic time. There even arises the question of the interest of homogenising the experience of time through the intermediary of constant, fixed units.

It is from this last point of view, from the angle of psychic causality, that T1 is:

- the first term of a series;
- the precedent term modified by the development of the series in the form of TX;
- the term through which the preceding terms are precipitated in order to constitute it as the first term in the series (T0–T1);
- the term of which certain elements can be found in the succession or in some of the other terms produced by the series;

- the term that is unrecognisable as the first term in the series mixed with the other terms of the series.

Thus the operation of successiveness becomes, in psychic causality, sequentiality. This implies freeing oneself from successiveness, from its connotations in terms of units, homogeneity, and direction. Psychic time can then be seen as a juxtaposition and palimpsest of diversified temporalities establishing a relationship between the harmonies of a dissected temporal system and the resonances of disordered or co-ordinated temporal systems the result of which reveals the relations between the time of the subject and the time of the Other.[34] The principal component of temporal inscription has to conform to the aleatory constraints of semantic intelligibility according to parameters which do not depend only on consciousness, but also on its relation with the unconscious.

This processual intelligibility can sometimes be identified in diversity, that is, by cutting up a sub-set which reflects the complexity of the ensemble sufficiently to serve as a selection of samples, notwithstanding what is sacrificed, in terms of the total understanding of the ensemble, to the interests of exemplarity. Although the nature of T remains mysterious – and must, perhaps, remain so, like Bion's alpha function, so that the system can go on functioning – it can at least be assumed that the passage of any one of the Ts to a later one reveals an active latency working on the interval. Here, as one deduces the phenomena underlying the surface continuity, one can identify, retroactively, an interplay of analogies and differences (Freud had already spoken of condensations and displacements), of erratic marks which are sometimes very close to the meanings that they 'impose', sometimes kept at a distance from them (acting as warnings for any future linking), and sometimes amalgamated in an indistinct way in the signs which they are supposed to mark until the moment when the mutation of T1 into T2 occurs. Once this change has occurred, the processes that have led to this transformation become visible, but only then. Unequal sequences, ample or precipitated rhythms – largely iterative – retroactions, the succession of times all conform to a division which is analogous to that which occurs spontaneously in listening, but not necessarily immediately, and which periodically gathers together certain components as the process unfolds. These components look, if not like constants, then at least like references, which are identifiable for a given duration, for all the Ts. Similarly, the nature of T will suggest the existence, in certain intervals of the sequence, of modalities that are foreign or even contrary to the process of successiveness (stases, repetitions, stretching, and regressive masking, varying tensions of conflictuality, and so on). These lead us to postulate the existence, alongside a vectorised temporal apprehension, of an activity that is opposed to the state of what is past for ever, where the effects can be felt of an over-determination concerning the reactions of psychic causality in the face of an internal pressure consuming its own production. This invites us to conceive of temporality as a resistance to the exhaustion of the energy of the living order in its conflict with meaning and thought, which are only compatible with a regime of the lowest level (Freud's 'small quantities').

A Model of Memory in Psychoanalysis

Memory has provided the opportunity for a reflection which sees in the exercise of its functioning the revelation, retrospectively, of networks of meaning which are organised in symbolic matrixes. These matrixes only refer to the past because they govern the whole of human experience from birth to death. What they owe to the past is the impossibility of their being unveiled immediately, or of being totally elucidated in the course of the development. No prior information, no prediction can circumvent the experience of being surprised by a retrospective truth. This only acquires the quality of a respectable experience (something that will be more than knowledge without claiming to be wisdom) when the motivating forces of human bonding have already played their part and can only be 'apprehended' retrospectively. It is not so much a question, then, of memory, strictly speaking, as of the undefinable change which affects anyone who, though present, considers himself in the past. And, just as memory, as such, does not escape intact from this retrospection, the present is no longer the same after it either. Psychoanalytically, one can consider as present everything in the psyche which is connected with actual, lived experience. One can even consider as present that which is not perceptible to someone who is questioning himself here and now, but which can be perceived by someone else situated spatially elsewhere: either what comes back from the reflection of the unconscious or what affects another vision of seeing things that is co-present. Memory and perception were only opposed in the early days of psychoanalysis in order to distinguish an actual time completely absorbed in the appreciation of the moment and a 'trans-actual' time which was held to be genuinely psychic as a result. But the very evolution of the issues raised by psychoanalysis led to this extratemporality of the actual being challenged, since many circumstances showed that the state could not be considered as evidence of a neutrality required by the work of recording experience. This is why I believed it was necessary to give a greater extension to the concept of negative hallucination, the importance of which Freud himself had sensed even though he did not pursue his own observations to their logical conclusion. At the end of his life, however, these became more insistent (from fetishism to the splitting of the ego), without creating the new perspectives that one might have hoped for. He remained caught between a new conception of the imagination as spatio-temporal transcendence and an embryonic theory of thought that was perhaps too imprisoned by its debt towards abstraction, encountering many difficulties in squaring it with the theory of the drives.

And yet the solution to the problems that had not been resolved by the lifting of infantile amnesia was to be found with a theory of binding (in its relation to unbinding). From then on perception could no longer be defined only by its relation to the present and to presence – closely related here to its philosophical, or purely phenomenological conception – unaffected by its connection with a conception of memory that had been fundamentally revolutionised. It should have been possible to base it on a conception of instituting binding as opposed to a conception of the psyche as instituted unbinding, a phase prior to rebinding which, phenomenologically speaking, is not a secondary synthesis, but the very manner in which psychic productions present themselves to us for analysis. The psychoanalytic conception of memory is a particular case of this operation of rebinding based on apperceptive unbinding. This is why all the criticisms that can be made of reconstruction, or of the conception of the past to which analysis gives rise, do not detract in the slightest from the necessity of the subject in analysis to relate to the non-present of which the past is the other modality of the elsewhere. However vain the undertaking may be, the aim cannot, without negating itself, allow itself to be deflected from its goal which is memory in process expressed by psychical activity.

There is no alternative, then, but to propose a model of memory that is adapted to psychoanalysis. It should include the constituents of mnemic organisation as a whole, while taking into account these amnesic forms of memory. We will be obliged, therefore, to make a generalising reduction in order to define the elements whose sequence is as follows: alteration, durability, resurgence.

(a) *Alteration* is what determines a change of state in the psyche that is noticeable immediately or retrospectively, without consideration of its origin or nature, and envisaged purely in terms of the effect which translates the modification. This is what, retrospectively, will constitute the trace of the historic in what can be historicised. This can be envisaged from different points of view (developmental or maturational, environmental, interactive, factual, etc.), entailing an entanglement of causalities which are not to be taken into account from the perspective I am adopting here, which subordinates them to the sequence which leads to change.

(b) *Durability* is what allows us to notice the non-disappearance of alteration (but not necessarily its preservation in the same state) depending on the characteristics of the psychical topography in which it is envisaged, so that it is enough to see signs of its presence (by observation, inference or deduction) in one of the topographical sub-spaces for it to be taken into consideration. Two factors will have to be taken into account here: meaningfulness, which justifies the perennity of alteration and often allows it to be recognised subsequently, and, secondly, the operations which have affected the preservation and which are an integral part of the mnemic matrix which combines, in such a way as to make them indistinguishable, the veiling and unveiling of alteration.

(c) *Resurgence* is the condition which can either make the signifying potential of alteration flow back through its two earlier phases or it can present itself as the only surviving indicator of the series, implicating the others through the feeling of resurgence alone – even if the terms suggested retrospectively are different from those of the process which led up to it. It will be assumed, then, that they are not contingent but result from modifications of the signifying potential of the earlier phase. Resurgence shows that durability is not sustained by an inert but rather a moving duration, for the reproduction which can be observed in it necessarily refers neither to alteration nor to durability, but can acquire, when it takes the form of resurgence, new characteristics compared with its earlier state. The consequences of resurgence on the systems for inscribing alterations modify the relations between what is inscribed and what is not, as well as the relations between the supports of what is inscribed and what is not, bringing into play the mechanisms of binding, along with their notation, their mobilisation, their conversion into other systems, their potentialisation, their capacity for disrupting topographical, dynamic, economic relations, and so on.

It is not only the different formulations given to the sequence alteration–durability–resurgence which give it its psychoanalytic validity. Above all, it is the way in which such a set-up proves to be sensitive to the parameters that psychoanalysis is particularly concerned with, both in the intercalation at the heart of their median phase (before and after it) and in the framework of the initial and terminal phases.

(d) *Inserted factors.*

Between alteration and durability, I place *association*. In his work on aphasia (1891), Freud makes a remark of fundamental importance. He defends the idea that sensation and association (in the course of the text 'sensation' is replaced by 'representation') should not be thought of separately, as each is located in the same place.[35] Representation and association can only be apprehended together; and, if one is led to consider them independently of each other, this is the result of a resistance and not a 'natural' observation.

It is the attraction by the pre-existing repressed that has been unduly considered as a 'late' phenomenon, whereas in fact the repressed only appears in this form. For primordial and primal repression are not a fact of experience but an epistemological deduction, just like primal phantasies. For the psyche, the alteration never entirely escapes the vicissitude of being absorbed by a production of associative relations which amass and weave themselves around it, allowing one to deduce retrospectively – by what follows – the semantics of the alteration which can sometimes triumph over its reduction to the state that existed before it emerged. Determining the effects of the alteration does not just involve noticing the changes produced, but is defined by appreciating the aims and consequences, concordant or discordant, between the events produced (intrapsychic and intersubjective), the effects of reality, the maintenance of the constancy of the psychic organisation in the face of the disturbing effects of mobilising significations, etc.

Likewise, between durability and resurgence, I will place the *transformation* that is implicitly present in the association that we have just taken into consideration. In this state, it is more active than passive; that is to say, the fact of association gives rise to transformations which result from combinations already established and which, to a certain extent, determine the particular vicissitudes of the process of resurgence. The latter only occurs if the modifications that have taken place lead to an imbalance which is sufficiently marked to make a new psychic event necessary. This occurs in such a way that this event does not unduly compromise the relations between the different aspects of the mnemic matrix. This can reach the point where resurgence appears in isolation; that is, the psyche then only takes into account the aspect of the return (true or false) of what is happening without knowing what this is a return of (*déjà vu, déjà vécu*, and so on). Resurgence is just one of the possible vicissitudes of the mnemic matrix, but it is the one that interests me here. The vicissitude of durability can be accomplished by going through certain sub-systems which can be grouped together under three headings:

(a)   maintenance (or even the attempt to suppress) in the state of latency: inhibition of resurgence;
(b)   the solution towards a 'placement' inserted in the cultural order, constituting an individual psychic disappropriation in favour of a collective re-appropriation (resurgence in a sublimated form);
(c)   isolation as a result of being disconnected from the cultural order (alienation).

In any case, two parameters are in competition or in synergy here: representation or realisation. The hesitations that one may have concerning the relations between association and transformation should be dispelled by the justification I am giving for the essential function that I am attributing to transformation. This is the indispensable condition for the accomplishment of resurgence. An arrow pointing in two directions unites association and transformation.

The hypotheses of the *surrounding framework* are situated at the beginning and at the end of the process.

In the position represented by resurgence, what is important is that resurgence be recognised as resurgence. Which does not mean being recognised as explicit memory but as repetition, the modalities of which still have to be determined. This recognition can pertain to the phenomenon of resurgence alone, as I have said, or to the connection between the latter and alteration. In no case, however, can resurgence imagine the state prior to alteration; it can only construct it *a posteriori* in ways that are sometimes contradictory.

Recognising resurgence as resurgence produces effects which can be traced back to the intervention of alteration: for anyone who has noticed it, or in anyone in whom it is noticeable, recognition becomes impossible to dissociate from a subjective position which existed before the moment of recognition. The process as a whole is marked by the adoption of a position of acceptance or rejection towards that which resurges. These choices have a retroactive effect on the apperception of the state of latency prior to the resurgence. This is why the subject is not only the subject who recognises resurgence, but also the subject of the Cogito. This observation has consequences for the eventual witness that the situation of resurgence may include, creating a supplementary determination for this resurgence. The linking up of the effect with the recognition of resurgence creates a second obligation of recognition duplicating the object of the resurgence – that is to say, of the subjective position where there is an encounter between the object of the resurgence and the objectifying witness, thanks to whom the phenomenon of recognition escapes from the purely subjective explanation, leading to the recognition of this recognition by the third party who finds himself included. This will constitute a decisive turning-point for the status of the subjective position which has to objectivise itself in relation to both oneself and to a fellow human being, who is just another version of oneself. The whole process of recognition makes it possible to reformulate the question as follows: 'Who says yes or no, to what or to the return of what, in relation to whom, recognised or not, in the place of who else?'

The state prior to alteration should be considered heuristically as an unknown,[36] even when it seems to be the end of another phase (resurgence). This unknown depends on the manner in which it can be envisaged through alteration which condenses the state of change and its substratum – the change being posited, hypothetically, not only as initiation but also as initial. Its signification as an unknown supports the idea that one can only envisage the process on the basis of the state of change, which sets in motion (thus making its apprehension possible) a psychic event that is intrinsically processual. Like psychoanalytic experience itself, this can only be thought about with reference to the transference on which it is constructed, including the state that exists before the transference has been established. The content of what was preparing itself to be altered, and its perpetuation, are the result of the invisible action which can only be spoken about in terms of its effects, thus inferring the existence of durability as a central phenomenon of the mnemic matrix, and inviting us to take into account the effects of radiance or the effects of the resonance of psychic causality in the relations between perception and memory and vice versa.

The coherence of this ensemble can only be guaranteed by envisaging the relations in the conflict between its general vector-isation and the retroactions occurring within it:

1. from alteration to resurgence and from resurgence to the recog-nition of resurgence;
2. interruptions of this process vectorised by the effects of inter-ference of association and transformation;
3. retroactions between transformation and association and between the recognition of resurgence and the retrospective con-struction of the unknown prior to alteration.

The work produced by the unfolding of this process is not to be seen as towering above, or dominating memory but as resurgence, which itself appeared when the concept of memory in psychoanalysis was created/constructed out of the convergence of multiple sources of experience, thereby constituting a true 'memography' which is to memory what historiography is to history.

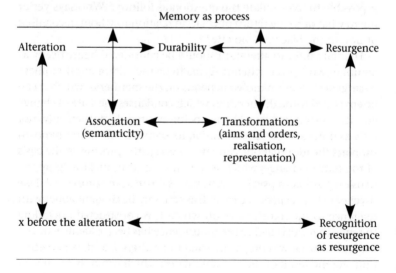

Figure 6.1

The Punctuation of Time

The questions raised here concerning memory are never more than a chapter of the treatise on the historical problematic of the relations between History with a capital letter (or should one now speak in the plural) and the historical dimension of the human condition to which psychoanalysis has added a supplementary factor of complexity.

Freud was, I think, one of the first to observe that a society does not make 'History' immediately. It must first reach a certain degree of development in order to be able to look back on what, only then, appears to be its past – a point of view that always tends to be idealised retrospectively. He made the remark simply to underline the identity of the positions which mark individual history and the history of peoples. On the other hand, it is easier nowadays to get a less distorted idea of what was described retrospectively about the beginnings of a society or of a human group than about the prehistory of an individual in spite of the illusions of psychology. The latter does not seem to realise that what these descriptions fail to embrace is the very essence of historicity; namely, the way an individual suffers or shapes temporality and, in any case, can do no other than construct it.

The suspicions cast on Freud's view of historicity have certainly taught us to be more cautious about our suppositions and more critical about what we take to be self-evident. They have done little to advance our conceptions of individual or personal history; for, though it has become necessary to recognise the role of construction, nothing has been said at the level of (or absence of) what is constructed, about the constraints imposed, the degree of variations authorised, the differences between what can be conceived and what is lived, and the role played in it not by fiction – of which one is easily persuaded – but of truth. It is easier to cast doubt on the truth than to purely and simply eliminate it from research, but one should not, however, succumb to absolute scepticism (otherwise what is the point in even beginning to do research?). Is it not enough to strive for even just a little exactitude? Behind Freud's grandiose project and his imposing fresco this was the basic and primary aim. Today, we are certainly not in a position to provide definitive conclusions. Perhaps we shall have to wait until time is more pressing in order to be able to see more clearly.

This relation to the non-present, which I have tried to elucidate, has probably not entirely done justice to our capacity to enjoy what is new – the stumbling block of every study centred on the persistent effects of the past in the present. In fact, the question is not just about appreciating the novelty – or even about the existence of such a possibility. Behind it there is also the possibility of detecting, in what assumes the characteristics of the absolutely new, the faculty of shaping what is yet to come and which is only seen as a future enigma. So difficult is it, in fact, for us to adopt, without having a sense of concern and reticence, the principle of *carpe diem* that, in principle, it does not even need formulating, since it should be applied as a matter of course. Especially after Freud had given it its letters, if not of nobility, at least of accreditation to thought, with the pleasure-unpleasure principle. Emancipation from a past, regarded as heavy and cumbersome, is never so liberating as when the non-present lies discretely in a latent state. Here, it is not so much forgotten, but lives in hope of the arrival of new norms under which it would either lose all its power or, conversely, make its return majestically. We can therefore assume that it is absolutely necessary for the psyche to have a 'second life', which serves not only as a warehouse for the undesirable but also as a reserve for its own posterity. This would safeguard the possibility of allowing, at an opportune moment, the transformation of what is undesirable into a new state which is able to satisfy the new norms of desire in which the old will pass unnoticed, disavowing, when necessary, its origins. Denuded of meaning, psychic life cannot survive; but may polysemy live in order to guarantee our flight ... in time.

There remains, finally, one aspect that cannot be passed over in silence. Though for a psychoanalyst, reflections on the passage of time or questioning of the distinctions between past–present–future meet with an indisputable echo in theses relating to the unconscious, they leave out of the picture one point which is more readily acknowledged by those who approach temporal matters from the angle of art rather than – unless I am mistaken – from the angle of science. The continuity of temporal experience or its reversibility are quite indifferent to a knot which is encountered in every psychoanalysis – that is, the possibility, whether it be through repetition or, on the contrary, through the emergence (real or illusory) of what is new, of giving density to the present by linking it up with the echo it arouses or that is created by the very fact of having acquired more density. It is thanks to this density that memory occupies, in the psyche, the position of an attractive pole that is always alive and very different from the pole it would occupy in a space which was only filled with ghosts. It is also thanks to this density that are woven, around memory, the thousand and one circumstances which are made the object of secret or shared commemorations calling for their renewal. 'Many happy returns ...',[37] say the English to celebrate a moment of origin: birth. Historicity is unthinkable without this sense of the present being perpetuated on the horizon, albeit unknown, of the future. What subsists in the way of mystery is not so much, 'What will tomorrow consist of?' as the way in which the present carries within it the germs of what will dislodge it from its situation as an occupant of the actual. And this is why the movement cannot be perceived in a purely natural way like the path of a torrent flowing down from the mountain into the valley, or like clouds being carried along by the wind. Rather it should be seen as the fruit of an opposition of wills which seem to be shaped by willing and counter-willing, both of which are uncontrollable and ignorant, basically, of what sets them in motion. It is time that gives psycho-analysis its best reason for only understanding retroactively (après coup) the articulated ensemble of determinations. Even if they have not all remained secret, it would never be possible to understand the woven tissue of their dispersed motifs, either because of chance, or because of the diverse contexts which cannot be brought together in order to form the coherent image of a meaning – a meaning which they do not so much carry but suggest, once everything has been accomplished. Everything?

'Time sees all ...', says the chorus to Oedipus.[38]

7 Life and Death in Incompletion (1994)*

In Memoriam N.R.P.

Let me fumble it gently and patiently out – with fever
and fidget laid to rest – as in all the old enchanted months! It
only looms, it only shines and shimmers, *too* beautiful and too
interesting; it only hangs there, too rich and too full, and with
too much to give and to pay; it only presents itself too admirably
and too vividly, too straight and square and vivid, as a little
organic and effective Action.

The Notebooks of Henry James, p. 348

To complete[1] something is to finish it, and there is a sense of
liberation especially when a goal has been attained. The projected
task has been realised in accordance with one's expectations, and
there is nothing more to be added. It has reached the point where it
finally exists by itself, and the sense of 'finish' it procures is a source
of felicity. Language, however, has strange short-circuits, since
achever also means to finish off, to kill. The same word is used both
to signify access to full, ripe, autonomous, existence, and to mark
the moment of passing from this world. The idea of completion
(*achèvement*) is thus understood either as the termination of a process
of growth, which is the equivalent of a new birth, or as a definitive
end of existence. One might think that the idea of ending is neutral
and that it applies indifferently to the work of life and to the work
of death. This would be to minimise, where the first sense is
concerned, the fact that completion brings with it a sense of
exalting, accomplished fullness, which is the very basis of this state.
Whereas, in the other case, one has to take the full measure of a
silence that falls like the blade of a guillotine, abandoning to nothingness that which hitherto had been animated with a potential for
being. It is not simply a question of contextual connotations, but of

---

* First published as 'Vie et mort dans l'inachèvement' in *Nouvelle Revue psychanalyse*, 50, 1994, pp. 155–84.

intrinsic, contradictory resonances which cannot be reduced to a single focal point.

Let us consider, for a moment, incompletion (*inachèvement*) as the interruption of a work that has not been pursued to its end. There are many circumstances in which this fate is encountered. The first, obviously, is if the worker dies: *An Outline of Psychoanalysis*, for instance, was interrupted by Freud's imminent death. The second, quite different, is a voluntary interruption, decided upon by the author, as a result of a sense of dissatisfaction with the result obtained, even if others find it marvellous; Leonardo da Vinci's *London Cartoon* is a case in point. This cartoon is one of a series of representations of the theme of the Metterza, most of which remained as sketches which culminated in the definitive solution of the painting of *St Anne* in the Louvre. Nevertheless, the *London Cartoon* is far from being a simple sketch, as the work is in fact in a very advanced state. It nonetheless bears the obvious marks of incompletion. The final choice, the *St Anne* in the Louvre, shows that Leonardo adopted other pictural solutions for the theme that he set out to treat. This work, albeit much more advanced than the one that preceded it, was also, in his eyes, unfinished (*inachevé*). Which is why he kept it with him until his death. Freud was right in thinking that, though incompletion was a symptom of Leonardo, this theme provided us with a special opportunity for understanding his inhibition. For although – its success notwithstanding – the work in the Louvre still awaits something from Leonardo's brush, the one in London is in charcoal, generally used in preparation for a painting, and was never transformed into a painted work. It was both unfinished and, apparently, disavowed by him. It is possible to give a different explanation for this than for the uncompleted *St Anne* in the Louvre. The work was abandoned, in my opinion, because it revealed too transparently Leonardo's unconscious phantasies regarding his infantile sexual theories.[2] Analysing the picture has allowed me to detect in it a strange optical effect, a real parapraxis of his creation, which creates the illusion that a member can be seen emerging between two widely-spread legs, erroneously attributed to St Anne, which is the counterpart of what may be interpreted as a pubis. This glimpse of Leonardo's unconscious – at least, this is how I understand this bizarre impression – is endorsed by the position of the Virgin on St Anne's knees. Moreover, she is wearing a masculine expression, which is very different from the other representations in the studies Leonardo made of her, as well as from the

painting in the Louvre; and it contrasts strongly with the gentle
expression on the face of Jesus' mother. Other indications support
this view, suggesting that the sexual theory about the existence of
the maternal penis managed to find its way into the painting. This,
then, helps us understand that the completion of a work does not
consist in exhibiting everything which is contained in the creator's
vision, but in achieving a balance between what is necessary in order
to make it alive, suggestive, mysterious, and what, depending on the
aesthetic criteria of the period, needs to be left out or at least
disguised.[3] Sometimes a piece of art is compromised because it has
been over-worked. This particular work is in fact neither unfinished
nor over-worked; it is quite simply *manqué*. The unfinished state of
the *Cartoon*, whose beauty is universally recognised – it has even
been considered by some to be superior to the *St Anne* in the Louvre
– is merely a mask which prevents one from seeing the 'too-much-
perceived', that is, the internal unconscious representation which
interferes in the work. Leonardo was a restless man, constantly
solicited by his curiosity and creativity which were not solely
pictorial. But, if it is in his paintings that we are struck by his
slowness and inhibition, it is because it involves his view of himself.
Although he dared to open up corpses in order to scrutinise their
anatomy more closely, his drawings of female genital organs,
observable to the naked eye, were executed badly, and showed little
interest for the *cosa mentale* that his eyes saw behind their projection
onto the canvas.

Let us now consider another situation, where the work begun is
impossible to pursue. This was the fate of Henry James' *The Sense of
the Past*.[4] This unfinished novel, whose title is significant (the hero
is a historian), is compared by James to one of his recent published
short stories, *The Jolly Corner*. In fact the path between the completed
and the uncompleted is more sinuous than it seems. The entry in
the *The Notebooks* dated 9 August 1900, refers to a real impasse in
the conception of *The Sense of the Past* which James had hoped would
be 'as simple' (!) as *The Turn of the Screw*. The parallel between the
two titles deserves, however, to be explored further. The cornerstone
of the work was supposed to reside in the revealed effect of 'terror',
making the hero who experienced it a source of terror himself, a
revelation that is much more important than the first. One is in
danger of going astray if one understands this relationship in terms
of a successive order in which the terrorised personage in turn
becomes terrorising. For James says clearly that the young man in

question had become a source of terror. The situation was taken up again six or seven years later; and, this time, it was pursued to its conclusion, apparently without difficulty, in *The Jolly Corner*.[5] What James had been unable to develop in the context of the voyage into the past which would have brought his hero into acquaintance with the family of his English ancestors of almost a century before, he was able, apparently, to accomplish in different circumstances, that is, by staging a terrifying encounter with the ghost of an ancestor which haunts a house he has inherited. The hero of *The Jolly Corner* returns to the United States after a voluntary exile. This ghost arouses anxiety and fright, not so much because it belongs to the kingdom of the dead, but because it is the representation of what the hero imagines he might have become if he had stayed amongst his own people instead of exiling himself – an aggressive, powerful and rich man. The ghost nevertheless bears the marks of suffering and amputation. This 'transcendence' might be attributed to the fact that here, the other is an ostensibly paternal figure, a possible source of identification, the difference of generation being preserved between the apparition and the hero; whereas at the end of Book II (written during the first attempt in 1900) of *The Sense of the Past*, this difference is suppressed. The hero observes a painting in which the personage seems at first to avoid his gaze, returning 'inside the picture'. At the end, the figure in the painting leaves the frame, moves around the room and turns towards the visitor, showing him his face which, 'he was astounded, was his own'.[6]

It is remarkable that James returned to his abandoned novel, while putting aside another work, *The Ivory Tower*, which he did not finish either. In 1914, as he was meditating once again on his project, he recalled that when he was writing *The Jolly Corner*, he had had the impression that he was filching the subject – which was merely adjourned – of *The Sense of the Past*, and that he might conceivably regret it subsequently. The goal of *The Sense of the Past* was, moreover, far more ambitious. Its subject was the dual consciousness – following the fusion of the identities of the narrator and the incarnated ancestral portrait – of each of the protagonists, that is, the consciousness of being both the other and themselves, accompanied by the confused and distressing impression that this anomaly makes on other people. In fact, James had left the literary world of ghosts to embark upon a world of alienated possession. The theme of the relations between the person of the author and that of the writer is not new. It becomes distinctly more complicated when one adds to it the historic dimension of the past which is resurrected, at the risk of alienating the hero, for he is haunted by a story which is not his own, but that of his ancestors. In fact, the excursion into the country of origins is initiatory. The reason for this return to the family cradle was that the hero had been rejected by a young widow for being too passive and so set out in search of adventure to prove the contrary in the hope of winning her back again. The long note of 1914 in *The Notebooks* explicitly shows the deliberate similarity of spirit between the two works: the completed short story and the novel that could not be brought to its conclusion.[7] The contents of this note betray an element of disdain. For the comparisons between the two works do not allow us at any stage to notice this triumph, albeit temporary, over the alter ego in the unfinished work. In order to discover the trace of such a situation, one has to turn to the account of the nightmare of the Galerie d'Apollon, related in the author's autobiography[8] with a note of triumphalism. While we know when the work was written, that is, in 1911, on his return from a trip to the United States after William's death, James does not record the date of the nightmare. It may have put an end to a period of depression. Edel supposes that it occurred in 1910, which was precisely when he was thinking, *a posteriori*, of situating the action of *The Sense of the Past*, as he was reworking it in 1914. James tried in vain to revise it completely according to a plan worked out in 1917, though he had not written any novels or stories for a long time. He did not manage to overcome the obstacle, and was still working on it the day before the onset of his illness which after causing him to suffer moments of delirious confusion, finally led to his death.

Incompletion is not always a sign that the creator has stopped working. In fact, the opposite occurs in the first stages of a creative work when, in a completely uninhibited state of mind, the artist deliberately works in a provisional manner. He uses his drafts, sketches and canvases to project ideas (literary, pictorial, musical, and so on) in order to explore the motif, leaving the field free for spontaneity, experimentation, just 'to see'. A precious spontaneous outpouring of material might occur in these experiments whose secret will not always be recaptured in the finished work. But is it not true that small miracles occur precisely because of the artist's relative disengagement?

As my first thoughts on this theme came to me – which were not quite the first, since I had already written on this subject with regard to Leonardo – I said to myself that 'incompletion', just like the 'unconscious' could be related to the idea of a work of the negative, and might have been included in the work I had written on that subject.[9] This supposes that we take into account the distinction between what has not been completed (*le non-achevé*) and the unfinished (*l'inachevé*), similar to that which exists between what is not conscious (*le non-conscient*) and the unconscious (*l'inconscient*). When speaking of what is unfinished, little thought is given to what is being referred to when evoking the unconscious. The negative connotation compared with the conscious is, in any case, largely masked by the positive content of the concept unconscious. Before Freud – notwithstanding a few rather vague, romantic intuitions – the unconscious denoted only that which was not conscious and surged up occasionally to present itself to consciousness. It may be, then, that there is a need to distinguish in the same way between what has not been completed – that is, simply the contrary of what has been completed – and what is unfinished/incomplete, understood as a latent form carrying within it a potential completion whose outcome, which is as unknowable as it is unknown, cannot be identified with what is suggested by the unfinished work. In this respect, a sketch is unfinished but its final form, its completed state, is inconceivable. Its virtuality makes any hypothesis concerning its outcome uncertain.

The work of the negative – the hypothesis of which I have developed – has the interest of not considering what is unfinished as a mere state, but of considering it as a stage of elaboration whose outcome is not determined.

If one puts aside the case of the project that is interrupted by death, one will see that the others must be appreciated in the light of the pleasurable or unpleasurable feelings aroused by the work. When the feeling is one of displeasure, the usual explanation given is one of disappointment caused by the discrepancy between the artist's intentions – which only exist in a virtual state – and their realisation. But in fact, one quickly notices that there is a conflict between two states within the artist. Moreover, when the work is brought to completion, the satisfaction obtained is short-lived. No artist ever considers his work to be finished – even when he has reached the summum of his art. Shakespeare did not stop after *Hamlet*, nor Watteau after *The Embarkation for Cythera* or Berg after *Wozzeck*. In other words, completion or incompletion do not concern the result of the work, the *opus*, as much as its author's thirst for work. Creating a work is not just about bringing a work to its conclusion, however difficult that is; it is about setting oneself the task of giving a certain order to the confusion of the world and the disorder of being (even if one wants to transmit an echo of it). And since these are less states of fact to be modified than mental states to be fostered – inasmuch as agitation constantly renews itself – completion is not possible, unless one gives up this preoccupation; and incompletion cannot, for long, play the role of a haven where one stops to have a rest.

Whatever the result achieved, creation only comes to an end with the creator's death, unless the source dries up, or is deliberately deserted (Rimbaud). We are then no longer dealing with the unfinished, for everything is consumed, and sometimes even disowned. There is thus something unpredictable in what is unfinished, but the same is true of the fate of the creation when it is brought to completion, for there is little chance that the whoever has pursued this chimera all his life can rest on his laurels once he has experienced success. These states cannot be defined according to fixed criteria, but only in terms of an exchange between the creator and the products created, engendering effects which can be unexpected owing to the relations between the unconscious sources which inspire the work and the conscious activity which imposes on them its formal choices, more or less in accordance with the treatment reserved for the former. It is thus on the side of the instinctual dynamic, and the disturbances it provokes, that the sustained effort to accomplish the work is to be appreciated. Whatever it is that nourishes the work can equally well poison it, just as the obstacles that are feared can, so as to avoid anxiety, impede the flow of nourishing blood which is indispensable to it.

When incompletion is the result of being forced to abandon a work out of unpleasure, it is a deviation of the conditions which governed incompletion as a stimulus for the quest to create with pleasure. How is this change to be explained? Whether the result of the work is finished or not is less important than the sense, the idea, of having gone 'further'. For, whether it is still being elaborated or has reached what is felt to be a very advanced state, a work can give its author the sense that it still holds something in reserve, which its admirers do not always suspect. The ensuing displeasure is caused by discord within oneself. It is the sign of the presence of a conflict that cannot be approached more closely. Nor can it be made the object of a compromise or occulted. What is interpreted as a sign of impotence, or as a fatal condition (this state of completion can never be attained, except by the gods), drowns, with this generalisation, the conflict at the heart of every creative work which is divided between what it claims to disclose in the way of novelty, and what, in the sources of creation, cannot cross the bar of silence.

In other words, the real criterion is the movement required by the agreement to pursue the dialogue with the object of the work as well as the resistance which opposes this commerce with oneself, and which has its roots in the unconscious. Ultimately, Braque ended up detaching himself even from that which was the centre of his fervent interest, the object, whose properties he had explored indefinitely, so as to interest himself only in the space from which it emerges.

To say of the unconscious that it is bottomless, limitless and formless means that the categories of finished and unfinished are not applicable to it. However, one cannot overlook the fact that its manifestations are animated by a desire which seeks to see its demands fully granted. If the drive is in search of satisfaction and does not stop until it has obtained it, and if, as Freud maintains, it is a 'demand for work', when such a work attains its goal, can one not speak of completion, even if it is temporary? For the paradox of the concept of the drive is that there are two aspects to it: there is the idea of an exigency that is all the stronger in that it is supposed to originate from a blind source (endosomatic excitation); and there is also the idea which sees the latter as the product of work. The urge of excitation changes according to the demand for work, the latter setting two heterogeneous dimensions in relation to each other – that is, the disturbance coming from the body or from the senses and the mind's mode of activity in the functions which connect it with the body. Plainly there is a need to render compatible the sensible bodily demand which wants to be obeyed and the implicit regulation of its partner which works on it. These reflections can also be applied to creative activity which is unquestionably inspired by the same sense of internal exigency but must, when this 'takes shape', be translated by the measure of the demand for work between the origin of the need to create and its translation into the specific language of art, which implies translation into another universe. Each of them can be conceived of separately, more or less easily. What eludes theoretical comprehension is the relation between them. Any demand for definitive satisfaction is thus an illusory quest for total completion, since it will not be long before desire reappears. The loss of the primary object makes it possible to account, retrospectively, for the origin of the quest undertaken with the hope of re-finding it, all satisfaction being measured by the phantasy of what would have been if the golden age, which is supposed to have existed prior to this loss, had not been interrupted. This mirage, marked by nostalgia, is a retrospective mythical construction. It can be found underlying the absolute thirsts haunting creation. We should be careful not to dissolve it too quickly, for it serves as a goad for crossing the barrier which opens the way to unlimited freedom. While diverting its course, modifying its aims, displacing the objects of its desire, and accepting to participate in the field of socially valued activities – which is little more than a means for allowing oneself to explore a series of questions relating to the world or himself – the subject accepts the compensations offered by the products of his research which also bring with them a bonus of pleasure. But the phantasy that the goal might be attainable one day remains active in the unconscious, animating, for better or for worse, the ongoing pursuit of the quest. What watches over the necessity of incompletion is the obscure feeling that completing the work might coincide with the end of all creation, leaving the creator no other alternative than that of drying up or of death.

*

Thus far we have only considered the model of artistic creation. But other models can provide a basis for reflection, too; for instance, science. When the scientist measures the extent of our ignorance and the very limited nature of knowledge, he cannot fail to be aware of everything that separates him from a total explanation of the world. Yet this aim has been abandoned. If science has no reason to be too unsatisfied with its acquisitions, it is precisely because it only gives itself the objective of resolving limited problems, which can be controlled and verified. It is this progression in small steps which has allowed it to acquire the formidable capital of knowledge on which it prides itself.

The scientist today can only carry out his work by effecting a split. He knows that his approach to reality is necessarily partial, incomplete. He even derives a certain glory from this, since he has thereby renounced the global explicatory systems which are all more or less religious in essence. And when he stands back from these temptations, he congratulates himself on having agreed to sacrifice a *Weltanschauung* in order to privilege his need for exactitude and rigour. Nevertheless, though he seems to accept what is unfinished (*l'inachevé*), he does so in a different way to the artist. He accepts it, but places no confidence in it. He does not expect anything from it; nor does he expect to receive a message from this beyond. He grapples with the unknown, an opaque and mute unknown, and not with the unfinished. For him, there is no intermediary between ignorance and knowledge. Each fragment won over from ignorance must, on the contrary, become the object of complete knowledge. When this is not possible, it must at least contain an inventory of what remains to be known. Here incompletion can never be a source of hope, a promise of richness to come. To see things otherwise would be to expose himself to great dangers. No theorem could be demonstrated, no experience verified, no reasoning generalised. Completion and objectivisation are complementary. By envisaging the question from a different angle, one understands that to objectivise it is to desubjectivise. It is for the subject to think about incompletion in terms other than those of insufficiency, recognising it as a positive attribute of the infinite.

Can we not take advantage of the fact that contemporary science has transcended this prejudice by introducing the role of the observer into the description of a phenomenon? A variable could thus be taken into account which has to be related to the subject. In fact the subject in question is only considered within the strict limitations of what occurs in the context of an experiment that is dependent on controllable parameters.[10] This, then, is where reflecting on the relations between the subject and the idea of completion leads us. The subject is neither complete nor incomplete, but he has the capacity either to close himself or remain open, depending on the situations related to the tasks he sets out to accomplish and the context in which they are situated. This enables us to understand that the only thing that matters is perpetuating the movement created by the impulsion to work; and, moreover, that this movement can make use of each stage, however much it complies or does not comply with the canons of its discipline, to sustain the pleasure of going further, towards the infinite. This has been the case ever since creative activity ceased to be restricted to the domain to which it was formerly confined. Not that it is necessary to begin singing the praises of creativity in general; it is just a matter of being aware that creating is an essential property of psychic activity.

It is probable that the euphoric effects of completion and incompletion alternate in artistic creation. It may come as a surprise that science, where details are concerned, and religion, where the totality of knowledge is concerned, pursue the same ideal of completion. It is not enough to recognise that the diversity of human activities all make use in turn of the goal of completion and incompletion. It is not so much the idea of a complementary unity that needs to be adopted as one that makes us attentive to all the opportunities their strategies have for deviating permanently. For the ascetic ethic of knowledge is far from enjoying an undisputed reign. Once the average conditions of experimentation have been left behind, many scientists openly proclaim their adhesion to such and such a religious system – which is not necessarily the one that was transmitted to them in their childhood. And those who openly acknowledge their convictions are far from representing all those who think in this way. Is it with a view to bridging the gap between scientific thinking and epistemological speculation that new parameters have been introduced in order to make it possible to think differently about the relations between completion and incompletion?[11] The idea of hyper-complexity endeavours to show the prematurely closed character of certain approaches.[12] In another domain, some religions, in contrast to others, emphasise the need to reject certain limitations – though they are scarcely seen as such by those who believe in them – connected with the too restricted, perhaps overly anthropomorphic character of Western religions, and the need to extend our intuition of the infinite. Might this not be an explanation for the current vogue of Buddhism in countries of Christian tradition?

Clinical analysis, a dimension that is lacking in this study, shows us that we cannot be satisfied with the ideas gleaned from art and science. This is because, more than any other approach, it allows us to observe the relation of the psyche to itself; and, more specifically, the way in which the latter, having no other way out, becomes the prisoner of its own treatment.

*

Let us now take, as examples, some cases where the analyst is faced with problems of incompletion. Before turning to clinical cases where incompletion is in evidence, it is worth recalling that it was also present, implicitly, at the origins of psychoanalysis. Hysteria was hidden for a long time behind the smokescreen of its exuberant pathology. 'It's stunning', as we say. Everything is an appeal to the other; and the latter rushes forwards, a victim of the illusion of the desire which seeks to make of him the object which is lacking in the hysteric's sense of wholeness and completion. And yet, after Freud, Lacan was to say, quite rightly, 'The hysteric is desire for unsatisfied desire.' And for good reason: as far as the hysteric is concerned, once it is over, it no longer has to be done; and, if it no longer has to be done, it means desire is dead. Hysterical conversion occurs when there is a need to prevent a phantasy from reaching the end of its course. The actual neuroses are the product of a stagnated process in which affect has been 'strangled'. But there are even more exemplary cases. How striking – and how constant its symptomology – is the clinical picture of obsessional neurosis (which Freud was the first to describe as a constituted neurosis; before that we only knew of obsessions). Today, with the denomination of 'constraint' neurosis (Laplanche), what is being stressed is the aspect of force underlying the obsessional ideas, over and beyond the character traits attributed to the obsessional individual, that is to say, of indecision or procrastination. Anyone who can recall the famous observations of Esquirol, Von Gebsattel or Freud – united by a similarity which surmounted the difference of epochs and explanatory systems – will appreciate that the expected sense of relief resulting from having accomplished one's duty, or of the measure of protection adopted, is thoroughly impossible to attain. The rituals of verification against all manner of dangers (intoxication, contagion, accident, and, ultimately, death) have no end. All attempts to put an end to such rituals by third parties – parents or spouses who consider that 'that's enough' – result in insurmountable anxiety. In religious orders, over-scrupulous novices who have never finished with their endless confessions are sent to the psychiatrist. In such cases, incompletion cannot be dissociated from questions related to aggressivity and death. This suggests – and Freud came to understand this – that the secondary defences of obsessionals, that is, the endless rites aimed at appeasing their pitiless superego, are in fact the expression of disguised satisfactions. Those satisfactions whose direct instinctual expression is prohibited have found refuge in this disguise. Without necessarily constituting an organised obsessional (or constraint) neurosis, incompletion can paralyse any task whose completion would entail a narcissistic or Oedipal satisfaction. All that remains, then, is the pleasure – unconscious – of masochism.

Y. was doing research. During her psychotherapy, she managed to bring her abandoned doctoral thesis to a successful conclusion. The result was so promising that it was recommended that, after making some revisions – concerning its form more than its content – she should try to publish it so that the thesis might be turned into a book. It was the most exasperating failure. I had a few ideas as to the reasons that might have been preventing her from completing the task. We had seen that this work had acquired a symbolic value designed both to repair her own self-image and to offend her colleagues. This book was an image of herself, without any metaphorical distance. It was supposed, moreover, to demonstrate to others that she was not as useless as she seemed; and it was even intended to become a weapon, as one could guess without much difficulty, to make others feel useless. In the sessions – face to face – she continually made the same complaints, though there was no possibility of entering into the details of what was going on with my patient and her work. Finally, I realised that nothing could be brought to completion because she subjected her text to the worst tortures – in a sterile manner. She wanted to improve the form but felt unsatisfied with any form she tried. If she wrote, *'It seems that'*, she would cross this out and write, *'It appears that'*. Needless to say, at a later stage of revision, she reverted to, *'It seems that'*. When she managed to make a little progress, she was soon struck by the idea that at the rate she was going, the content of her book would cease to be of any topical interest. I was made responsible for having allowed her to hope that she would be able to complete her project.

There was no shortage of memories of sphincter training, which had been particularly conflictual and highly eroticised by the mother. But it seemed to me that I was dealing here with a form of primal anality whose conflicts referred to something quite different from the classical anal relationship.[13] Narcissism played a much greater role here. When the patient was ready to say a little more about the anxieties she felt when she was working, two major situations became noticeable. The first was related to the idea that, if she accomplished her work by herself, she risked losing me. During one session, she said to me: 'Yesterday, I made some progress with one chapter. But I was upset because I didn't have you behind me and I could no longer imagine you supporting me and encouraging me by saying: "Go on, that's good, keep going!"' Separation anxiety and fear of loss can easily be detected here; but there is also a fear of autonomy, of being free from all authority. One should not underestimate, however, behind the appearances of a dual relationship, the triangulation which introduces the third party, represented by the work, between the analysand and the analyst. Identification with the father could only take place in the form of failure. The other type of anxiety was more persecutory. The mother's presence in her took the form of someone who turned to her daughter only when there were unpleasant tasks to be done. In her own work, my patient jealously guarded her ideas, and their written expression, being constantly preoccupied by the obscure intrigues of her exploiting and dishonest colleagues who were just dreaming of dispossessing her of it; or, of adding, unduly, their name to a publication whose merit was hers alone. She reminded me of those birds of prey which, having captured an animal, assert their ownership of the victim's body by placing a paw on it, but never begin to savour it until they have scrutinised the surroundings to make sure there is no other bird of prey in the vicinity, ready to rob the ephemeral victor of its prey. Once again, one suspects a fear of loss, but in a different way. What is in danger of being lost is what has just been won. Gaining something exposes one to losing it; whereas if one has nothing, there is scarcely any danger of being dispossessed. Likewise, by expecting nothing, one does not suffer from any lack, or disappointment. Because she felt incomplete on all levels, she barricaded herself behind the duty to complete everything.

Something is always in danger of being lost – that is, the object on whom one depends and to whom one's own existence is attached, or the object to whom one has oneself given existence. In both cases, what is threatened is the unity of a couple: either one is in the position of someone who, being capable of accomplishing his separation by becoming the subject of a task to be accomplished, in so doing, 'kills' the object from which he has only just barely distinguished himself; or, of someone who, giving birth to a separate object, condemns the latter to be 'killed' by a third party.

One of my patient's childhood memories was that she used to suffer from the fact that, when she was carrying out some task (often a chore) for her parents, which she was having difficulty in completing, they would say to her, just as she was on the point of finishing it, 'Leave it; we'll do it.' By taking over like this at the last moment, they gave her the impression that everything she had herself accomplished was of no value, and that they themselves were laureates of accomplishment. In short, she was condemned to preliminary (un)pleasure for life.

The most remarkable thing was undoubtedly her absolute incomprehension concerning the meaning of the verb 'to associate'. She would say, 'I cannot do two things at once, think and speak.' For her, associating freely meant losing the mastery and control that she exercised over herself in order not to allow space for a freedom that would betray her – except for very rare moments when she did so spontaneously, without realising it. The only thing that mattered for her was the pleasant or unpleasant character – depending on how she experienced it – of the interpretation that I was led to give her. I should add that she had come to me after having read one of my works on narcissism which, she said, was the only book on psychoanalysis that spoke to her. She had never openly expressed envy towards me on this subject – nothing but a slightly sad admiration, which made her aware of how far she felt she was from achieving a comparable result – but it was difficult not to think that her painful failure was related to envy. A painful failure: yes, it is the most fitting word for it – for how many times did she tell me that, faced with her sense of impotence – she was capable of spending hours and hours looking for the right word, without success – she would cry day and night. One cannot fail to interpret this as suffering caused by being unable to live up to her ego-ideal. Its counterpart was a total lack of awareness of the pleasure of suffering derived from offering herself as an expiatory victim of a sadistic object of whose presence there was no trace, but which was given, as it were, a timeless existence through this negativity. One can surmise here that completion has no relation either with the necessity of reaching a goal or with maintaining a momentum that would open up new fields of research or investigation. I had even asked myself whether the inhibition could be interpreted here solely in terms of the displacement of a prohibited action, given that any form of accomplishment was regarded as transgressive. But I felt more that I was witnessing a kind of dual to the death in the only domain of her existence where there were signs of prospective activity. Apart from her psychotherapy, everything else seemed immobile and limited to strictly codified obligations. The aim was to show me just how far her more personal commitments were threatened by this shadow of death whose existence one could surmise in the phantasies about her work. This was, perhaps, precisely because all activity that is strictly creative involves accepting a process of mourning: mourning the identity of the creator and of his creation. But this clinical vision also shows us that, with respect to this issue which is not always so transparent, any task that is likely to be seriously invested is constantly solicited by unpredictable currents; and, in return, calls for all sorts of manoeuvres in an attempt to avoid catastrophe or, at the very least, to control its trajectory which can go astray at any moment.

The links between obsessional neurosis and melancholy have been well established since Abraham. Who is not familiar with those cases of mourning which seem to go on and on forever, where life only returns to normal long after more ordinary cases. And contemporary clinical psychoanalysis has made us only too familiar with cases where, although there are no signs of it in the surface symptoms, the transference reveals the existence of a wound from which the individual concerned has never recovered. Can one set these forms of incompletion in opposition to others which are their contrary? Is it not true that this completion which the obsessional is chasing after is achieved by the paranoiac in his delusional state? The systematisation of his intellectual construction might suggest this, but one cannot fail to notice, in this titanic effort to sustain the coherence of the delusional vision, a desperate attempt to make up for the ego's weaknesses, to ward off the return of those 'fruitful moments' of delusion on which Lacan rightly insisted, in which reality vacillates, and, lastly, to push away as far as possible this sense of the end of the world which opens up the abyss of annihilation under the delusional patient's feet. And though they do not all reach this point, we would do well to recall the yells uttered by Schreber, which tells us enough about the worm-eaten pedestal on which his delusion was constructed.

In considering the various situations of incompletion that creative activity allows us to observe, we have already noticed that they acquire a different meaning depending on whether they are accompanied by a sense of pleasure or unpleasure. Psychopathology presents us with situations in which this unpleasure goes as far as suffering, even though the signals of anxiety, designed to prevent psychic pain, have not been triggered. In this respect, it is worth recalling that Freud opposed inhibition to symptoms and anxiety; for, when this phenomenon remains in moderate forms, it only manifests itself in the form of a hindrance which avoids conflict with the superego, since the movement pushing towards the satisfaction of desire is lacking.

*

What tools are required for thinking about incompletion in psychoanalysis? I have already referred to the unconscious as an inexhaustible source of desires which seek accomplishment, that is, the end of dissatisfaction, however much this is a phantasy which has scarcely any chance of being realised. Nevertheless, this general situation can become more complicated and engender additional suffering. What are the reasons for this?

The easiest reason to mention is fixation. The stronger the fixation, the more tempting regression will be, finding refuge at this point of arrest, and the more difficult it will be for the process of development to get going again. It should not, however, be concluded too hastily that the allusion to fixation and regression necessarily imply a normative view of things. Access to the Oedipal level goes hand in hand with a greater freedom of choice, orientations and perspectives, whereas anal fixation, for example, restricts the possibilities and increases the constraint. Constraint neurosis is a neurosis where the obligation to act or to think in a certain way – something that is always imposed – is a prominent feature, bringing in its train, as a measure of retortion, sterilising doubt.

There are other aspects involved which we have noticed in passing. Among them is narcissism. We know the importance, for the narcissist, of considerations related to the idea of a self-sufficient, complete and perfect totality. The *belle forme* is an ideal to strive for which exerts a magnetic attraction on the mirror of narcissism. This is its most classic version. But there is another, more subtle version, which seems to express quite the contrary. For some narcissistic subjects, it is the idea of completion that is menacing. For to complete or finish something is, at the same time, to determine an established form, once and for all; and, consequently, to render it entirely and definitively identifiable by its contours, and therefore more exposed – like a target to be destroyed. Thus by showing what one is and how one is, one lays oneself open to being grasped, caught hold of, questioned, doubted, and perhaps annihilated. It also means tracing one's frontiers, saying that one is only 'that', no less and no more. Borges used to say that it was intolerable to be only what one is.

Finally, there are the more pernicious forms, though they were not immediately recognised. They emerged once Freud had decided to accept the existence of the death drive, condemning the subject to transform Penelope's admirable trickery into a blindly, self-destructive project.

All the symptomatic configurations mentioned here occur in a context where the dominant idea is that the completion of the act is the displacement of the fulfilment of the prohibited, 'specific action'. Incompletion is evidence of a compromise between the desire to realise the prohibited wish and the defence against it. Between the wish and the tendency to act out the desire completely, there are many intermediate factors obstructing the process. The more the propensity for action is pronounced, as in obsessional neurosis, the stronger will be the expression of the conflict, manifesting itself in incompletion.

Nevertheless, beyond the pleasure principle, Freud was to countenance a bold hypothesis requiring the observation of phenomena which do not avoid unpleasure, but seem not to be stopped by its occurrence, or indeed even seek it. This is the case of the compulsion to repeat. But the analysis of situations where it is dominant suggests that the recurrence of repetition could be interpreted as resulting from the fact that their causal nucleus has not been exhausted. A long time ago, Lagache likened transference to the *Zeigargnik* effect described in psychology, which attempted to explain the repetition of interrupted, uncompleted tasks.[14] Though it is true that the transference is a much more mysterious phenomenon, incompletion, in this case, shows us that nothing of what has marked our immaturity can ever be entirely transcended. It is as though we were condemned to relive our unsatisfied desires, to be continually confronted with the same causes of failure, to seek, in vain, satisfaction of the same fundamental desires, and, to attempt, day after day, to liberate ourselves, as much from their untiring resurrection as from the suffering caused by the sense that we are still just as impatient, obstinate, and difficult to satisfy. We are not only born incomplete, but remain so throughout our lives in order to have a reason to reach back to our inaccessible origin.

We have just seen the ontological significance of incompletion which is so tangible in the attitude of human beings towards death. We find it unacceptable when one of our loved ones disappears forever; when he or she no longer exists, definitively. This suffices to explain the almost indispensable character of all religious ideas concerning life after death. At the other extreme are the odd situations that can be observed in psychopathology. It should be noted that in the two principal examples I have taken, obsessional neurosis and melancholia, death is at the heart of the issue. Whether a task has been completed or not, it serves each of these two possibilities equally well – for what counts is not the point at which the project stopped, but the point at which it will take off again.

In both cases, it is life, in its indetermination, which does not stop. On the other hand, that which is unfinished and destined to remain so for ever because the movement of life has deserted it, is well and truly dead. It seems, in fact, that incompleteness is one of the forms of the work of the negative. For whether one is thinking of its biological effects or of the long dependence of the small human being in comparison with young animals, there is always the idea that a supplement of work is necessary in order to reach a state that can be considered as mature. However, what is lacking in the notion of human completion is not only the fact that certain of our vital functions are dependent on the assistance of others, but also that this assistance only acquires meaning if it is motivated by love. What we can see is that there does indeed come a moment when this dependence gives way to a certain autonomy; but, on the other hand, love never arrives at a stage at which it can do without others definitively. Has sufficient thought been given to Freud's synonymy: instincts of life or love? If the *raison d'être* of love resides in this incompleteness, then one cannot dissociate the latter from a permanent elaboration which links past and future, expectations of survival, and the hope of abolishing every form of incompleteness. As I said with regard to the definition of the drive, what is important is the idea of work. And when we come to the question of symptomatology, we will have no difficulty in finding, behind the idea of constraint, that there is an obligation in obsessional neurosis to carry though an incessant work of defence against anxiety and destructiveness. In melancholia, this will be even more obvious: a work of mourning.

Very well, but why the negative? The negative is an inescapable aspect of the psyche. This is because, though it is grounded in instinctual life, what we perceive of it in ordinary existence only allows this instinctual life to subsist in a form that is filtered through repression and the defences whose role is to put an end, in their own way, to an unacceptable demand. The vision that we have of ourselves presents itself, then, in a negativised state, and can only be re-established in its positivity by imagining what we would be if all repressions were lifted – which is just as inconceivable as imagining the final, completed state of what is unfinished. At best, desire has aligned itself on the side of life, having opted for the hope of satisfaction, even if incomplete, which it is the task of the primary processes to realise and of sublimation to relay. What is essential is to ensure that investments are maintained. In other words, that the movement of the appropriation of the sources of pleasure, of the sharing which divides and multiplies them, and of the bindings carried out by the ego – a task that is intrinsic to its own activity – is pursued.

There are other cases where the negative of what is prohibited or impossible is never overcome, where no consolation is acceptable, where all frustration is at once intolerable and unforgettable and where, through a strange inversion of values, only the negative is real (Winnicott). Consequently, and quite unconsciously, the psyche is irresistibly attracted by the negative. Assisted by the compulsion to repeat, negative and unfinished become synonyms, because incompletion will be the solution whereby everything will at last come to an end. Incompletion, which has now become the ordinary state of things, is no longer the state which simply impedes progress, but anticipates an irremediable collapse. When faced with such a malediction, one can imagine the temptation to cut the Gordian knot. What will 'sustain' the transference is the double movement whereby the instinctual pressure seeks again to realise that which is unaccomplished in it and, simultaneously, that which is at work negatively in the unconscious structure and can ultimately completely subvert the project of Eros.

Suicide is the paradigm of incompletion, since the subject is driven to withdraw from life before the end determined by nature or destiny. Notwithstanding everything that has been said, argued and written about it, its mystery has not been exhausted. When the suicidal individual is on the verge of committing the terminal act, then one can only surmise that he must be floundering in the most impenetrable darkness, under the influence of the most irrevocable and implacable vision of his situation. His suffering is such that, being unable to imagine any respite or hope of alleviation, he equates his sense of being closed in with the trajectory of his life. There are good reasons for suspecting psychic murder here. Psychopathological studies of suicide have noted the link between suicide and the subject's sense that time has stopped and become lifeless, long before his actual death. But this can still be interpreted as a defence. Stopping time is a way of controlling what is uncontrollable, of preventing pain from getting worse and one's self-image from becoming even more hateful. Putting an end to time is a way of avoiding a rapid descent into the abyss, which is worse than death, and of resisting an unremitting decline. Suicide may be seen, then, as putting an end to time in order to fend off the terror of what is even worse.

What is worse, more terrifying than any other danger? One cannot imagine all the possible torments assailing someone who decides to cut his life short.

Two ideas come to me here. According to Freud, analysis is interminable – and thus indefinitely unfinished – due to the repudiation of femininity in both sexes. If I try to interpret the meaning of such a statement today, I make sense of it by linking the feminine with the idea of passivity – even though these terms are far from being synonymous. And Freud's clarification 'in both sexes' becomes intelligible when one considers that both sexes have a woman – the mother – as their first object, on whom they depend absolutely. The repudiation of 'passivity' could signify, then, the fear of returning to a situation of total dependence on the mother.[15] This would be the ultimate regression, the antechamber of a kind of annihilation of any personal will. Thus what was once evocative of the lost paradise of childhood here takes on an infernal colouring. Is it a question of avoiding a situation where the imposition of the mother's will alone abolishes any form of initiative which gives the subject the feeling he exists? Or is it a question of avoiding the danger of living a relationship that is felt to have been excessively bad? Or should one think, on the contrary, that this fear of going so far down the path of regression coincides with the fear of repeating what may have been suffered when separation from the primary object occurred, as well as the sense of dereliction which was felt at its loss. Or, alternatively, as a last hypothesis, perhaps we are dealing here with a colossal counter-investment which negates the most exquisite joys that man has ever experienced? These remain open questions.

The other thought that comes to me is this. In his article 'Fear of Breakdown',[16] Winnicott contends that the feared catastrophe has already been experienced (without reaching its term), and that, in fact, what is feared is its return – that is, the prevailing feeling at the time that no object was reliable and capable of 'holding' the child, who thus felt he was falling for ever in a void. The hypotheses of Freud and Winnicott seem to me to coincide. They give incompletion a new meaning, since it is such an outcome that has to be delayed, or even compensated for, by giving oneself the illusion that one is able to decide for oneself, avert a disaster, or escape from it. But, owing to a reversal of the balance of forces, induced by despair, it is precisely by means of an act which decrees once and for all the suspension of any continuation that by ending his life the subject has preferred the incompletion of life (identified here with distress) by putting an end to it prematurely. Suicide can be regarded as the repetition of a situation restraining one from rushing into the gaping crack of the earth which, having trembled, opens up in order to engulf you.

P. was the son of a doctor of great renown who had made a name for himself in the non-psychoanalytic treatment of hysterics whom he healed by authoritarian means, as was customary at the time. He had friends who had crossed the bridge separating medicine and psychoanalysis. As a child, P. remembers having been deeply impressed by the sight of patients entering the house, where the surgery was situated, on stretchers, before leaving again on their two feet. He was born during the occupation and the mother had been obliged to hide from the Germans in the provinces on account of her origins. He had therefore only seen his father intermittently and fleetingly in his early childhood. Subsequently, the dissension between his parents had grown constantly, resulting in violent disputes during which the father sometimes resorted to racist arguments against his wife. When P., who until then had been an only child, was about ten, his mother took into their home a boy from among her close relatives who had been made an orphan, and who was presented to him as an example in all matters. When he reached adolescence, his father was in a state of depression. This had long been treated unsuccessfully with the means available at that time, and ultimately proved to be the inaugural manifestation of Alzheimer's disease. The illness developed slowly, but in the most catastrophic manner, resulting in a lamentable decrepitude and growing impotency. What is more, he was hospitalised in a nursing home abroad, which meant his family was only able to visit him intermittently until his death. P. had kept a good memory of his father during his childhood years, even though their relations were quite distant. From time to time he accompanied his father when he went hunting and had a feeling of complicity with him. So the memory of his father in a state of physical and mental decline, walking with his nurse at his side, did not fail to make a most distressing impression on him. Although he did not go through a marked period of mourning, he was very affected by this loss.

He was highly intelligent, but from university on his behaviour was characterised by failure and abdication. One day, in a philosophy exam, he wanted to hand in a blank copy and leave the hall prematurely. The assistant, who was invigilating, and who knew him, stopped him, obliging him to stay at his table and to write something; of course, he got an excellent mark, but one does not always benefit from such fortunate circumstances.

His father had left him an inheritance, which meant he had a lot of money at his disposal. He proved incapable of finding a profession and led a dissipated life related to alcoholism, which various therapies were unsuccessful in curbing. He had been followed by several psychotherapists who had dropped him after a few months. They had been recommended by a family friend, a psychoanalyst, who, knowing him too well, could not take him into care himself.

Soon it was my turn. This same colleague, who had been my teacher, referred him to me. Having established a relationship with P. which seemed to me to be better than those he had had hitherto, and once I felt he was interested by what was happening in the therapy, I took the risk – one I would probably not take today – of suggesting he use the couch, while reassuring him of my presence by making regular interpretations. I was then able to witness the unfolding of a highly defended homosexual transference, as well as the appearance, in his relationship with the young woman he was seeing, of pathological jealousy. Soon his behaviour became so unbearable that the young woman with whom he was living had a relationship with another man, abroad, and divided her time between these two lovers, all the while remaining very attached to him and very touched by the intensity of his anxiety. In addition, the conflicts with his mother intensified and their relations were somewhat reminiscent of those his father had had with her. When I took him into treatment, he was already divorced from a woman who bore the marks of an oedipal choice, and he was the father of a little girl whom he cherished enormously. He was obliged, very reluctantly, to entrust her education to his own mother, which gave him the feeling that his daughter would be subject to the same errors of which he considered himself to have been the victim. Soon he began missing sessions more and more frequently, and eventually broke off the treatment. After a two-year interval, he came back to see me in what seemed to me to be a worse state. I recommended that he continue with someone else. It was a gross error, I realise – no doubt due, in large measure, to my counter-transference; and, partly, too, to circumstances which left me no other choice. He did not follow up my suggestion. He continued to remain in contact with me, telephoning me from time to time at the most unpredictable hours, sometimes even in the middle of the night, no doubt in a state of great anxiety: 'Green? This is P. How are you? How are you doing?' Conversation of a rather general nature followed. When I had the possibility, and when I felt he 'needed it', I told him to come and see me, giving him an appointment as soon as possible. I noticed his progressive deterioration. He had a glazed look in his eyes, a sallow complexion, and lit his cigarette with the butt of the previous one. He said, 'I'm not smoking, I'm bottle-feeding.' Following a serious accident, he had his driving licence taken away and he was hospitalised in order to dry out. There were worrying signs that he might be developing polyneuritis. Once he was out, he came to see me in this pseudo-friendly mode, but refused any form of ongoing therapy – and I think I was included in this rejection. He still had no professional activity, though he expressed a certain interest to his close friends in avant-garde theatre, and was still capable of speaking in a brilliant, but disconnected way, on this subject. He told me that he had made a decision. If, in the future, he found that he was unable to walk, as result of the onset and development of the polyneuritis threatening him, he was determined to disappear. Under no circumstances, he told me, would he tolerate being reduced to the condition of a baby. That he drank like a toddler was something he could accept about himself, on the condition that he had his autonomy and that he was free to come and go. But once again to be a prey to mothering – never! I was, of course, attentive to the over-determination that was pushing him towards this outcome. How could I not have in mind the terminal dementia of his father walking with short steps, dependent on his nurses – a tragic evocation of a man who, in his childhood, had incarnated the image of the hunter, the thaumaturge and magician who made the dying stand on their feet again and gave them back their faculty of mobility? 'Stand up and walk!' How, after what his transference had revealed of his homosexuality, would I have not seen the link between his phantasised paralysis and that of his father's patients? But all these causes hinted at his uncontrollable and irremediable dependence on alcohol, his incapacity to acquire autonomy, his way of hanging on the object which was only equalled by his way of taking flight, when he did not provoke the other to do so first. Basically, it was as if all the earlier pathological behaviour patterns had been characterised by incompletion, leading up to the event that was going to provoke the end of his regressive process.

One day, when he was out walking, a car grazed him. He inter-preted the incident as the result of a loss of his reflexes. Interpreting this as a sign that the polyneuritis was setting in, he went to a gunsmith, bought a gun 'for shooting big game', entered a bistro – no doubt to drink his last beer – with his gun wrapped in newspaper, shut himself in the toilets and then shot himself through the mouth. In so doing, he had stopped the regressive process which was taking him back to the initial stages of his life by a symbolic act in which several meanings were condensed.

Had time stopped? Yes. But behind him even more than ahead of him. Incompletion can serve to fend off the worst – the worst thing being to relive the beginnings as an ultimate completion.

*

After exploring the fields of artistic creation, scientific discovery, and psychopathology, we have seen in the transference an ontological figure of incompletion, and finally, in suicide – which is perhaps outside the scope of clinical analysis – its most paradoxical outcome. Nothing would be further from my intentions than to conclude by opposing a salutary incompletion that is promising and open, and a state of incompletion seen as a symptom of helplessness. Even if, at first sight, things may look like this on the surface, the manifes-tations of incompletion can only be classified in this way if one refuses to analyse them thoughtfully. Incompletion is neither a fixed state nor an isolated entity; and the mere evocation of the word shows that it is a notion that must be evaluated in terms of its relation to the movement of time. Since that which is unfinished cannot be dissociated from the idea of a goal to be reached or an end point towards which a process tends, how can it be thought of inde-pendently of this horizon, which lies beyond it, however much it remains in the state of pure virtuality? It is, then, the way we fill this future that has not been realised which retro-acts on what is unfinished. In other words, the idea of incompletion cannot be confined to a situation in which the course, the process of something which, in one way or another, still had possibilities ahead of it, comes to a stop. This being so, the problem ceases to concern incom-pletion alone, and becomes one of the relations between completion and incompletion. Any positive or negative qualification can become subject to a reversal; so, rather than staying with those cases in which one of the two terms can be seen slipping into its opposite,

I would prefer an approach which sets out to evaluate their mutual relationship. What does this mean? Certainly not that we should adopt an attitude of sceptical relativism which would invite us to think that everything is possible as well as its contrary. This is what is suggested, perhaps, by defending the idea that incompletion, far from being the symptom of an incapacity is, on the contrary, the sign of an infinite availability, careful never to impede – something that always happens too quickly – the accommodation of that which is still to be; and, that conversely, far from marking the culmination of a fruitful work, the traditional values associated with completion are a sign of the premature closure of a discourse which still has something to say. One would end up by being immobilised by uncertainty, always fearful of coming to a conclusion, of whatever kind. One of the two terms of the alternative always seems capable of prevailing over the other. The relations of the couple, thus exposed, are not simple. We are not dealing here with an ordinary pair of opposites, placing the accent now on one, now on the other. Nor should we conceive of their relationship in terms of Freud's contrasting pairs. For, as we have seen in many different ways, what determines this relationship is its relation to time.

Though the psychoanalytic conception of time still has many shortcomings, one thing is, however, certain: under no circumstances can an exclusively linear conception of temporal development resolve the questions at issue. But one cannot simply turn one's back on it either. What causes the difficulty is that such a psychological experience really does exist and – it hardly needs stating – is the first intuitive apprehension, as well as the most resistant to examination, of conscious psychic manifestations. The problems begin when one tries to conceive of the relations between this fact of conscious life and everything else that can be learnt from investigating the psyche – with which we can link up the alternative completed-uncompleted – revealing the existence of other models of functioning (retroactive meaning, repetition, the timelessness of the unconscious, and so on). The exposition of a conception representing all these aspects will have to be left for another occasion.[17] Nevertheless, it is already possible to subsume them under the umbrella of a path of development oriented by the arrow of time, to which both completion and incompletion belong (in fact, only completion is to be taken into consideration here, as incompletion is just one of its forms). This conception will be contrasted with another that transcends this outlook marked exclusively by its orientation towards an end, surpassing the limitations of the earlier vectorisation. This, I think, is what is suggested by the couple progression-regression, all aspects of which deserve full consideration. Freud was the first to recognise it, in the context of dreams, in the model presented in chapter VII of the *Traumdeutung*. Let me remind you of it: during sleep, a certain number of ideas try to make their way towards the motor pole, with the aim of becoming acts. The shutting down of this pole obliges these thoughts to regress, taking the form of visual memories. Instead of experiencing the fulfilment that would give them access to motricity – the completion of conscious activity – they make a virtue of their incompletion and, under the influence of the dream work, are fulfilled in a different way and obey other exigencies than those of conscious life. Though psychoanalysts are very familiar with this, not enough importance is given to the fact that the starting point of the dream is to be found in the refusal of a certain number of excitations to be abolished when the ego regresses, leaving a residue of excitations linked to wishful phantasies repressed during the waking state which sleep cannot overcome. But as a consequence, during the waking state, that is, when progression is in full swing, some elements will have a tendency towards retro-gression retroactively. The duality pro-gression and retro-gression cannot be limited to the opposition between the waking and sleeping states. The waking state accepts that discrete formations exist within it, which are not identified as such but will subsequently be organised in a retrogressive mode; and, that sleep will also comprise progressive tendencies – which are also not identifiable as such – transporting ideas towards the destination which, in the waking state, would be considered as the term of their itinerary, ideas culminating in acts.

Whence the notion that, in the couple incompletion-completion, each includes within itself a part of what is constitutive of the other. This, therefore, is why, as I said at the outset, one cannot consider the two senses of *achever* (reaching maturity and dying) as simple determinants affected to a neutral term (the end), but as belonging to their intrinsic nature. Likewise, completion and incompletion should be thought about simultaneously. A consequence of cardinal importance is that, if one accepts, as I have just suggested we should, the solidarity between the two elements of the couple, while also recognising their fundamentally complementary nature (which does not mean to say in equal proportions, but which prohibits any idea of components unaffected by their opposite), and if we subject it to the category of a divided, bidirectional time, we can then hope to get out of the impasse menacing reflection. Here again, the paired structure should not entail the idea of a reciprocal neutralisation of the two elements, blocking the relations between them. This coupled form should give rise to interesting contrary, if not contradictory, relations. Similarly, the defence of bidirectional time does not refer in any way to immobile time. It does not suffice to substitute bidirectional time for oriented time; and it is important never to lose sight of the fact that, what we are dealing with is a conflictual relation between two temporalities: one oriented by the arrow of time and the other which is the timelessness of the unconscious, of which the dream is a dialectical figure. What is more, such conflictuality is itself the expression of the relations between binding and unbinding, as well as between creation and destruction. The reference to life and death is indirect here; for, first of all, it is the life and death of psychic activity that is in question. And when in certain cases – in psychosomatic illnesses for instance – psychic death is involved, one is struck by the similarities that can be noticed in certain psychical organisations marked by still-born intrapsychic associative processes, which, moreover, can be compatible with creative activity, preserved by splitting. We will thus be attentive to the fact that the organisers of the living order are subject to the irreversibility of the arrow of time, but that the human psyche is able to elude it on account of the unconscious. It does not, however, break its ties with what links it to living systems, but transcends certain limits, thereby creating original phenomena.

In considering the domain of creation, we have left on one side those cases where incompletion is due to the author's death. And yet, when we look at the death of certain great figures of cultural patrimony who died when they were still young, we cannot avoid the impression that some of them have paid a heavy price for the temerity of their prospective effort. The fact that we dispose today of better medical and scientific means for preventing death makes us attribute – by a process of simplistic reasoning – the premature deaths of these creators to medical, pathological causes which are thought to have shortened their lives. We do not dare to think that they may have died from something other than the effects of known lethal causes. It is possible to imagine, for instance, that there was no longer anything in them resisting a work of death which resulted in their swelling the ranks of the funeral battalions. And when, subsequently, we mentioned the imposed or voluntary cases of incompletion, we thought that it was impossible to understand them independently of the conflict underlying feelings of pleasure and unpleasure. *Basically*, the state of unpleasure, when it accompanies creative incompletion, is scarcely any different from the neurotic state of unpleasure. The only thing that changes is the relation of these affects with the centrality of the unconscious conflict and its mediations. *Basically*, does not mean that they are identical, but that they depend on the same processes, organised differently. Above all, we realise that creation is not an activity which progresses or stops for no reason; on the contrary, it is at every moment a risky, hazardous activity, each stage of which can lead to a regression which stagnates the process, or even stops it. It assumes the form of a game where, advancing, while it resolves certain formal problems, can lead one to encounter, without being aware of it, the conflictual knot.[18] This resists any subsequent elaboration of what, from a distance, allows creation to emerge from an obscure blend of instinctual forces, unconscious phantasies, and repressed memories of everything that likens them to the day residues endowed with regressive and semantic capacities which will be at the origin of the dream construction.

What are we to say then about those who make incompletion a pattern of behaviour? Anyone who has had the opportunity of frequenting artists cannot fail to be aware of the fact that their major anxiety – no other, even when much more invalidating, is feared more – is that of seeing their creative capacity dry up. It matters little here what the unconscious meaning underlying this anxiety is; let me simply point out, for the moment, that it is their essential preoccupation. Even if their work shows no signs of weakening, they are dogged by their own evaluations of their production. Should one be surprised, then, that they try to ruse with the danger by imposing on themselves a line of aesthetic conduct which tends in this direction? The main point, for them, in acting in this way, is to accumulate a reserve of desires, to compare the association between the finished status of a work and the possible end of all creative activity. For there is a permanent temptation to see a shift occurring which gives a meaning to the idea of what is being completed which brings it closer to the end signalling the exhaustion of creative capacity. So the solution is to seek incompletion. This ruse can be so effective that the unfinished products that they produce sometimes create the illusion that they are even more consummate achievements. This is because incompletion does not involve a refusal to follow the work through to its end; but it is another way of seeing the work or of presenting it to others who then have the onus of determining what its meaning is. Stopping short of any form of accomplishment is a way of averting the anxiety of facing the most unpardonable sanction – one that can only be imputed to oneself; to what one is, even more than to what one does. To preserve one's self-love, all that remains is the prudence that prevents one from falling when one has taken the risk of throwing everything one has into the equation – because one has put one's faith in the project. This is what the artist does again *each time*, and never just once and for all, with the desire not only to finish, but also to ward off the shadow of what he fears, which is that he will never again be able to pursue his quest. And when it is the very ones who defend incompletion who take their preoccupation with finishing what they are producing to extremes, it is as if we were faced with a latent hybris from which emerges the fear of unleashing the anger of a god?

And since we know that there are psychic structures 'beyond the pleasure principle', and that some of them are interpreted by the analyst as a search for the unconscious pleasure of suffering – ferociously denied by those concerned – should we be surprised by the attitude which imposes incompletion as an elected, chosen and acknowledged aim, thereby deflecting the awareness of suffering and making one blind to anxiety? Can one not detect a whiff of superstition here? For no creator, as I have said, ever considers his task to be finished. And he has little need of a theory, or even a justification, of whatever kind, to find reasons for pursuing his work. From the moment he feels the need to create fetishes, which is at the very basis of his creative attitude, it undoubtedly means – notwithstanding all explanations of an artistic order – that some sort of menace is lurking, which is perhaps inseparable from the transgressive process of creation.

The possibility of drifting can therefore apply as much to incompletion, to the point of making one feel the effects of a painful paralysis, as to completion, after the labour has insidiously taken leave of the perilous, fascinating paths along which it had ventured, to become no more than the shadow, or a caricature of its original aim. Where the question of the couple completion-incompletion is concerned, one should not commit the error of mistaking the *act* related to it with the *movement* which sustains, transcends and survives it. Subtle exchanges will take place between the movement and the act. But what we sense about incompletion has no more than an indirect relation with the act: progression and retrogression do not exist without the movement which animates meaning.[19]

Is it possible, on the basis of these reflections, to draw a few conclusions about the vocation of the writings of psychoanalysts? We are obliged to note that psychoanalytic literature has witnessed the blossoming of a great number of genres, from the most poetic to the most prosaic. Questions only arise here because the diverging opinions among psychoanalysts sometimes lead to their adopting positions which are not always free of a sort of moralising prescription concerning either what it is fitting to think or which theory should be adopted. And sometimes there is even an attempt to decree what the 'truly psychoanalytic' way of expressing oneself is. I shall confine myself here, though, to the issue that is of immediate concern to us.

There is no doubt that, within the psychoanalytic movement, there exist dogmatic writings coming from militant groups. There is no need to dwell for long on the content or the form of the ideas they convey – their style is enough to condemn them – even if they are right; for the poison of militantism only succeeds in destroying the portion of truth they may contain, since their movement is only concerned with nourishing their faith. They are in fact closed systems.

Psychoanalytic theory is at once a product of creation, scientific knowledge (even though psychoanalysis is not a science) and clinical experience. The coexistence of these three orders of knowledge acts as a balance for them taken in isolation and gives the ensemble a necessarily open perspective. It is a product of creation owing to the gap between theory and practice which constructs these ideas, at a distance from facts which are always registered by consciousness, but understood according to the co-ordinates of the unconscious. This creation must, however, be clearly distinguished from artistic creations which, though they are rich with a certain knowledge of the unconscious, can do more than point one towards it. This is because the comprehension that they solicit depends on an intuitive correspondence or on a sensibility towards their truth, but not on knowledge, or even recognition, of the unconscious.

For it is necessary for intelligence to discover its sources, aims, thrust and object, indeed everything that has called for the construction of a psychical (theoretical) apparatus, as a fiction that is destined for work which goes beyond the mere effect of resonance. There are many today who think that this language is, in fact, detrimental to the psychoanalyst because of its dangers of sclerosis. It is difficult to see how one can undo the link which ties the advance of knowledge to a set of organised ideas. The psychoanalyst adopts neither the procedures nor the methods of science; but it is perhaps important, nonetheless, not to stop thinking about them, so as to set limits to the potentially arbitrary nature of the creative imagination of psychoanalytic action. It is only too true that in its practice psychoanalysis is similar to art, so it must hold firmly to a mode of thinking which resists formal seduction, the mysterious charms of reading or listening, in order to offer the intellectual progression of ideas a consistency and rigorous conceptualisation whose articulation gives a coherent and convincing image of psychic functioning. Finally, the psychoanalyst's work needs to be related to clinical experience; for, just as much as that of the artist or scientist, it is prone to 'blockages' or 'excesses' (over-achievements), and to driftings against which we are very badly protected. There again, this balance between the artistic, scientific and clinical approaches should prevent the psychoanalyst from lapsing into the excesses of unilateralism.

One cannot pass over in silence the fact that there exists in the current psychoanalytic movement an anti-theoretical tendency which inclines overtly or insidiously towards a psychoanalytic phenomenology. Nothing can resist the incomparable effect of this way of addressing oneself to the minds of those to whom one is speaking, offering them the 'dressed-up' version of what has been perceived, felt and evoked by the psychoanalyst's consciousness. I am speaking here of a phenomenology in the broad sense, going beyond its philosophical meaning. What I am referring to reflects a mistrustful attitude towards ideas, always suspected of putting the seals on what psychoanalytic listening teaches us or of exercising a tyranny of abstraction. '*Ça n'empêche pas d'exister*', Freud had heard Charcot remark. One forgets to add that there is a codicil to this judgement: If only one knew *what* exists! It is not this precaution which is open to criticism but, in my opinion, what is preferred to it. Instead of hegemonic ideas as a means of elucidating the discourse of the unconscious as perceived through the analysand's words, there are those who would prefer another way of expressing things. This 'other way' is just as marked by ideology, even though this is masked.

A false theory can be refuted, amended, rectified and replaced. An absence of theory – where preference is given instead to a certain style – is not a question of completion or incompletion. It is, in fact, 'outside time'; its productions, whether successful or unsuccessful, are only temporary wonders, and, in any case fade as soon as they are finished.

It has often been pointed out that Freud professed to be mistrustful of global systems. Though it is true that the unconscious can only be examined on the basis of fragments, Freud never failed in his duty to give as much order as possible to his discoveries. What was he working on at the moment of his death? Well, on his *Outline of Psychoanalysis*, each line of which only acquires meaning when considered within the context of the whole work, whose aim was clearly to construct a reduced and complete model of psychoanalysis. Freud's capacity for synthesis is stunning for a man of his age. And when did illness force him to stop? At the point when, having just written a particularly substantial chapter on the external world, he was preparing to give an account of the progress of our knowledge about the internal world. This was, I believe, a case of incompletion because, given the novelty of the unusually wide scope of the chapter before, I think that the formulations that he was about to advance contained some disconcerting propositions for readers who were familiar with his ideas.[20]

What better way is there to conclude than to recall the definition in three parts that he himself gave of psychoanalysis in his article in the *Encyclopaedia Brittanica* in 1922. The first two are written in a lucid style and their content is self-evident: they deal with its status as a method and its therapeutic applications. The third is written in a particularly circumspect manner and, for my part, I can see no better way of concluding: psychoanalysis is, then, also the name of 'a collection of psychological information obtained along those lines, which is gradually being accumulated into a new scientific discipline'.[21]

Notes

Chapter 1

1. In an earlier work ('La psychanalyse devant l'opposition de l'histoire et de la structure', *Critique*, no. 194, July 1963), I had begun to tackle the opposition between history and structure, taking as my starting point the debate between Lévi-Strauss and Sartre on diachrony in its relations with structure. Corresponding currents of thought could be found in the psychoanalytic field (so-called genetic psychoanalysis versus structural psychoanalysis) reproducing the same debate. My opinion, which saw this as an illustration of the major questions of the contemporary movement of ideas, seems to have been confirmed by the large number of studies which have since been devoted to it and the positions taken by the main protagonists (see 'J.-P. Sartre répond', *L'Arc*, no. 30: 'A dominant tendency [in the attitude of the young generation] at least, for the phenomenon is not a general one, is the rejection of history ... But structuralism, as it is conceived and practised by Lévi-Strauss, has contributed considerably to the current discreditation of history inasmuch as it only applies to already constituted systems – myths, for example'). The different studies that have examined the problem further have taken a variety of directions. Either the authors have contributed to thinking about the contradiction between history and structure in terms of the theoretical systems of Sartre and Lévi-Strauss (cf. P. Verstraeten, *Les Temps modernes*, nos 206–7, July and August 1963, and Jean Pouillon, *L'Arc*, no. 26), or they have dealt with it more or less implicitly within the context of a re-examination of the interpretation of Marx and Marxism (cf. Louis Althusser, '*Pour Marx* and the critique of N. Poulantzas', Paris: Maspéro), or within the framework of the religious hermeneutics of myth (cf. Paul Ricoeur, 'Structure et hermeneutique' *Esprit*, new series, no. 11, pp. 597ff. and the reply of the late L. Sebag: 'Le mythe, code et message', *Les Temps modernes*, no. 226, March 1965); or, it has been studied within the context of a work on the archaeology of human sciences (Michel Foucault (1966), *Les Mots et les Choses* [*The Order of Things*, 1970]). This dispersion is evidence of the general nature of the problem; but it is more apparent than real. Is it not still pivoted on the socio-anthropological point of view? And if linguistics was, and remains, one of the essential poles of the discussion, it is inasmuch as it is regarded as a social science (Greimas, 'La linguistique, science sociale, s'il en est ...'). Similarly, the concept of history is still linked up with its collective expression: the history of societies, modes of communication and ideas. While the recent article by Greimas, 'Structure et histoire', *Les Temps modernes*, no. 246, November 1966, has the merit of tackling the problem head on, it clearly shows that the confrontation remains confined to historians, sociologists and linguists. It is as though the impact of the opposition between structure and history did not concern

the subject, whom one is nonetheless obliged to refer to from time to time (as a 'translinguistic' subject, ibid., p. 825). The merit of this work is that it no longer confines the problem within an irreducible opposition. It has no doubt been left to psychoanalysts to deal with this aspect of the problem, as they are in a privileged position to do so. However, psychoanalysts are not very inclined to join in the debate. A recent gathering (Congress for Psychoanalysts Speaking Romance Languages, 1964, *Revue française de psychanalyse*, 1966, XXX, nos 5–6), devoted to the examination of genetic psychoanalysis, enabled us to become aware of the complexity of the concept of history in Freud and the divergences of opinion to which his interpretation gives rise today. It is not possible to summarise these discussions here. I refer the reader to the reports presented by R. Loewenstein and E. and J. Kestemberg. It is worth drawing attention, though, to a potential source of confusion in the text of these authors: they refer to psychoanalysts who espouse Hartmann's conceptions as structuralists, though his conceptions have nothing to do with anthropological or linguistic structuralism.

2. 'The disappearance or, as Lacan says, the de-centring of the subject, is linked to the discrediting of history' (*L'Arc*, no. 30, p. 91, 1966).

3. And, to a certain extent, collective (cf. *Totem and Taboo* [1912–13] *S.E.* XIII, and *Moses and Monotheism* [1939] *S.E.* XXIII, pp. 1–137).

4. Here we are merely witnessing a re-hash of the argument – even though it seemed to have served its time – that what the psychoanalyst infers from the material derived from observing neurosis only has meaning within the framework of psychopathology. The neurotic has no history; the normal man has one. Psychoanalysis, then, can tell us nothing about history; so it is not surprising to find it among the components of this structuralist movement. It is as if the contribution of psychoanalysis could be reduced to its interpretation of illness and did not concern the general nature of human psychic activity. Are dreams, Freudian slips, parapraxes and fantasies restricted to neurosis? I will not mention the Oedipus complex, since Sartre thinks he has been lucky enough to escape it (*The Order of Things*). See A. Green, 'Des mouches aux mots' in *La déliaison*. Paris: Les Belles Lettres, 1992 [note added in 1999].

5. Greimas, 'Structure et histoire' perhaps it is not a coincidence that this author, who attaches great importance to the structural semantics of psychoanalysis, particularly in the chapter on 'actant' models, feels concerned by the problem. Nevertheless, Greimas wishes to 'go beyond' – a never-ending argument – Freudian psychoanalysis.

6. See note 1.

7. See B. Brussset (1992) *Le développement libidinal*. Paris: Presses Universitaires de France (Que sais-je?).

8. Letter dated 6 December, 1896. J.M. Masson (ed.) (1985) *The Complete Letters of Sigmund Freud to Wilhelm Fliess, 1887–1904*, pp. 207ff. London: The Belknap Press.

9. S. Freud (1923b) *The Ego and the Id. S.E.* XIX, pp. 3–66.

10. Though quite recently certain discoveries (apoptosis) plead in favour of cellular suicide. See J.C. Ameisen (1999). 'Le suicide cellulaire ou la mort créatrice'. *La sculpture du vivant*. Paris: Le Seuil [note added in 1999].

11. Cf. *Totemism Today*, trans. R. Needham. Merlin, 1964. (*Le totémisme aujourd'hui*, Presses Universitaires de France, 1962.)
12. *S.E.* XXIII, p. 43.
13. Translator's note: this article was written at a time when the two concepts *coupure* and *suture* were widely used in French epistemological circles, the former standing in opposition to the latter. As there is most probably an allusion to castration involved, we have translated this term as the 'cut'; otherwise, usually translated as 'break', as in an 'epistemological break'.
14. J. Lacan (1977) *Ecrits: A Selection*, p. 52. Translated by Alan Sheridan, London: Routledge.
15. J. Laplanche and J.-B. Pontalis, *The Language of Psychoanalysis*, trans. D. Nicholson Smith, London: Hogarth Press, 1973.
16. E. Jones (1957) *The Life and Work of Sigmund Freud*, vol. 3, p. 445. New York: Basic Books.
17. 'Our attention is first attracted by the effects of certain influences which do not apply to all children, though they are common enough – such as the sexual abuse of children by adults, their seduction by other children (brothers or sisters) slightly their seniors, and, what we should not expect, their being deeply stirred by seeing or hearing at first hand sexual behaviour between adults (their parents) mostly at a time at which one would not have thought they could either be interested in or understand any such impressions, or be capable of remembering them later.' *An Outline of Psychoanalysis*, *S.E.* XXIII, p. 187.
18. It should be added here that Freud saw in these phylogenetic contents of the superego the specificity of the human species. He refused to attribute this specificity to the structure of the human ego, inasmuch as the latter can be distinguished from the id for example. The ego–id differentiation does not qualify man but more rudimentary organisms. It is the human superego, itself born of the experiences linked to totemism, that is thus seen as the foundation of human life (see *The Ego and the Id*, *S.E.* XIX p. 37ff). Is there not a similarity here between Freud's view and the conclusions of Leroi-Gourhan on the existence of a 'religion' in prehistoric man? It is necessary, though, to be clear about the sense that Leroi-Gourhan lends to the word religion (which he declines to distinguish from magic on account of the lack of objective data): 'it is purely founded on the manifestations of preoccupations that seem to go beyond the material order' (*Religion de la préhistoire*, p. 5); 'showing evidence of a behaviour which surpasses vegetative life' (ibid., p. 143). This should be sufficient to pre-empt any eventual criticism for introducing, *a priori*, spiritualist elements. The main issue is to explain the link between the material order and the symbolic order. It is certainly no coincidence that this 'religion' expresses itself primarily on the basis of data concerning death and graphic symbolism. That graphic symbolism draws on the representation of the difference between the sexes comes as no surprise to the psychoanalyst.
19. Cf. his correspondence with Jones on this subject and his justification for maintaining his thesis in spite of the invalidating arguments of science presented in *Moses and Monotheism*.

20. In *On Narcissism: An Introduction*. *S.E.* XIV, p. 78.

21. The lines that follow develop a line of thinking centred on anaclisis, even though the word is not pronounced [note added in 1999].

22. I am leaving aside here the aspect mentioned above concerning the loss of the object of satisfaction which makes all repetition impossible, *stricto sensu*, and bars desire.

23. Letter, dated 10 January 1910. *Psychoanalysis and Faith. The Letters of Sigmund Freud and Oskar Pfister*, p. 31. Eds Heinrich Meng and Ernst L. Freud. Trans. E. Mosbacher, London: Hogarth Press and the Institute of Psychoanalysis, 1963. I refer the reader to the theme of repetitive scansion in a previous article (*Critique*, no. 194, 1963).

24. 'In my first crude attempt, made at a time when I was still trying to take the citadel by force, I thought it depended on the age at which the sexual trauma occurred – the person's age at the time of the experience [an allusion to the letter of 20 May 1896]. That I gave up long ago ...'. (Letter of 9 December 1899. J.M. Masson ed. [1985]. *The Complete Letters of Sigmund Freud to Wilhelm Fliess, 1887–1904*. London: The Belknap Press.)

25. Cf. S. Freud (1937b). 'Constructions in Analysis'. *S.E.* XXIII, pp. 255–69.

26. J.A. Miller, 'La suture'. *Cahiers pour l'analyse*, no. 1, pp. 39–51. Paris: Le Graphe.

27. C. Lévi-Strauss (1967) 'La notion de structure en ethnologie'. *Sens and usage du terme structure*. Mouton: La Haye.

28. To which Jacques Derrida devoted an insightful commentary (cf. 'Freud and the Scene of Writing', in *Writing and Difference*. Trans. Alan Bass, London: Routledge & Kegan Paul, 1978). In my text, the terms 'spacing' and 'difference' were suggested by my reading of this commentary.

29. This point needs clarifying, for things are not like this if one looks at things more closely. Cf. my article 'Primary Narcissism: Structure or State?', in *Life Narcissism, Death Narcissism* (2001). Trans. Andrew Weller. London: Free Association Books.

30. *Moses and Monotheism*. *S.E.* XXIII, pp. 1–137.

31. Sebag gives no value to the distinction conscious–unconscious.

32. 'Le mythe: code et message' (in *Les Temps modernes*, March 1965, no. 226, p. 1605). See also A. Green, 'Le mythe: un objet transitionnel collectif', republished in *La Déliaison*. Paris: Les Belles Lettres, 1992 and Hachette, 1998 [note added 1999].

33. A.J. Greimas (1970, 1983) *Du sens*. Vols I and II. Paris: Le Seuil.

34. J. Derrida (1967) *De la grammatologie*. Paris: Minuit.

Chapter 2

1. Sophocles (1962) *Antigone, Oedipus the King, Electra*, p. 62. Trans. H.D.F. Kitto. Oxford World Classics, Oxford University Press.

2. Ibid., p. 63.

3. On several occasions, in his *Studies on Hysteria*, Freud exculpates the father by attributing the seduction to the uncle, something he was to rectify in later editions.

4. F. Gantheret (1988). 'Habemus Papam!' *Nouvelle Revue de psychanalyse*, 38, pp. 61–70, letters dated 8 and 11 February 1897.

5. Crimes (parricide and incest) have already occurred in Sophocles' play; moreover, their theatrical presentation on stage refers the spectator to a story that was thought to be true, or one that had been so in heroic times.
6. Myth is a story circulating in the community which is no more than the object of suppositions: 'It is said that ... .'
7. M. Delcourt 'Oedipe ou la légende du conquérant'. Psychanalyse à la Université, 1983, vol. 8, no. 32, pp. 633–52.
8. A. Green (1992b) 'Oedipe, Freud et nous'. La déliaison. Paris: Les Belles Lettres.
9. S. Freud (1937a) 'Analysis Terminable and Interminable'. S.E. XXIII, p. 245.
10. Translator's note: Green uses the standard French translation of the German term Nachträglichkeit. Strachey's usual translation was 'deferred action', but this term is felt now by many to be unsatisfactory. I have opted here for the term 'retroactive meaning', that is, the attribution of meaning, retroactively, to an earlier event. Jean Laplanche has also proposed the English neologism 'afterwardsness'.
11. K. Obholzer (1981) Entretiens avec l'Homme aux loups. Trans. Romain Dugas, Paris: Gallimard.
12. S.E. XI, p. 83.
13. M. Detienne (1981) L'invention de la mythologie. Paris: Gallimard.
14. Ibid., p. 93.
15. S.E. XVII, p. 97.
16. Without necessarily agreeing on its corollories. The drawback of this theorisation is that it makes no distinction between maternal seduction (already described by Freud, moreover: the mother is the child's first seducer, he says in the Outline) and seduction experienced as a trauma, introducing, among others, the economic point of view.
17. G. Dumézil (1952) Les dieux des Indo-Européens. Paris: Presses Universitaires de France. My italics.
18. Ibid., p. 95. [Citation from The City of God.]
19. J. Laplanche and J.-B. Pontalis (1964) 'Fantasme originaire, fantasme des origines, origines du fantasme'. Les Temps modernes, no. 205, pp. 1833–68.
20. S.E. XVII, p. 119.
21. S. Freud (1987) A Phylogenetic Phantasy – Overview of the Transference Neuroses. Cambridge, MA: Harvard University Press.
22. S.E. XIV, p. 195.
23. Ibid., p. 119.
24. In Paula Aulagnier's work, though, the conception 'primal' refers to primitive forms of psychic development with the pictogram.
25. Page 238. Trans. Alan Sheridan. London: Routledge, 1999. First published as Le Discours vivant, Paris: Presses Universitaires de France, 1973. This work was presented in the form of a report entitled 'L'affect' read to the Congress of Romance Languages in 1970 and published the following year in the Revue française de psychanalyse.
26. B. Juillerat (1992) Oedipe chasseur, vers une ontologie. Presses Universitaires de France. I should point out, in passing, that there is a large area of consensus between my own views and those of the author who believes

- which is rather rare for anthropologists – in the dialogue between anthropology and psychoanalysis [note added in 1999].
27. A. Green (1986) 'Réponses à des questions inconcevables'. *Topique*, 37, pp. 11–30.
28. See Freud's letter to Fliess dated 21 December 1899. 'Buried deep beneath all his phantasies, we found a scene from his primal period (before twenty-two months) which meets all the requirements and in which all the remaining puzzles converge', p. 391.
29. It seems to me, although I am not sure, that the concept of *prégnance* recently advanced by René Thom could find an echo here.

Chapter 3

1. *The Complete Letters of Sigmund Freud to Wilhem Fliess, 1887–1904*, p. 207. Translated and edited by J.M. Masson. London: The Belknap Press, 1985.
2. S. Freud (1914a) 'Remembering, Repeating and Working-Through'. *S.E.* XII, p. 147.
3. It would be necessary to cite the text in full. I am referring to the translation of Laplanche and Pontalis. Cf. S. Freud *Essais de psychanalyse*. Paris: Petite Bibliothèque Payot, 1981, pp. 51ff.
4. On this point, though, we can note that Freud made a denial in order to affirm the ordinariness of the situation, with a view to defending a mechanism that has nothing exceptional about it.
5. Interjection. *Littré*: 'Grammatical term. A part of the discourse expressing the passions, such as pain, anger, joy; a word that is uttered abruptly, which bursts out, as it were, in spite of ourselves, and which the passions wrench from us.' The connection with affect should be noted here. *Le Robert*: '(13th cent. from the Latin *interjectio(n-)* "interpose", from *jacere* "to throw")'. Grammar; 'Invariable word, capable of being employed alone, and as such (Lat. "interjectus") inserted between two terms of the utterance ... in order to express in a lively manner an attitude of the speaking subject' (Marouzeau). 'Strictly speaking, an interjection, which is as unintellectual as possible and always clear by virtue of the circumstances and tone, is, in a way, formless. But, by studying interjections, one can see the transition from the cry to the sign, from the *animal reflex* to *human language*' (Brunot and Bruneau, *Grammaire historique*, para. 418). I am employing the term interjection here in spite of the fact that Freud rejected it, saying that the 'mother and the writer of this present account were agreed in thinking that this was not a mere interjection' on account of its meaningfulness. But we have just seen that meaningfulness is not absent from the interjection. Along with Freud, I want to stress this meaningful and symbolic value by giving this term an even wider meaning. In my opinion, what we have here is an inter-jection because it unites the child and the mother with the wooden reel in a significant way. In the relation uniting him with the wooden reel, the child combines the cry with the act and with the object's appearance-disappearance. The interjection provides the vocal *analogon* for the throwing of the wooden reel (its pro-jection) and for the action which brings it back, just as this *analogon* accompanies the observation of the absence

and presence of the object. The expressive utterance is thrown between these operations, just as it is thrown between the child and those around him who witness what has been accomplished.

6. But the specific characteristic of this functional unity is that multiplicity is involved at all levels: multiplicity of the elements of the montage, of the parts involved (the child and the wooden reel, the child's relationship with the adults who pick up his toys, and with his mother), of the situations evoked (the game as a game and as a representation of his mother's departures and returns).

7. 'He compensated himself for this, as it were, by himself staging the disappearance and return of the objects within his reach' (S. Freud (1920) *Beyond the Pleasure Principle*, Chapter II. *S.E.* XVIII, p. 15).

8. This abreaction can be found in an analysand who escapes the distressing situation of the transference by attempting to fulfil his wish to become the analyst himself.

9. Unless I am mistaken, this is the first time I have introduced this term into my theoretical vocabulary [note added 1999].

10. The objection will no doubt be made that what makes the game possible is that it is invested with meaning, and that, logically, the meaning cannot be expressed *nachträglich*, after the event. At the most it could be argued that the unconscious meaning can only be revealed in a differed fashion. But is this really so, and are we not prisoners of a reflective tradition? And what if the meaning were only the justification for the phantasy? And the phantasy itself – is it not conditioned by meaning? It will be seen that I believe that the phantasy can only be meaningfully invested after it has been constituted.

11. It is worth recalling here Jean Cocteau's words: 'Since these mysteries are beyond us, let's pretend that we are the ones who organise them.'

12. In fact, with respect to the totality, the compulsion to repeat has an ambiguous function. To the extent that it strives to reconstitute the ensemble that it repeats, it proposes it as a totality. But, because it repeats the ensemble, it does not allow a stoppage, the stasis by which the stabilised totality opposes the change of becoming. The totality can only be expressed as a totalisation in course during the process. This is what the game indicates. Later, we will notice the reasons for this ambiguity in its relations with unity. Each repeated unity presents itself both as memory and as an absolute beginning. Each of these two positions inevitably encounters its limit in the other.

13. This should attract our attention to the role of the mirror in narcissism as a third party between the character (or characters) who is looking at himself and his image. If the child turns towards the mother who is looking at him in her arms, if he tries to catch his mother's image, we need to take account of this surface which is necessary for creating this situation which is both a lure and a copy of reality.

14. Later I proposed the term 'excorporated' to describe the situation [note added 1999].

15. On the other hand, if the bad object is lost, the object is found, since Freud attributes the birth of the object to its unavailability for the subject. The object is known in hate – this locution of Freud's has often,

in my opinion, been misinterpreted. What Freud means, I think, is that it is through hate that the object is known as an object which is henceforth distinct from the ego, ceasing to be at its disposal; but it does not mean that the object thus known is invested with hate. Hate appears because such an object is now a non-possession of the child, the first sign of the subject–object separation. On the contrary, here again, splitting continues between hate ('a determining condition for knowing the object'), and this object. For the object known is necessarily an object to be introjected and, as such, cannot be an object of hate to be vomited. It is precisely because hate makes its return, in spite of the introjection of the object, that what has been excluded outside will have to suffer the same fate again on the inside through repression. When this occurs, it will not be hate alone that is repressed, but everything undesirable entailed in object-investment, that is, sexual violence as well as hate. Accordingly, hate incarnates here a prototype of violence which will be denounced in all the registers where it cannot be contained; that is to say, not only in the expressions of the erotic libido but also in those of the destructive libido.

16. *S.E.* XIX, p. 237.
17. 'An essential component of this experience of satisfaction is a particular perception (that of nourishment, in our example) the mnemic image of which remains associated thenceforward with the memory trace of the excitation produced by the need. As a result of the link that has thus been established, next time this need arises a psychical impulse will at once emerge which will seek to re-cathect the mnemic image of the perception and to re-evoke the perception itself, that is to say, to re-establish the situation of the original satisfaction. An impulse of this kind is what we call a wish; the reappearance of the perception is the fulfilment of the wish ...' (*S.E.* V, p. 565). Thus desire is produced during an experience of repetition by going back over a trace, a fold. The path traced by this fold is a reproduction of the primitive furrow owing to a re-investment aimed at producing perceptual identity. Let me underline the repetition in this text: re-invest, re-evoke, re-establish.
18. In *The Language of Psychoanalysis*, Laplanche and Pontalis point out that we tend to overlook the fact that the ultimate aim of thought-identity is to re-establish perceptual identity. There is no denying this. But, by completing the loop, what has been accomplished is a dissociation of effects between the aim and the process. Achieving the desired result becomes much less important than the manner in which this achievement has occurred. Paraphrasing Freud, I would say that the secondary route (of detour) has acquired a fundamental importance. The introduction of a return in the communication changes not only the structure of the communication but its meaning, opening up a new field ahead. The heuristic value of this result resides less in the 'progress' accomplished than in the dialectical conflict thus made possible between perceptual identity and thought-identity.
19. Concerning the notion of serialisation, cf. Gilles Deleuze, *Logic of Sense*, trans. Mark Lester, ed. C.V. Boundas. New York: Columbia University Press, 1995. (*Logique du sens.* Paris: Editions de Minuit, 1969.)

20. Cf. Jacques Derrida, 'Freud and the Scene of Writing' in *Writing and Difference*, trans. Alan Bass, Chicago: University of Chicago Press; London: Routledge & Kegan Paul, 1978. Originally published in 1967 as 'Freud et la scène de l'écriture', in *L'écriture et la différence*. Paris: Le Seuil. This text was presented for the first time at my seminar at the Paris Institute of Psychoanalysis in 1966 [note added in 1999].

21. J.M. Masson (ed.) *Complete Letters*, p. 207.

22. I would ask the scientifically informed reader to show indulgence here and to bear in mind that the following pages were written in 1970 [note added 1999].

23. In the present situation, the risk of making an error of interpretation seems less important than the dangers of systematic ignorance. At least such errors can be an opportunity for fruitful rectification, whereas the silence shrouding these studies works in favour of unacknowledged speculations which do not even have the merit of being based on scientifically established facts.

24. Cf. *Entretiens sur la sexualité* (Cerisy Colloquium, 1965). Paris: Plon, 1969. In *Beyond the Pleasure Principle*, Freud notes that Darwin held a similar opinion. It is worth noting that in some species certain somatic cells have the possibility of becoming germ cells.

25. E. Wollman, 'La sexualité des bactéries'. *Entretiens sur la sexualité*, Paris: Plon, 1969, p. 10. It should be noted that at this level the descendants of a receptive layer acquire the characteristics inherent to a layer that differs from the first owing to certain hereditary characteristics. In 1964, it was shown that it was possible to observe mechanisms of genetic recombination in bacteria – mechanisms that were thought to be specific to species which reproduce themselves sexually. We must not forget, however, that the cell of a mammal contains a thousand times more DNA than a bacterium.

26. It goes without saying that, here, I am only taking into consideration – in order to clarify the discussion – memory structures, leaving on one side fundamental points of biological organisation: organisers, receivers, enzymes, mediators, hormones and numerous regulating constituents. More recently, light has been thrown on the relations between the nucleus and the cytoplasm, challenging the idea of a genetic whole. [This last sentence was added in 1999.]

27. This problem needs to be distinguished from the heredity of acquired characteristics in that it is by virtue of singular experience that the potentialities acquired become the object of an individual appropriation. What might be facilitated is the transmission of homologous cases of conditioning.

28. It has long been thought that the regulation of sexual processes depended ultimately on nervous structures. In the light of recent works, it would seem that the order of the processes should be inverted: C. Aron refers to studies by F. Bariassov 'which have established beyond doubt that, in the very days following birth, a sexualisation can be observed of the hypothalamic structures which determine hypothyseal activity' (1969, p. 342). H. Charniaux-Cotton points out that 'animals have a sexual gender before they have a nervous system'. This statement is all

the more interesting in that, with certain non-vertebrates which she is studying, the investigation leads her to suppose that the secretions of the androgen gland are not steroids but probably proteins (*Entretiens sur la sexualité*, p. 343). For the relations between emotional life and sexuality, cf. 'Le rhinencéphale dans l'organisation cérébrale' by J. de Ajuriaguerra and C. Blanc, pp. 297–336 in *Les grandes activités du rhinencéphale*. Paris: Masson, 1960.

29. *S.E.* XVIII, p. 257.

30. It has been debated whether DNA reproduces itself or if it gives birth to RNA, which then reproduces itself (messenger RNA, transference RNA) in protein synthesis. Recent studies have demonstrated the existence of self reproduction at the level of DNA.

31. DNA differs from RNA in its location (the first is located in the nucleus, whereas the second is found in the ribosome); in its composition (the pentose of DNA is deoxyribose whereas that of RNA is ribose); in its base (the thymine of DNA is replaced in RNA by uracil); and, finally, the stability of DNA can be contrasted with the greater speed of renewal found in RNA.

32. Following the studies of M. Delbrück, S. Luria and J. Hershey on phages and viruses and the elucidation of the genetic code by M.W. Nirenberg, H. Khorana and D. Hollberg, it seems increasingly likely that we are dealing with a universal system of information that is applicable both to micro-organisms and macro-organisms.

33. The importance of this discovery lies in the fact that it was the fruit of the inventive, rigorous and imaginative spirit of investigators who were not 'specialists' in these matters; in any case, much less so than many of their colleagues. See J. Watson, *The Double Helix*. London: Simon and Schuster, 1968.

34. J. Lamotte and P. L'Héritier (1965) *Biologie générale*, Paris: Dion, p. 86.

35. In a photographic sense.

36. Or of a division as is the case of twins.

37. I am thinking here of the substitution of one of the bases of DNA in RNA, that is, thymine by uracil. This 'normal' difference stands in contrast to the serious anomalies resulting from errors in reading the genetic code.

38. That which separates the two base groups: purine and pyrimidine.

39. The concept of the absent cause was proposed by J.A. Miller. (An echo from Lacan's seminar at L'Ecole Normale which, however, I stopped attending after 1967.)

40. *S.E.* XVIII, p. 39.

41. *The Symposium*, V, 1916.

42. In *Entretiens sur la sexualité* (pp. 305–15), H. Charniaux-Cotton points out that the word 'sex' is probably derived from the Latin verb '*secare*' meaning to cut, separate. For though it is true that what characterises sexuality is a genetic recombination, this presupposes mitosis and fertilisation, constituting the universal cycle of sexual reproduction. However, mitosis is a succession of two cellular divisions of one diploid cell (that is to say, of a cell containing a pair of each chromosome of the species). The second division occurs after a normal mitosis (new

division), the final result of which is to transform the diploid cell ($2 \times n$ chromosomes) into four haploid cells (with n genetic chromosomes) and only comprises one single replication of the genetic material. At all stages, then, we have the following series: the division, reduplication and reconstitution of new units, either from the same half or from two halves, one of which 'resembles the other yet differs from it' – as is the case during fertilisation. It is only at this last stage that, by means of the process of *crossing-over*, random combination occurs through the exchange of segments between similar chromosomes of $2 \times n$ special haploid cells, the male and female gametes. Finally, it is worth noting that hermaphroditism seems to be a manifestation of sexual differentiation (in non vertebrates), disappearing thereafter in vertebrates (these pathological cases excepted). When all is said and done, it would seem that sexuality can be defined in terms of the encounter between *separation-division* and *genetic recombination*, of which the Platonic myth is an allegory. I should add, though, that Plato's myth is much more complex than this, and I am only citing the part of it that concerns my present work.

43. It is worth noting that what scientific truth reveals is – if I dare say so – more mythical than the myth. The intuitive insight of the myth attains a degree of complexity that intuitive imagination would not have produced. In Plato at least. One would have to go back to Empedocles and Heraclitus to find myth placed on the same level as science.

44. I am using the word subject for convenience, in its ordinary sense. I will have occasion to make allusion to it again later with the same meaning.

45. Or, to be more exact, pre-genital.

46. I cannot go into details here which would involve an exposition of the problem of psychosis.

47. *S.E.* XVIII, p. 63.

48. *S.E.* XVIII, p. 63. I will return later to the importance of these remarks in my article 'Sur la discrimination et l'indiscrimination affect-représentation', a paper given at the XXI Congress of the International Psychoanalytic Association in Santiago, Chile. *Revue française de psychanalyse*, 1999b, LXIII, pp. 217–72 [note added 1999].

49. In his article 'Le jeu comme structure' (1947) E. Benveniste shows how myths and rites dislocate the unity of the sacred operation: 'It can be said that play exists when only half of the sacred operation is accomplished by translating the myth alone into words or the rite alone into acts. Moreover, the specific characteristic of play is to recompose fictively the absent half in each of its two forms: in word play one acts as if a factual reality should follow; in bodily play one acts as if it were motivated by a rational reality.' Cited by J. Ehrmann in his excellent study, 'L'homme en jeu', *Critique*, no. 266, pp. 599–607.

50. O. Rank (1932) *Don Juan, une étude sur le double*, p. 104. Trans. S. Lautman, Paris: Denoël and Steele, p. 104. [Translator's note: I have translated this passage from the French as it does not appear in the English version, *The Double: A Psychoanalytic Study*. London: Karnac, 1989.] See my study 'Le double double' in *La déliaison*, Paris: Les Belles Lettres, 1992c.

51. Let us recall that Freud points out in a footnote of a late edition of *The Interpretation of Dreams* that the child enacts a similar game the day before his father was due to leave for the front.
52. J. Lacan (1977) *Ecrits*. London: Routledge, pp. 313–20.
53. This is the term used by Plato: 'Each of us when separated, having one side only, like a flat fish, is but the indenture of a man, and he is always looking for his other half' (*The Symposium*, 191d).
54. 'It is interesting that in connection with early experiences, as contrasted with later experiences, all the various reactions to them survive, including of course contradictory ones. Instead of a decision, which would have been the outcome later.' 'Findings, Ideas, Problems' (1941 [1938]) *S.E.* XXIII, p. 299.
55. *S.E.* XXIII, p. 76.
56. In addition to modern psychoanalytic works, the reader might wish to refer to the commentaries of J. Derrida ('Freud and the Scene of Writing' in *Writing and Difference*, translated by Alan Bass, London: Routledge, 1978) and of G. Deleuze in *Différence et répétition*, Paris: Presses Universitaires de France, 1968, pp. 26–30 and especially pp. 128–53.

Chapter 4

1. Translators note: *'après coup'* is the standard French translation for the German term *Nachträglichkeit*. 'Deferred action' is the usual translation in the *Standard Edition*, but has been the subject of much criticism. The question of which term to use in English is a matter of current debate. What is meant, in any case, is the attribution of meaning, retroactively, to a past event.
2. Raymond Devos.
3. M. Milner (1969) *In the Hands of the Living God*. London: Hogarth Press.
4. To use C. David's expression.
5. Milner, *In the Hands of the Living God*, pp. 253–4.

Chapter 5

1. Translator's note: the complete saying in French is: *'Dis-moi qui tu hantes … et je te dirai qui tu es.'*
2. Resolutely atheistic hermeneutics, I hardly need to add.
3. See A. Green (1995) *La causalité psychique*. Paris: Odile Jacob.
4. Translator's note: the French reads *'une méconnaissance d'une méconnaissance'*; in other words a double misrecognition.
5. G. Cobliner has made a useful study of the relations between Piaget and psychoanalysis in the appendix (pp. 233–71) of *De la naissance à la parole* (R. Spitz). Trans. L. Flournoy, Paris: Presses Universitaires de France, 1968.
6. G. Canguilhem (1968) 'Qu'est-ce que la psychologie?' *Etudes d'histoire et de philosophie des sciences*. Paris: Vrin.
7. Even Melanie Klein, who was very concerned to stay within the field of strictly analytic interpretation, with the neutralty it implies, is not entirely free of normative references. One simply has to refer to *The*

Psycho-Analysis of Children, trans. A. Strachey, London: Hogarth, 1949, p. 12 note 1 and p. 29 note 3, to see this. I do not wish to reproach her, for the question that needs to be asked is the following: since the child has to live in a given cultural environment and needs it in order to be able to grow up and live in it later, can one ever avoid being 'normalising' with him, even if one refrains from being normative?

8.   It is striking that there have been so few studies in the literature on child psychoanalysis on the state of being in love.

9.   Once again, let us turn to Melanie Klein, because she claims to be a purist in the matter. Her claim that the psychoanalysis of children is just as 'pure' a psychoanalysis as that of the adult does not withstand examination. To convince oneself of this, it is sufficient to refer to the first two chapters of *The Psycho-Analysis of Children* where we have a shining illustration of Melanie Klein's interpretative genius. But under what conditions? What we find (pp. 26–7) is an analyst seeking to soothe the child's anxiety, to reassure her, to play with her in the first instance. And then the analyst who is playing by herself while describing what she is doing to the terrified child. She puts a doll to sleep, says that she is going to give it something to eat (themes of the last session), invites the child to choose what food it should be, and then invites her to suck her fingers as if she was trying to make herself fall sleep. The child lies down on the sofa, on the analyst's suggestion, while the latter continues to play with the dolls. It is not only the child's games which take the place of her free associations, but also the games of the analyst who participates in the games which the child cannot play on account of her anxiety, by inducing the material until the point when she introduces the father's penis.

10.   The psychoanalytic community as a whole was not mistaken in rejecting the eventuality of an autonomous status of child psychoanalyst distinct from that of psychoanalyst without a label. The choice was all the more difficult in that the option 'child psychoanalyst' was defended by the daughter of the founder of psychoanalysis.

11.   See the recent stir in psychiatric circles aroused by the law on disabled people.

12.   There are those who will say I am exaggerating. Just to take one example, consult the summary of the last issue of the *International Review of Psychoanalysis* (1978, 5, no. 4). Five articles out of six contain in their title the word 'development' or 'developmental'. Let us refer to the corresponding issue of the *International Journal of Psycho-Analysis*: an article by Emmanuel Peterfreund, 'Some Critical Comments on Psychoanalytic Conceptualization in Infancy' (1978, 59(4), pp. 427–42) does not pull its punches; in his conclusions, he writes: 'I have attempted to demonstrate that many typical psychoanalytic characterizations of early infancy have no logical foundation, little basis in observation, and are not truly useful for any theory about the infant's world' (p. 440). The author concludes that psychoanalytic theorisations concerning the child, to the extent that they come within the general psychoanalytic framework, have no meaning in other frames of reference such as neurophysiology, biology, the theory of evolution, or informational models. The author taxes them

with being adultomorphic and pathocentric. Margaret Mahler, from this
point of view, is a dangerous speculator. Needless to say, the author
thinks that salvation will come from the disciplines cited above. We are
slipping from the unconscious towards the 'evolutionist continuum' and
'psychophysical parallelism', that is, the reference to the central nervous
system. Hence the path to be followed, he argues, is neurophysiology,
ethology and, of course, 'the theories of Piaget and contemporary
psychology in general'. (Since this article was written, the situation has
got worse – the contingent of 'scientists' having increased in size [note
added in 1999].) Peterfreund is not alone in his genre; far from it. The
works of D. Freedman and S. Furst, just to mention two, tend in the same
direction. But what needs to be emphasised is their power of contami-
nation. Thus Harold Blum, who directed with tolerance and openness
the conference on symbol formation at the Congress of the International
Psychoanalytic Association in 1977 in Jerusalem, where Guy Rosalato
and Hanna Segal presented respectively a Lacanian and Kleinian point of
view on this theme, published in the same issue a paper on symbolism
entitled 'Symbolic Processes and Symbol Formation', in which the developmental point of view, the autonomy of the ego, and the notion of
adaptation dominate. Here again, Piaget is drawn on to make up for what
is supposed to be missing in Freud and demonstrates a less realistic point
of view: 'Before turning to some important psychoanalytic developmental studies, I shall refer to the very valuable work of Piaget (1951) on
the origins of symbolism' (article cited p. 461). The preliminary question
of the compatibility of Freud's and Piaget's theoretical systems is not even
raised. The concordance is taken for granted, even if some divergences
exist. Yet the discordance between Lacan, Rosolato and Freud is
underlined. It is necessary, however, to find a better ally than Piaget if
one wants to make a critique of Lacan. And though help is finally found
by drawing on Winnicott, it is, above all, for the purpose of clarifying
chronology: the Winnicottian symbol emerges in the second semester
of life; gestual negation, according to Spitz, is present at fifteen months,
and the nomination of objects at eighteen ... Chronology serves here as
a protection against any theoretical imagination, with the backing of a
science of observation – whose limits are never pointed out – always
more credible than a metaphorical conceptualisation.

13. An expression used by Freud in order to designate psychoanalytic elucidation.
14. In his book *Le champ des signes* (1978), Roger Caillois argues that one of
the most remarkable elements of the scientific spirit is the taste, or the
quest for implausible truths or of obvious facts that have been veiled or
hidden, 'those which seem at first to defy common sense and accredited
opinions. Between what is plausible and what is obvious, it is the
obvious that must always prevail; that is, the well-established coherence
of an ensemble of extremely wide-ranging data. If deluded reason or
misleading logic are scandalised by this, it is up to them to reform
themselves. Implausibility is, of course, not a sign of truth, but it must
never lead away from it' (p. 38).

15. For 'infantile' is linked to the most precious possession: 'I swear with my hand on my heart' and is also the stigma of backwardness: 'What an infantile way of behaving'.

16. D.W. Winnicott (1958a) *De la pédiatrie à la psychanalyse*, pp. 310–24. Paris: Payot. ['The First Year of Life', *The Medical Press*, vol. CCXXXIX, no. 6201, 1958, and *The Family and Individual Development*. London: Tavistock, 1965.]

17. Exposed at length in Winnicott's *Therapeutic Consultations in Child Psychiatry*, 1971b, but described as early as 1953; cf. 'Symptom Toleration in Paediatrics: A Case History' in *Through Paediatrics to Psychoanalysis*, chapter IX. London: Karnac, 1958b.

18. In *The Psycho-Analysis of Children* (1932), Melanie Klein does not seem to make any structural difference between instincts, unconscious phantasy, play and dreams. See p. 11 where the relating of a dream of Trude (three years and nine months) receives no particular commentary with regard to its transference value in terms of psychic functioning. Melanie Klein is above all concerned – surprisingly enough – with the child's relationship with reality.

19. It is a pity that Lacan was unable to follow the same path, owing to the distortions he imposed on the analytic setting. These distortions which the neurotic can accept – or even solicit masochistically – are intolerable in borderline cases, or for psychotics who react to them very brutally by breaking with the setting or by breaking off the analysis, when they cannot constitute an 'analytic false-self', which is often the case.

20. Translator's note: a term forged by Lacan which condenses *la haine* and *l'amour*. It is also homophonically evocative of *énamourer*: to be enamoured with.

Chapter 6

1. The clinical material presented during the oral presentation has been suppressed from the definitive version. This work no doubt loses much from this amputation which deprives it of its means of demonstration. The requirements of professional ethics are, however, equally important.

2. M. Proust (1996) *In Search of Lost Time*, vol. 1, p. 51 [*A la recherche du temps perdu*, Pléiade, vol. I, p. 43].

3. Ibid., p. 54 [Pléiade, p. 47].

4. Ibid., vol. 6, p. 223 [Pléiade vol. III, p. 872].

5. Ibid.

6. Cf. A. Green (1982a) 'La réserve de l'incréable' in N. Nicolaïdis and E. Schmid-Kitsikis (eds), *Créativité et/ou symptôme*. Paris: Clancier-Guenaud.

7. Proust, *In Search of Lost Time*, vol. 6, p. 451 [Pléiade, vol. III, p. 1048].

8. The note in French here is: We are familiar with the difficulties of translating the word *insight* which is not the same as *prise de conscience*. 'Introspection' possesses a precise meaning which does not correspond to what is signified by insight. 'Internal vision' is heavy and 'introvision' does not exist. So I am keeping insight.

9. *S.E.* XXIII, pp. 257–8.

10. Cf. my article 'Temps et mémoire' (1990b), *Nouvelle Revue de psychanalyse*, pp. 179–205. See later in this chapter.

11. *S.E.* XII, p. 151.

12. Ibid., p. 154.

13. *S.E.* XVII, p. 94.

14. K. Obholzer (1981) *Entretiens avec L'Homme aux loups*. Trans. from the German by R. Dugas, with a preface by M. Schneider. Paris: Gallimard.

15. Obholzer, *Entretiens*, p. 176.

16. A. Green (1982b) 'Travail psychique et travail de la pensée'. *Revue française de psychanalyse*, XLV, p. 425.

17. M. Gardiner (ed.) (1971) *The Wolf Man by the Wolf Man*. New York: Basic Books.

18. L. Guttieres-Green (1990) 'Problématique du transfer douloureux'. *Revue française de psychanalyse*, LIV, p. 407.

19. 'Use every man after his desert and who should escape whipping?' (*Hamlet*, act II, scene 2).

20. *S.E.* XIV, p. 246.

21. A. Gibeault (1989) 'Destins de la symbolisation', Congrès des psychanalystes de langue française des pays romans, Paris. *Revue française de psychanalyse*, 53, no. 6, pp. 1517–1618.

22. See above.

23. Cervantes (2000) *Don Quixote*, p. 977. Trans. John Rutherford. London: Penguin Classics.

24. Ibid., p. 979.

25. Hence the habitual reference to the direct influence of Brentano does not generally mention that, unlike many other eminent minds of the period, the latter respected Darwin, in spite of his religious convictions. Cf. *Freud* by Peter Gay, London: Anchor, 1988, p. 29. Feuerbach's influence could account for a certain latent Hegelianism in Freud, which later flourished in Lacan's writings.

26. The expression had not yet acquired its definitive meaning.

27. S. Freud (1937b) 'Constructions in Analysis'. *S.E.* XXIII, p. 258.

28. I. Rosenfeld (1988) *The Invention of Memory: A New View of the Brain*. New York: Basic Books.

29. S. Freud, Letter of 6 December 1896. This letter is the principal document for any study on the Freudian conception of memory, as J. Laplanche has understood. (For a detailed analysis see my *The Chains of Eros*, 2000a.)

30. I am alluding here to those theories which, taking Freud literally, conceive of repression exclusively as 'translation', a view he never adhered to himself. The defence of this point of view overlooks the context of this comparison which relativises its significance considerably (cf. *The Chains of Eros*) [note added in 1999].

31. That is to say, after the elaboration of the final theory of the drives and of the second topography.

32. D. Stern (1985) *The Interpersonal World of the Infant*. New York: Basic Books.

33. A. Green (1990a) 'La remémoration: effet de memoire ou temporalité à l'oeuvre', *Nouvelle Revue de psychanalyse*, LIX, pp. 947–72.

34. A. Green (1975) 'Le temps mort', *Nouvelle Revue de psychanalyse*, 11, pp. 103–11.
35. S. Freud (1891) *On Aphasia*. London: International Universities Press, 1953.
36. Here, of course, I am alluding to G. Rosolato's *la relation d'inconnu* or unknown relation (Rosolato [1978] *La relation d'inconnu*. Paris: Gallimard).
37. Translator's note: in italics in the original.
38. Sophocles (1962) *Oedipus the King* (l. 1212). Trans. H.D.F. Kitto. Oxford: Oxford World Classics. [The French and English translations differ slightly. The French reads: *Il t'a retrouvé, le temps qui voit tout.* In English, the passage reads: 'Time sees all, and Time, in your despite, Disclosed and punished your unnatural marriage'.]

Chapter 7

1. Translator's note: the reader should be aware that the French text plays on different possible meanings of the *one* word *achever* which in English may be translated variously, according to the context, as (a) to finish, end (reach an end) or complete; and (b) as to kill, as in finish off.
2. See A. Green (1991b) *Révélations de l'inachèvement*. Paris: Flammarion.
3. Hans Bellmer would have been delighted by this oversight. But it is true that he would have provoked it.
4. H. James (1991) *Le sens du passé*. Trans. John Lee. Paris: Editions de la Différence. [Original title: *The Sense of the Past*, 1917.] The first three books were written in 1899–1900; the fourth in 1914–15, shortly before the writer's death. Léon Edel finds that the work is impregnated with autobiography. And John Lee adds: 'Whatever connections may be established with the man Henry James, it is certain that the writer invested his characters with a problematic and approach similar to his own' (p. 23). Perhaps one can imagine an 'aesthetic counter-transference' when the artist sees emerging from his work the man whom it contains, but who should melt or be dispersed in it and, in all respects, in all senses of the word, be unrecognisable ... even for him.
5. H. James (2001) *Ghost Stories of Henry James*. Ware: Wordsworth Classics. See my analysis of this book in 'Le double fantôme' (1980) pp. 139–55, *Corps et création*, under the direction of J. Guillaumin Lyon: Presses Universitaires de Lyon.
6. Ibid. p. 107. In Book II, the relationship between the two works is indisputable. Though the theme of the relation between the model and its painted translation is treated by James on many occasions, nowhere is it accompanied, as it is here, by the theme of going back in time. James' stay in America in 1905 awakened his desire to reconsider his years of youth. 'The question, however, is with, is of, what I want now, and how I need to hark back, and hook on the past' (H. James (1947) *The Notebooks of Henry James*. Ed. F.O. Mathiessen and K.B. Murdock. Chicago: University of Chicago Press. 29 March 1905, p. 318). According to Edel, the idea of *The Jolly Corner* dates from the beginning of August 1906, one year after his return.

7. *The Notebooks*, p. 367. 'The most intimate idea of *that* is that my hero's adventure there takes the form so to speak of his turning the tables, as I think I called it, on a "ghost" or whatever, a visiting or haunting apparition otherwise qualified to appal *him;* and thereby winning a sort of victory by the appearance, and the evidence, that this personage or presence was more overwhelmingly affected by him than he by *it*. That is what the analogy amounts to ... .' The other side of the coin is that he feels cut *off*, lost.

8. H. James (1990) *Memoirs d'un jeune garçon*. Trans. Christine Bouwart. Paris: Rivages, pp. 274ff. [Original title: *A Small Boy and Others*, 1913.]

9. A. Green (1993a) *Le travail du négatif*. Paris: Minuit. [*The Work of the Negative*. Trans. A. Weller, London: Free Association Books, 1999.]

10. On the other hand, scientific epistemology does not fail to draw attention to problems related to the effect of closure. See the works of F. Varela.

11. A. Green (1991c) 'Méconnaissance de l'inconscient', in *L'inconscient et la science*. Directed by R. Dorey. Paris: Dunod, pp. 140–220.

12. See F. Fogelman-Soulié, *Les théories de la complexité, autour de l'oeuvre de H. Atlan* (1991) Paris: Le Seuil, and E. Morin (1990) *Introduction à la pensée complexe*, Alençon: ESF, 1990.

13. A. Green (1993b) 'L'analité primaire dans la relation anale', in *La névrose obsessionelle*, Monographies de la Revue française de psychanalyse, pp. 61–83.

14. D. Lagache (1952) 'Le problème du transfert', *Revue française de psychanalyse*, XVI, p. 102.

15. It is clear that 'passivity' is better rendered by *Hilflosigkeit*. However, I think that if Freud preferred to emphasise passivity, it was because *Hilflosigkeit* can be overcome with development. There are situations where passivity no longer plays any obvious part, but where its presence can nonetheless be anticipated. Once again, Freud preferred to refer to a constant – even if it was necessary to take into account important modifications – than to invoke a 'primal' cause which is only active at one stage however early it may be. Likewise, recent ideas on the baby's activity from birth on contest this passivity inferred by Freud as well as the possibility of a primary narcissistic state. This, though, is to attach little importance to the original situation of helplessness of which incompletion is the correlate. (I have since clarified the relations between passivity and 'passivation', a situation of helplessness linked to the distress imposed on the child. A. Green (1999a) 'Passivité, Passivation: jouissance et détresse', *Revue française de psychanalyse*, 63(5), pp. 1587–600 [note added 1999].)

16. D.W. Winnicott (1971a) 'Fear of Breakdown'. *International Review of Psychoanalysis*, 1, pp. 103–7.

17. A. Green (2000b) *Le temps éclaté*. Paris: Minuit. [Translated into English as *Time in Psychoanalysis – Some Contradictory Aspects*. London: Free Association Books, 2002.]

18. I have tried to analyse this nucleus in Proust in connection with a maternal nucleus. See my 'La réserve de l'incréable' (1998b) in *La déliaison*. Paris: Hachette, 1998.

19. In *Connaître les sciences cognitives* (trans. P. Lavoie, Paris: Le Seuil, 1988), F. Varela points out that the only organisms to possess a nervous system are those that are endowed with motricity. One could apply this observation to the existence of a psyche which has internalised motricity, and then make the hypothesis that the psyche of man has acquired the property of freeing itself from the limits of irreversible time by attributing bidirectionality to representational movements.

20. I have found a trace of this in the text – also unfinished – of 'Some Elementary Lessons on Psychoanalysis', where he describes how psychoanalytic concepts were becoming increasingly far-removed from ordinary modes of thought. I think that here Freud was anticipating the future. See my *La folie privée* (1991a), chapter 1 [translated as *On Private Madness*, London: Karnac, 1997].

21. S. Freud, *S.E.* XVIII, p. 233.

Bibliography

Ajuriaguerra, de, J. and Blanc, C. (1960) 'Le rhinencéphale dans l'organisation cérébrale', in *Les grandes activités du rhinencéphale*. Paris: Masson.

Althusser, L. (1965) '*Pour Marx* and the Critique of N. Poulantzas'. Paris: Maspéro.

Althusser, L. (1990) *For Marx*. Translated by Ben Brewster. London: Verso.

Ameisen, J.C. (1999) 'Le suicide cellulaire ou la mort créatrice', in *La sculpture du vivant*. Paris: Le Seuil.

Anzieu, D. (1980) *Corps et création: entre lettres et psychanalyse* (under the direction of J. Guillaumin). Lyon: Presses Universitaires de Lyon.

Aron, C. (1969) 'La ponte ovulaire chez les mammifères', in *Entretiens sur la sexualité*, Colloquium of Cerisy. Paris: Plon.

Atlan, H. (1986) *A Tort et A Raison, Intercritique de la Science et du Mythe*. Paris: Editions du Seuil.

Benveniste, E. (1947) 'Le jeu comme structure', *Deucalion*, 2, pp. 161–7.

Blum, H.P. (1978) 'Symbolic Processes and Symbol Formation', *International Journal of Psycho-Analysis*, 59(4).

Borges, J.L. (1941) 'Funes, the Memorious', in *Labyrinths*. Translated by James Irby, 1964. New York: Basic Books.

Brunot, F. and Bruneau, C. (1969) *Précis de la grammaire historique de la langue française*. Paris: Masson.

Brusset, B. (1992) *Le développement libidinal*. Paris: Presses Universitaires de France (Que sais-je?).

Caillois, R. (1978) *Le champ des signes*. Paris: Hermann.

Canguilhem, G. (1968) 'Qu'est-ce que la psychologie?', in *Etudes d'histoire et de philosophie des sciences*. Paris: Vrin.

Cervantes (2000) *Don Quixote*. Trans. J. Rutherford. London: Penguin Classics.

Congress for Psychoanalysts Speaking Romance Languages (1964) XXVI Congres des psychanalystes de langues romanes, *Revue française de psychanalyse* (1966), XXX(5–6); Paris: Presses Universitaires de France.

Delcourt, M. (1994) 'Oedipe ou la légende du conquérant', *Psychanalyse à la Université*, 1983, 8(32), pp. 633–52.

Deleuze, G. (1968) *Différence et répétition*. Paris: Presses Universitaires de France. (*Difference and Repetition*. Translated by Paul Patton. New York: Columbia University Press, 1994.)

Deleuze, G. (1969) *Logique du sens*. Paris: Editions de Minuit. (*Logic and Sense*. Translated by Mark Lester. Edited by C.V. Boundas. New York: Columbia University Press, 1995.)

Derrida, J. (1966) 'Freud et la scène de l'écriture', *Tel Quel*, 26, pp. 10–41. ('Freud and the Scene of Writing', in *Writing and Difference*. Translated by Alan Bass. London: Routledge & Kegan Paul, 1978.)

Derrida, J. (1967) *De la grammatologie*. Paris: Minuit.

Detienne, M. (1981) *L'invention de la mythologie*. Paris: Gallimard.

Dumézil, G. (1952) *Les dieux des Indo-Européens*. Paris: Presses Universitaires de France.

Ehrmann, J. (1969) 'L'homme en jeu', *Critique*, 266, pp. 599–607. Paris: Editions de Minuit.

Fogelman-Soulié, F. (1991) Les théories de la complexité, autour de l'oeuvre de H. Atlan. Paris: Le Seuil.

Foucault, M. (1966) *Les mots et les choses*. Paris: Gallimard. (English translation, *The Order of Things: An Archaeology of the Human Sciences*. London: Tavistock, 1970.)

Freud, S. (1891) *On Aphasia*. London: International Universities Press, 1953.

Freud, S. with Breuer (1895) *Studies on Hysteria*, in *The Standard Edition of the Complete Psychological Works of Sigmund Freud* [hereafter *S.E.*], XXIV vols. Edited by James Strachey. London: Hogarth Press, 1950–74. *S.E.* II.

Freud, S. (1905) *Three Essays on the Theory of Sexuality*. *S.E.* VII, pp. 123–243.

Freud, S. (1908) 'On the Sexual Theories of Children'. *S.E.* IX, p. 207.

Freud, S. (1910) 'Leonardo da Vinci and a Memory of His Childhood'. *S.E.* XI, pp. 57–137.

Freud, S. (1912–13) *Totem and Taboo*. *S.E.* XIII, pp. 1–161.

Freud, S. (1914a) 'Remembering, Repeating and Working-Through'. *S.E.* XII, p. 147.

Freud, S. (1914b) *On Narcissism: An Introduction*. *S.E.* XIV.

Freud, S. (1915) 'A Case of Paranoia Running Counter to the Psycho-Analytic Theory of the Disease'. *S.E.* XIV, p. 263.

Freud, S. (1915–17) *Introductory Lectures on Psycho-Analysis*. *S.E.* XV–XVI.

Freud, S. (1917) 'Mourning and Melancholia'. *S.E.* XIV.

Freud, S. (1918 [1914]) 'From the History of an Infantile Neurosis'. *S.E.* XVII, pp. 1–122.

Freud, S. (1919) 'A Child is Being Beaten'. *S.E.* XVII, p. 177.

Freud, S. (1920) *Beyond the Pleasure Principle*. *S.E.* XVII.

Freud, S. (1923) *The Ego and the Id*. *S.E.* XIX, pp. 3–66.

Freud, S. (1924) 'The Economic Problem of Masochism'. *S.E.* XIX, p. 157.

Freud, S. (1925a) 'Negation'. *S.E.* XIX, p. 235.

Freud, S. (1925b [1924]) 'A Note Upon the Mystic Writing-Pad'. *S.E.* XIX, p. 227.

Freud, S. (1926 [1925]) *Inhibitions, Symptoms and Anxiety*. *S.E.* XX, pp. 75–175.

Freud, S. (1937a) 'Analysis Terminable and Interminable'. *S.E.* XXIII.

Freud, S. (1937b) 'Constructions in Analysis'. *S.E.* XXIII.

Freud, S. (1939) *Moses and Monotheism*. *S.E.* XXIII, pp. 1–137.

Freud, S. (1940 [1938]) *An Outline of Psychoanalysis*. *S.E.* XXIII, p. 187.

Freud, S. (1941 [1938]) 'Findings, Ideas, Problems'. *S.E.* XXIII, p. 299.

Freud, S. (1981) *Essais de psychanalyse*. Trans. Dr S. Jankéléwitch. Paris: Petite Bibliothèque Payot.

Freud, S. (1987) *A Phylogenetic Fantasy – Overview of the Transference Neuroses*. Harvard University Press.

Gantheret, F. (1988) 'Habemus Papam!', *Nouvelle Revue de psychanalyse*, 38, pp. 61–70.

Gardiner, M. (ed.) (1971) *The Wolf Man by the Wolf Man*. New York: Basic Books.

Gay, P. (1988) *Freud*. London: Anchor.

Gibeault, A. (1989) 'Destins de la symbolisation', Congrès des psychanalystes de langue française des pays romans, Paris, 1989, *Revue française de psychanalyse*, 53(6), pp. 1517–1618.

Green, A. (1963) 'La psychanalyse devant l'opposition de l'histoire et de la structure', *Critique*, 194, July 1963.

Green, A. (1973) *Le Discours vivant*. Paris: Presses Universitaires de France. (English translation, *The Fabric of Affect in the Psychoanalytical Discourse*. Trans. A. Sheridan. London: Routledge, 1999.)

Green, A. (1975) 'Le temps mort', *Nouvelle Revue de psychanalyse*, 11, pp. 103–11.

Green, A. (1980) 'Le double fantôme', in *Corps et création*, under the direction of J. Guillaumin. Lyon: Universitaires de Lyon.

Green, A. (1982a) 'La réserve de l'incréable', in N. Nicolaïdis and E. Schmid-Kitsikis (eds) *Créativité et/ou symptôme*. Paris: Clancier-Guenaud.

Green, A. (1982b) 'Travail psychique et travail de la pensée', *Revue française de psychanalyse*, XLV.

Green, A. (1986) 'Réponses à des questions inconcevables', *Topique*, 37, pp. 11–30.

Green, A. (1990a) 'La remémoration: effet de memoire ou temporalité à l'oeuvre', *Nouvelle Revue de psychanalyse*, LIX, pp. 947–72.

Green, A. (1990b) 'Temps et mémoire', *Nouvelle Revue de psychanalyse*, pp. 179–205.

Green, A. (1991a) *On Private Madness*. London: Karnac, 1997.

Green, A. (1991b) *Révélations de l'inachèvement*. Paris: Flammarion.

Green, A. (1991c) 'Méconnaissance de l'inconscient', in *L'inconscient et la science*, directed by R. Dorey. Paris: Dunod.

Green, A. (1992a) 'Des mouches aux mots', in *La déliaison*. Paris: Les Belles Lettres; Hachette, 1998.

Green, A. (1992b) 'Oedipe, Freud et nous', in *La déliaison*. Paris: Les Belles Lettres; Hachette, 1998.

Green, A. (1992c) 'Le double double', in *La déliaison*. Paris: Les Belles Lettres; Hachette, 1998.

Green, A. (1993a) *Le travail du négatif*. Paris: Minuit. (*The Work of the Negative*. Trans. A. Weller. London: Free Association Books, 1999.)

Green, A. (1993b) 'L'analité primaire dans la relation anale', in *La névrose obsessionale*, Monographies de la Revue française de psychanalyse, pp. 61–83.

Green, A. (1995) *La causalité psychique*. Paris: Odile Jacob.

Green, A. (1998a) *La déliaison: psychanalayse, anthropologie et littérature*. Paris: Hachette.

Green, A. (1998b) 'La réserve de l'incréable', in *La déliaison*. Paris: Hachette.

Green, A. (1999a) 'Passivité, Passivation: jouissance et détresse', *Revue française de psychanalyse*, 63(5), pp. 1587–600.

Green, A. (1999b) 'Sur la discrimination and l'indiscrimination affect-représentation', *Revue française de psychanalyse*, LXIII, pp. 217–72.

Green, A. (2000a) *The Chains of Eros*. London: Rebus Press.

Green, A. (2000b) *Time in Psychoanalysis – Some Contradictory Aspects*. London: Free Association Books, 2002.

Green, A. (2001) 'Primary Narcissism: Structure or State?', in *Life Narcissism. Death Narcissism*. Trans. Andrew Weller. London: Free Association Books.

Greimas, A.J. (1966) 'Structure et histoire', *Les Temps modernes*, 246, November.

Greimas, A.J. (1970, 1983) *Du sens*, Vols I and II. Paris: Le Seuil.

Guttieres-Green, L. (1990) 'Problématique du transfer douloureux', *Revue française de psychanalyse*, LIV.

James, H. (1947) *The Notebooks of Henry James*. Edited by F.O. Mathiessen and K.B. Murdock. Chicago: University of Chicago Press.

James, H. (1990) *Memoirs d'un jeune garçon*. Trans. Christine Bouwart. Paris: Rivages. [Originally published in English as *A Small Boy and Others*, 1913. Reprinted New York: Turtle Point, 2000.]

James, H. (2001) *Ghost Stories of Henry James*. Ware: Wordsworth Classics.

Jones, E. (1957) *The Life and Work of Sigmund Freud*, Vol. 3. New York: Basic Books, p. 475.

Juillerat, B. (1992) *Oedipe chasseur, vers une ontologie*. Paris: Presses Universitaires de France.

Klein, M. (1932) *The Psycho-Analysis of Children*. Translated by Alix Strachey. London: Hogarth Press and the Institute of Psycho-Analysis, 1986.

Kris, E. (1956) 'The Recovery of Childhood Memories in Psychoanalysis', in *Psychoanalytic Study of the Child*. New Haven: Yale University Press.

Lacan, J. (1977) *Ecrits: A Selection*. Translated by Alan Sheridan. London Routledge.

Lagache, D. (1952) 'Le problème du transfert', *Revue française de psychanalyse*, XVI, p. 102.

Lamotte, J. and L'Héritier, P. (1965) *Biologie générale*. Paris: Dion.

Laplanche, J. and Pontalis, J.-B. (1964) 'Fantasme originaire, fantasme des origines, origines du fantasme', *Les temps modernes*, 215, pp. 1833–68. (English translation, *International Journal of Psycho-Analysis*, 1968, 49, pp. 1ff.)

Laplanche, J. and Pontalis, J.-B. (1967) *The Language of Psychoanalysis*. Translated by Donald Nicholson Smith. London: Hogarth Press, 1973.

Leroi-Gourhan, A. (1964) *Religion de la préhistoire*. Paris: Presses Universitaires de France.

Lévi-Strauss, C. (1967) 'La notion de structure en ethnologie', in *Sens and usage du terme structure*. Mouton: La Haye.

Masson, J.M. (ed.) (1985) *The Complete Letters of Sigmund Freud to Wilhelm Fliess, 1887–1904*. London: The Belknap Press.

Meng, H. and Freud, E.L. (eds) (1963) *Psychoanalysis and Faith. The Letters of Sigmund Freud and Oskar Pfister*. Translated by E. Mosbacher. London: Hogarth Press and the Institute of Psycho-Analysis.

Miller, J.A. (1966) 'La suture', *Cahiers pour l'analyse*, 1, pp. 39–51. Paris: Le Graphe.

Milner, M. (1969) *In the Hands of the Living God*. London: Hogarth Press.

Morin, E. (1990) *Introduction à la pensée complexe*. Alençon: ESF.

Neruda, P. (1991) 'Ode to a Watch in the Night', in *Elemental Odes*. London: Libris.

Nietzsche, F. (1911) 'Philosophy in the Tragic Age of the Greeks', in *The Complete Works of F. Nietzsche*, Vol. 2. Chicago: Henry Regnery Publishing.

Obholzer, K. (1981) *Entretiens avec L'Homme aux loups*. Translated from the German by R. Dugas, with a preface by M. Schneider. Paris: Gallimard.

Peterfreund, E. (1978) 'Some Critical Comments on Psychoanalytic Conceptualization in Infancy', *International Journal of Psycho-Analysis*, 59(4), pp. 427–42.

Plato (1871) *The Symposium*. Translated by Benjamin Jowett. Dover: Thrift Editions.
Pouillon, J. (1965) 'Sartre et Lévi-Strauss', *L'Arc*, 26, pp. 60ff.
Poulantzas, N. (1966) 'Vers une théorie Marxiste', *Les Temps modernes*, 240.
Proust, M. (1996) *A la recherche du temps perdu*. Pléiade, Paris: Gallimard. (English translation, *In Search of Lost Time*, by C.K. Moncrieff and T. Kilmartin. London: Vintage Classics, 1996.)
Rank, O. (1989) *The Double: A Psychoanalytic Study*. London: Karnac.
Ricoeur, P. 'Structure et hermeneutique', *Esprit* (new series) 11, pp. 597ff.
Rosenfeld, I. (1988) *The Invention of Memory: A New View of the Brain*. New York: Basic Books.
Rosolato, G. (1978) *La relation d'inconnu*. Paris: Gallimard.
Sartre, J.-P. (1966) 'J.-P. Sartre répond', *L'Arc*, 30, pp. 87–96. Aix-en-Provence.
Sebag, L. (1965) 'Le mythe, code et message', *Les Temps modernes*, 226, March.
Shakespeare, W. (1986) *The Sonnets and A Lover's Complaint*. Edited by John Kerrigan. London: Penguin Classics.
Sophocles (1962) *Antigone, Oedipus the King, Electra*. Translated by H.D.F. Kitto. Oxford: Oxford World Classics, Oxford University Press.
Spitz, R.A. (1958) *The First Year of Life. A Psychoanalytic Study of Normal and Deviant Development in Object Relations*. New York: International Universities Press, 1965.
Spitz, R.A. (1968) *De la naissance à la parole*. Trans. L. Flournoy. Paris: Presses Universitaires de France.
Stern, D. (1985) *The Interpersonal World of the Infant*. New York: Basic Books.
Strauss, L. (1962) *Totemism Today*. Boston: Beacon Press, 1963.
Varela, F. (1988) *Connaître les sciences cognitives*. Translated by P. Lavoie. Paris: Le Seuil.
Verstraeten, P. (1963) 'Lévi-Strauss ou la tentation du Néant', *Les Temps modernes*, 206–7.
Watson, J. (1968) *The Double Helix*. London: Simon & Schuster Trade, reprint 1998.
Winnicott, D.W. (1941) 'The Observations of Infants in a Set Situation', in *Collected Papers: Through Paediatrics to Psychoanalysis*. London: Tavistock, 1958.
Winnicott, D.W. (1958a) 'The First Year of Life', *The Medical Press*, CCXXXIX(6201). Also in *The Family and Individual Development*. London: Tavistock, 1965.
Winnicott, D.W. (1958b) *Through Paediatrics to Psychoanalysis*. London: Karnac.
Winnicott, D.W. (1971a) 'Fear of Breakdown', *International Revue of Psychoanalysis*, 1, pp. 103–7.
Winnicott, D.W. (1971b) *Therapeutic Consultations in Child Psychiatry*. London: Hogarth Press and the Institute of Psycho-Analysis.
Wollman. E. (1969) 'La sexualité des bactéries', in *Entretiens sur la sexualité*, Colloquium of Cerisy. Paris: Plon.

Index

Compiled by Sue Carlton